D0845108

PSYCHOLOGY ON THE STREETS

Recent titles in the

Wiley Series on Personality Processes

Irving B. Weiner, *Editor*
University of South Florida

Psychology on the Streets: Mental Health Practice with Homeless Persons *Thomas L. Kuhlman*
The Working Alliance: Theory, Research, and Practice *edited by Adam Horvath and Leslie S. Greenberg*
Handbook of Developmental Family Psychology and Psychopathology *by Luciano L'Abate*
A Theory of Personality Development *by Luciano L'Abate*
Anxiety and Related Disorders: A Handbook *by Benjamin B. Wolman, Editor, George Stricker, Co-Editor*
Social Origins of Mental Ability *by Gary Collier*
Symptoms of Schizophrenia *edited by Charles G. Costello*
The Rorschach: A Comprehensive System. Volume I: Basic Foundations (Third Edition) *by John E. Exner, Jr.*
Symptoms of Depression *edited by Charles G. Costello*
Handbook of Clinical Research and Practice with Adolescents *edited by Patrick H. Tolan and Bertram J. Cohler*
Internalizing Disorders in Children and Adolescents *edited by William M. Reynolds*
Assessment of Family Violence: A Clinical and Legal Sourcebook *edited by Robert T. Ammerman and Michel Hersen*
Handbook of Clinical Child Psychology (Second Edition) *edited by C. Eugene Walker and Michael C. Roberts*
Handbook of Clinical Behavior Therapy (Second Edition) *edited by Samuel M. Turner, Karen S. Calhoun, and Henry E. Adams*
Psychological Disturbance in Adolescence (Second Edition) *by Irving B. Weiner*
Prevention of Child Maltreatment: Development and Ecological Perspectives *edited by Diane J. Willis, E. Wayne Holden, and Mindy Rosenberg*
Interventions for Children of Divorce: Custody, Access, and Psychotherapy *by William F. Hodges*
The Play Therapy Primer: An Integration of Theories and Techniques *by Kevin John O'Connor*
Adult Psychopatholody and Diagnosis (Second Edition) *edited by Michel Hersen and Samuel L. Turner*
The Rorschach: A Comprehensive System. Volume II: Interpretation (Second Edition) *by John E. Exner, Jr.*
Play Diagnosis and Assessment *edited by Charles E. Schaefer, Karen Gitlin, and Alice Sandgrund*
Acquaintance Rape: The Hidden Crime *edited by Andrea Parrot and Laurie Bechhofer*
The Psychological Examination of the Child *by Theodore H. Blau*
Depressive Disorders: Facts, Theories, and Treatment Methods *by Benjamin B. Wolman, Editor, and George Stricker, Co-Editor*
Social Support: An Interactional View *edited by Barbara R. Sarason, Irwin G. Sarason, and Gregory R. Pierce*
Toward a New Personology: An Evolutionary Model *by Theodore Millon*
Treatment of Family Violence: A Sourcebook *edited by Robert T. Ammerman and Michel Hersen*
Handbook of Comparative Treatments for Adult Disorders *edited by Alan S. Bellack and Michel Hersen*
Managing Attention Disorders in Children: A Guide for Practitioners *by Sam Goldstein and Michael Goldstein*

Psychology on the Streets

Mental Health Practice with Homeless Persons

Thomas L. Kuhlman

A WILEY INTERSCIENCE PUBLICATION

John Wiley & Sons, Inc.

New York • Chichester • Brisbane • Toronto • Singapore

This text is printed on acid-free paper.

Library of Congress Cataloging in Publication Data:

Kuhlman, Thomas L.
Psychology on the streets : mental health practice with homeless persons / Thomas L. Kuhlman.
p. cm. — (Wiley series on personality processes)
Includes bibliographical references and index.
ISBN 0-471-55243-7 (cloth : alk. paper)
1. Homeless persons—Mental health services. 2. Homeless persons—Mental health. 3. Mental health personnel and patient. I. Title. II. Series.
[DNLM: 1. Homeless Persons—psychology. 2. Mental Disorders—diagnosis. 3. Mental Disorders—therapy. 4. Psychotherapy. WA 305 K955p 1994]
RC451.4.H64K84 1994
362.2'2—dc20
DNLM/DLC
for Library of Congress 93-40003

Printed in the United States of America

10 9 8 7 6 5 4 3 2 1

Series Preface

This series of books is addressed to behavioral scientists interested in the nature of human personality. Its scope should prove pertinent to personality theorists and researchers as well as to clinicians concerned with applying an understanding of personality processes to the amelioration of emotional difficulties in living. To this end, the series provides a scholarly integration of theoretical formulations, empirical data, and practical recommendations.

Six major aspects of studying and learning about human personality can be designated: personality theory, personality structure and dynamics, personality development, personality assessment, personality change, and personality adjustment. In exploring these aspects of personality, the books in the series discuss a number of distinct but related subject areas: the nature and implications of various theories of personality; personality characteristics that account for consistencies and variations in human behavior; the emergence of personality processes in children and adolescents; the use of interviewing and testing procedures to evaluate individual differences in personality; efforts to modify personality styles through psychotherapy, counseling, behavior therapy, and other methods of influence; and patterns of abnormal personality functioning that impair individual competence.

IRVING B. WEINER

University of South Florida
Tampa, Florida

Preface

This book represents a synthesis of my seven years of experience as a psychologist working with and on behalf of homeless persons in Madison, Wisconsin, and the Twin Cities area of Minnesota. This involved approximately three thousand face-to-face contacts during two thousand hours spent visiting various shelters, drop-in centers, and other urban sites where homeless persons congregate. Sixty percent of this work was performed on a salaried basis and 40 percent as a volunteer.

I have written this book to supplement the burgeoning research literature about homeless people in the United States. A bibliography of abstracts published by the American Psychological Association lists almost 500 articles on the subject of homelessness between 1967 and 1990 (Shinn, Burke, & Bedford, 1990). Most of this literature is cross-sectional, epidemiological, and/or nomothetic in nature. The present work is more longitudinal, ecological, and idiographic in nature. The prevalent survey and structured interview methods have generated a good picture of "the forest" of the homelessness problem, while the present work emphasizes the individual trees and the grounds from which they spring. A final difference is that the products of survey and interview approaches address the interests and needs of policymakers, planners, program directors, academics, and researchers. This book addresses the interests and needs of practitioners who would provide mental health services to homeless persons. These include the "street practitioner" and case manager who do outreach and treatment work amidst the street culture on a regular basis, the volunteer practitioner who performs *pro bono* work on a periodic or irregular basis, and office-bound practitioners who are limited to working with homeless persons in clinics, mental health centers, emergency rooms, and the like. My intent is to impart knowledge and to stimulate practitioners' modes of thought in ways that will make homeless persons and street cultures more comprehensible to them.

I also wrote this book so that practitioners from fields other than mental health would find it useful, for many of them are also confronted with mental health issues in their street work. To this end, I have minimized the use of specialty terms and have taken some pains to explain any specialty terminology that could not be avoided. Those whose major interest is homeless families and children will be better served by other works. The emphasis here is upon the adult individual and how he or she is to be understood against the backdrop of a street culture.

This work includes 60 vignettes that involve interactions between practitioners and street persons. Descriptor variables have been introduced, altered, and/or deleted from each vignette to preserve anonymity in accordance with ethical standards governing right to privacy.

I would like to thank Renee Reed for her careful perusal of this book and her helpful suggestions as to its style and contents. Irving Weiner, Herb Reich, and Toni Williams made up the support system that this author required. Informal contributions of my colleagues from both inside and outside of mental health fields were appreciated.

This work is dedicated to the homeless persons of the Twin Cities and Madison areas. They are also its co-authors.

THOMAS L. KUHLMAN

Eden Prairie, Minnesota

Contents

Introduction

Because most mental health practitioners come from the middle class, their backgrounds, belief systems, and cognitive biases will be at some variance with those of homeless persons.

Statements like the preceding one commonly appear in books about interacting with racial, cultural, and religious minorities. In fact, cultural diversity is now put forth as cause for celebration as well as respect in the current sociopolitical climate. The culture of homelessness is certainly no cause for celebration, but respect for and understanding of this culture is a basis for effective mental health intervention. To that end, the first vignette of this book does not portray a proverbial "bag lady" nor a schizophrenic man talking into the air through a scraggly beard matted with week-old ketchup. It comes instead from the author's first exposure to a street culture, a humbling experience but one that demonstrates the potential for culture shock that comes from meeting street people on their territory rather than in the familiar surroundings of the practitioner's own office culture.

> My wife had volunteered our family to help provide and serve a supper to homeless people at a soup kitchen along with our church group. I arrived late at the soup kitchen from my office, thus missing a brief orientation to the soup kitchen and its rules. I had given the evening little forethought beyond its being another wearying, weekday evening commitment, but I hoped that I would derive some spiritual nourishment from the altruism of it all.
>
> The serving of the meal along a cafeteria queue went smoothly enough. However, the exchanges of eye contact, gratitude, and small talk between servers and served across the stainless steel barrier were more variable and muted than I had expected. The situation turned awkward after all of the homeless people had been served and it was our turn to dine. I was disappointed that most of my fellow church members sat down together at an empty table rather than mingle with our "guests." Wishing my children to see otherwise, I led them to one of the other tables that had open seats at its far end. I sensed a begrudging silence as we set down our trays. The ongoing conversations that had paused at our arrival resumed with less volume and animation. The man sitting next to

> me and the one sitting across from him ate their soup in a robotic fashion without so much as a sidelong glance or a look at each other. My asking them for the salt and pepper brought no acknowledgment of me beyond the shakers themselves. I resorted to that universal ice-breaker, the weather. We had been enduring a hot, dry spell in central Wisconsin at the time but there had been a steady drizzle most of that particular day. So I offered the observation that it surely had been a good thing to get some rain for a change. The man next to me made a slight turn of his head and a momentary pause in the descent of his spoon to answer, "Folk who sleep outside need it to stop raining earlier (in the day) so it's got a chance to dry out before dark."
>
> With this even my seven-year-old could sense the awkwardness growing worse. She tried to engage me in an account of the day's swimming lessons and a bike ride to the creek behind the new houses. The men to my right started up their own conversation about a pair of women who regularly took too much clothing from the free stores and whether or not these two women were selling the stuff to flea markets.
>
> Thus we resumed our two sets of reality at the table. The twain had not met. As my son talked, I nodded on, still pensive about my faux pas. To change my cognitive set, I got up and went back to the cafeteria line for seconds. I paid no heed to the fact that no one else in the room had yet done this. One of the women from our church group whom I had only just met came over to the queue from a dish caddy. She addressed me as "Doctor" but then seemed flustered by my simple request. She hesitated, looking one way and then the other, until I sensed more awkward silence around me. The nun in charge of our group suddenly appeared at my right side. She squeezed my wrist in a reassuring way, then reached up for my shoulder and bent my ear down to her level. I was quietly informed of one of the soup kitchen rules that I had missed: there were no seconds for anyone here. Whatever was left over would be trucked to a meal site on the other side of town where they were scheduled to start serving supper an hour after ours closed.

Several themes of this incident will echo through this book. The first is that the essence of homelessness is not one of being without something as the suffix "-less" normally connotes. Homeless persons become part of a culture different from that of "homed" persons. It will be referred to as *street culture* here in order to emphasize that which is possessed over that which has been lost. (The terms "homeless" and "street" will be used interchangeably as adjectives throughout this book.) Within this culture, mundane events like light rain take on different meanings. Many practitioners are inclined to overlook these meaning shifts among people who read the same newspapers, grouse about the same politicians, root for the same home teams as themselves. At the same time, homeless persons are asked to respect rules like "no seconds" when they can see that food is still available, and to stay in congregate shelters when homes foreclosed upon by HUD sit vacant. Such meanings are easier for the middle class practitioner to appreciate.

A soup kitchen belongs more to the street people who use it regularly than to a fourth-Thursday-of-the-month church group. Thus, this was "their" territory and we who served them were more guests than hosts. On their territory, my behaviors of arriving late and requesting seconds are to be judged against different standards than those of an office culture. Consider lateness first: homeless persons are often late due to lack of personal control over most of their sources of transportation. As a result, lateness is typically overlooked and readily forgotten. But my ignorance of a "no seconds" rule was another matter among a group whose members have known hunger and are often forced to abide by rules designed to accommodate others, for example, shelter closes at 7:00 AM; drop-in serves lunch from 11 AM to 1 PM. The hesitation of the woman who came over to serve me and the pregnant silence around us asked which standard would be applied here: the one that applied to doctors versus the one that applied to street people. Practitioners who work amidst street cultures can expect to be scrutinized for "double standard" behaviors.

Consider next the treatment that I received at the table. Based upon my subsequent observations and experiences, my receiving the "cold shoulder" here was atypical. Most street persons react cordially if not warmly when volunteers join them for meals. But exceptions can prove important rules: by what license did I sit down uninvited and expect to be assimilated into their conversation? If my children and I had been in a restaurant and a group of Minnesota Twins (professional baseball players) had also been there with empty spaces at the end of their table, would I have behaved in the same way? This same behavior in the other context would have been patently inappropriate even though I could muster a similar justification for it, that is, my ticket purchases provide ballplayers with meals and I wanted my children to have an opportunity to meet them, too.

The consideration that makes these two situations different is the relative status positions assigned to celebrity athletes versus street persons. This points up a theme that is critical to the mental health practitioner who would serve street people. In order to promote a homeless person's self-esteem, positive identity, and self-empowerment, it is important to behave in ways that neither condescend nor otherwise reinforce the individual's low status position. A visit by a street person to the office or clinic evokes responses that reinforce that low status long before the street person is actually seen by the practitioner. Some overlook this while others choose to be noncompliant with future treatment appointments. In outreach work at street culture sites, the practitioner observes a street person's resentment more directly because the interaction occurs on the street person's territory.

These considerations also apply to the psychotic membership of the street culture. These people must be met and understood in the context of their culture as well as that of their diagnosis. As will be seen later, the sorts of schizophrenic persons who subsist in the street culture are different from those whom one meets in supportive housing facilities and aftercare programs.

Chapter 1 develops the postulates and implications of the ecological perspective that is introduced. The alienated, estranged character of street culture calls for an outreach stance that merges the roles of mental health practitioner and ethnographer. Chapter 2 is a literature review of studies of the New Homelessness, as Peter Rossi (1990) has labeled it. As part of this review, that segment of the New Homelessness which is of major concern to mental health practitioners is artificially divided into a social selection component (psychotic persons and others who would have been institutionalized 40 years ago) and a social causation component (persons whose mental impairments are caused or catalyzed by homelessness rather than vice versa).

The next two chapters are intended to prepare the practitioner for the interactional stressors of outreach work. Chapter 3 focuses on the homeless person's side of the dyad: it reviews the varieties and vicissitudes of resistance among homeless persons to the prospect of mental health intervention. The sources and remediation of resistance are also addressed. Chapter 4 focuses on the practitioner's side of the dyad: the varieties, sources, and remedies of countertransference and burnout reactions among practitioners who would attempt to ally themselves with resistant people.

Chapters 5 and 6 deal predominantly with the social selection component of the street culture. Chapter 5 explores the specific resistance, assessment, and intervention issues specific to psychotic persons of the streets. Chapter 6 addresses disability programs that were designed to support and maintain these people, with special reference to the federal SSI program and how practitioners can best deal with it. The complexities of the "disability" label and problematic responses to it are highlighted as important matters to be considered in all outreach and intervention work.

Chapters 7 and 8 emphasize the social causation component of the culture and interventions that address their needs. Chapter 7 explores the vehicle of single session psychotherapy and Chapter 8 the longer term, intermittent psychotherapy. Although these intervention concepts originated within managed care models, their raison d'etre in street work is not cost containment but the street person's inherent control over the occurrence, frequency, and duration of sessions that take place in street culture sites. A session-by-session analysis of one psychotherapy is provided to dramatize its differences from office culture work that goes by the same label.

Chapter 9 briefly introduces other segements of the street culture with whom the street practitioner will be called upon to intervene. These include persons who are chemically dependent and those who are both chemically dependent and mentally impaired (the so called "dually diagnosed"). The importance of tending to the training and burnout needs of other health care practitioners and service providers are also promoted. Chapter 10 is both a summary of the previous chapters and a caution about the iatrogenic effects that practitioners and researchers have generated while bringing their skills to bear upon the problem of homelessness in the United States.

CHAPTER 1

The Ecologist-Practitioner

It is difficult for a mental health practitioner to read the academic or popular literature about homelessness in the United States without experiencing sympathy, indignation, and/or outrage. Guilt and shame may be added to this mix when one reads Torrey's (1988) fiery indictment of the mental health professions for their contributions to the problem.

Such sentiments have helped to motivate both salaried and volunteer mental health practitioners to work with street persons. Unfortunately, there is no combination of motives to insulate one from street work's rude awakenings. Few street people value mental health practitioners and many resent their presence. Clergy and nurses receive more respect and better treatment on the streets than do mental health practitioners. In part this reflects the greater social acceptance that is afforded these other professions by society as a whole. But equally important is the fact that these others provide services that have more here-and-now validity to street persons. Such is seldom the case with mental health services, and this adds to existing credibility problems among a fearful and resentful culture. Many street persons even construe the mental health practitioner as an agent of oppression from mainstream society.

To counteract such problems, Project Help in New York City searches for psychotic street people by van and station wagon (Cohen & Marcos, 1992). Staff offer them food, clothing, medical care, and so on with no strings attached, and this might go on for weeks or months before the subject of mental health is broached. Even so, these efforts are not always rewarded and some "recruits" remain intransigent throughout.

Some practitioners have evoked responses that are beyond intransigence, for example:

> Once a psychiatric nurse was leaving a shelter and had to walk fifty yards from the back of the building to the front. On his way, he was compelled to walk through a small group of shelter guests who were

> jawing loudly with each other about something. They quieted down and made a space for him to pass through. As he did so, the first man whirled and waved his flattened hand about the nurse's face karate-style. He made several passes from different angles with great speed and precision; he came close to striking a blow but never did. His speed was such that it was all over before the nurse knew it; the nurse walked through the group before stopping to turn around. Three of them broke into laughter as the nurse hesitated to say something. After they had quieted down he smiled and shrugged and asked if there was anything else he could do for them that night. The men smiled back and shook their heads and waved him off as they walked in the opposite direction.

This parting did not seem an unfriendly one to the nurse, who interpreted the incident as something of a hazing ritual or initiation rite. Because the membership of a street culture is in constant flux, such hazings do not necessarily end after one's first month or first year on the streets. It is an unwanted strain of the work to have to find and calibrate a response to such hazings.

THE ECOLOGICAL PERSPECTIVE

The interpretation of such experiences as initiation rites of the street culture is more typical of social anthropology than mental health. Indeed, there is much which sociology, anthropology, and related disciplines have to say about modern day homelessness that can inform the mental health practitioner's work (Koegel, 1992). However, Koegel has further observed that these other approaches call for a level of practitioner involvement that stirs "reactivity" (better known to mental health practitioners as *countertransference reactions*). They also lend themselves to romanticism and complacency about the adaptive strengths that homeless people display as they eke out survival on the streets.

On the other hand, the American Psychiatric Association Task Force on the Homeless Mentally Ill has scarcely paid lip service to the possibility that street culture might influence the manifestations and adaptations associated with severe mental impairments. Although Susser, Valencia, and Goldfinger (1992) likened serving homeless people to crosscultural work, the word culture does not appear in either of the Task Force's two sets of recommendations for mentally impaired homeless persons (Lamb, 1984; Lamb, Bachrach, & Kass, 1992). Among these authorities, Bachrach (1992) has come closest to endorsing the crosscultural perspective in her statement that "life circumstances act like intervening variables in altering service needs" (p. 459). That a psychotic person might develop a sense of identity and fit within a street culture which makes that person more resistant to treatment warrants more serious consideration than it has been given thus far.

An approach that blends the best of both worlds is the ecological perspective articulated by Toro, Trickett, Wall, and Salem (1991). Although advanced primarily as a framework to shape research, policy, and community-focused interventions, its dual emphasis upon the homeless person (figure) and the street culture in which the homeless person is embedded (ground) is recommended to all street practitioners. The day-to-day adaptational successes and failures of homeless persons must be observed and appreciated beyond the individual's symptoms and deficits, and beyond the societal forces that rendered the individual homeless. Resistance and rejection behaviors toward mental health practitioners must be viewed as part of adaptation rather than as a basis for rejecting them back as untreatable.

The first step for the practitioner who wishes to adopt this approach is to depart the office culture in favor of regularly scheduled visits to various street culture sites. This makes one accessible to street people on their territory. Once one's "tour schedule" becomes general knowledge in the culture, street persons will know when and where to go for service at various times during the day/week/month. Abandoning the office culture practice of scheduled appointments means that there will be occasions at these sites when the demands upon one's time will exceed the supply of time that one has to offer. At such times, people will simply have to wait their turn or postpone the contact until later. Fortunately, the practitioner will soon learn that street people tolerate delays and waiting better than office culture people who have been shaped by the concept of appointments.

There will also be times when the practitioner arrives at a site and no one wishes to be seen. It is at such times that the practitioner should engage in more casual outreach and networking sorts of activities with members of the culture. One need not be distracted by the ongoing debate among researchers and academics as to how homelessness should be operationally defined (e.g., Bachrach, 1992; Fischer & Breakey, 1991). An ecological perspective permits a culture to define itself. People who frequent shelters, drop-in centers, labor pools, free stores, plasma centers, Greyhound bus depots, public libraries, and other such "found spaces" (Rivlin & Imbimbo, 1989)—all people who use these street culture sites—thus qualify themselves for the street practitioner's attention. Some are psychotic persons who reside in board-and-care facilities or halfway houses but reject the demands of day treatment centers or the stigmata of clubhouses for the mentally impaired. Other people move among a series of ephemeral housing arrangements that are described as "living with friends." Those who live in "doubled up" households with relatives ease the stress of overcrowding by coming to street culture sites. Some occupy the remnants of the single-room-occupancy (SRO) housing stock that has dropped precipitously during the last two decades. Others may even have stable residences and do not meet prevailing technical definitions of homelessness, but can be considered "one paycheck away" from homelessness for various reasons. Perhaps a "beater" car breaks down or an extended illness causes job loss; perhaps a series of government checks becomes lost in the mail, or a psychotic person takes a nonprescribed holiday from medications, or a kindly landlady dies and her heirs decide to increase her building's rental income. Any of these unfortunate circumstances (and other less honorable ones) can send at-risk people into homelessness. The fact that domiciled people frequent street sites at all attests to the fact that many forms of housing are experienced as tenuous and marginal. For the street practitioner, homelessness is better grasped as a state of mind than as a demographic trait.

Street cultures and sites include an array of nonhomeless people trying to meet the day-to-day needs of homeless persons. Some of the paid and volunteer staff of shelters and drop-in centers are newly emerged from homelessness themselves and were hired as employees after first becoming known as patrons. This is one example of the "boundary blurring" that pervades the culture as a whole, practitioners included. Other staff are middle class, many of them college educated. They come initially because of their ideals, but low pay, unchanging squalor, and the incessant needs, demands, and provocations of the patrons promote their burnout and rapid turnover. Add to this mix the once-a-week altruists and volunteers, social service outreach workers, advocates, health care providers, day-labor recruiters, plus the occasional tours by politicians and dignitaries, journalists, surveyors and researchers, choir groups performing at Christmas time—it all makes for a rich and complex milieu. The mental health practitioner who visits sites regularly becomes part of this milieu.

Street cultures from different geographic areas cannot be assumed to be identical. Local and regional forces influence the evolution of both a street culture and the resources and support systems that sustain it. Generalizations made about homelessness in one community lose validity when they are applied to another community. Thus, there are many contrasts between the nature of homelessness and street culture in New York City versus that which exists in the Twin Cities of Minneapolis and St. Paul. New York operates large, congregate shelters, some with the capacity to serve more than a thousand people per night at full occupancy. Writing about New York's Project Help, Cohen and Marcos (1992) observed that the congregation of young, predatory, substance-abusing people in these poorly supervised shelters drove psychotic and other "prey" persons out of the shelters and onto the streets in search of safety, thus creating the need for a mobile outreach service like Project Help. One reads Grunberg and Eagle's (1990) richly detailed account about life and culture in the Fort Washington Men's Shelter and finds it easy to understand the large role played there by security guards. By contrast, the largest shelter in Minneapolis has a maximum capacity of 250, and some effort is expended to identify and segregate predatory types of people from those upon whom they are likely to prey. The need for security guards, metal detectors, and so on has evolved much more slowly in the Twin Cities. Hopefully, it will never be as complete: there are few encounters with inanimate objects as appalling as the sight of a state-of-the-art metal detector gleaming at the entrance to a drab, decaying building that has been put into its final service as a shelter for homeless people.

Sociopolitical factors in Wisconsin and Minnesota have made some impact upon how homelessness has evolved there compared to other regions. The political climate of the Upper Midwest has long been dominated by liberal and progressive philosophies. This has been translated into greater respect (more resources) allotted to state and local governments than is the case in many other states. High rates of taxation have yielded better economic and social service support for homeless persons. One would logically expect few homeless persons to migrate to the Upper Midwest because of its climate. However, relatively large welfare stipends and benefits, plus lax residency requirements to qualify for these benefits, has helped to foster abnormally high rates of migration to the Upper Midwest until recent legislation removed these incentive properties. Cultural and linguistic diversity is not as great in the Upper Midwest as it is on the coasts, but it does include an atypically large presence of Native Americans. Political activism on behalf of both homeless persons and mentally impaired persons is as sophisticated and organized in the region as it is anywhere in the country. For both better and worse, it is sometimes characterized by factionalism, in-fighting, and civil disobedience.

With regard to mental health services per se, there is no shortage of professionals willing to work with homeless persons in the Twin Cities. In fact, mentally impaired persons are sometimes perplexed by duplication of effort involving multiple providers who are not well-coordinated or in good communication with one another. Part of that coordination problem is abetted by data privacy laws that are among the most stringent in the country. On a more positive note, Madison, Wisconsin, is internationally renowned for its community-based mental health system (Thompson, Griffith, & Leaf, 1990), and Wisconsin has been ranked first among all states in providing such services to the severely impaired (Torrey & Wolfe, 1986). Minnesota's programs are not as good, but they did earn a seventeenth place ranking in 1991. Neither Madison nor the Twin Cities has yet needed to rely upon mobile outreach programs to the extent that New York City and other large cities have done.

To summarize the impact of these regional factors, it is probably accurate to characterize the plight of homeless persons (including the mentally impaired) as being somewhat better in the upper Midwest than is typical for urban areas in the country as a whole. This statement is not made to stake a claim to provincial pride, nor to suggest that the region can serve as a model for the rest of the country. It *is* to suggest that the street cultures of these cities (and the practitioners' involvements with them portrayed in this book) evolved under somewhat more propitious conditions than exist in the rest of the country. Even so, the following theme bears repetition: this "better" homelessness in the Upper Midwest grants no blessings to its street people, nor does it give cause for practitioners and programs to take any bows.

STAGES OF HOMELESSNESS

Homelessness does not appear in many stressful life event inventories. It was not identified as a pathology-inducing stressor in the American Psychiatric Association's *Diagnostic and Statistical Manual of Mental Disorders,* 3rd ed. (DSM-III) (APA, 1980) nor in its revision of same (DMS-III-R) (APA, 1987). These oversights have now been remedied (DSM-IV) (APA, 1994). Homelessness is now a V-code condition that is assigned to Axis IV of that multi-axial system.

As a state of mind, homelessness does not occur at the same rates and through the same pathways for all people. It may help the practitioner to conceive of it as a developmental process involving three less-than-distinct stages, each with its own implications for a practitioner's decision whether and how to intervene with a person. The stage descriptions that follow owe something to Snow and Anderson (1987) and Hertzberg (1988) but assume labels that have long been associated with Hans Selye (1976). Selye's classic work on the *General Adaptation Syndrome* emphasized the biological adaptations of an organism to generic stress; the present description emphasizes psychological adaptations of an individual to the specific stressor of homelessness.

In the first stage (Selye's Alarm Stage), homelessness is experienced as an acute event. Suddenly, episodically, or temporarily, one has been made homeless in the wake of financial or psychosocial stressors, coupled with an absence of a support system that is willing and able to provide one with a safety net of temporary shelter and its attendant benefits. In this stage, being on the streets is experienced as a traumatic threat and an abject misery. A person in this first stage will seldom hesitate to approach a mental health practitioner in full view of the street culture. This violates a taboo, but because the person neither feels nor wants to be a part of the culture, this is of little concern at the time. In fact, such a person's request for help from the practitioner often includes an unsolicited assertion as to how "I'm not one of them." The person's continuing identification with the mainstream culture is strengthened by distancing from street persons (Snow & Anderson, 1987). Such a person displays gratitude for small favors—a meal, a lift, a package of cigarettes. Such expressions of gratitude are often intense and effusive reflecting the person's need to strengthen ties to and identifications with benefactors from the mainstream at a time when such ties seem threatened.

Mental health interventions with people who are in the first stage have a good chance for success if relevant resources are available. The person is highly motivated to leave the street culture; if the episode ends quickly, he or she may look back on the experience as a watershed life event. Such a person generally retains some coping skills and perhaps an ambivalent support system that can be shifted back into the person's favor. When these factors are absent, as occurs with many psychotic persons who are newly discharged from a hospital, intervention becomes more difficult. The proverbial revolving-door syndrome of psychotic persons clamoring and begging and manipulating for readmission to the hospital reflects good reality testing as to the dangers and other miseries of living as potential prey amidst the street culture.

If no quick and enduring remedy to an episode of homelessness is found, the person drifts into the second stage, which is analagous to Selye's Resistance Stage. Now one's dependence on mainstream benefactors becomes an ambivalent one. The numbing everyday realities of the street erode self-esteem. A soup kitchen meal may meet or exceed marginal standards but its lukewarm temperature and the way that different foods are piled up or flooded together on a collapsing paper plate echo internal dialogue about the self. Used clothing marked by the stains or t-shirt identity of its previous owner has a similar impact, as does sleeping nightly on a thin cot amidst a crowded gym floor and sharing stenchy bathrooms with anonymous others. As a way of life rather than an episode, such provisions come to evoke shame, resentment, hostility, guilt, and bitterness in complex combinations. One is no longer traumatized by being on the streets but still tries a range of flight and fight behaviors to end the episode or reduce its pain. The range of flight behaviors includes alcohol, drugs, and other hedonistic pursuits of a here-and-now lifestyle. Some people in this second stage avoid street culture sites. They prefer to scavenge railroad yards or dumpsters behind restaurants and grocery stores, or take to stealing and shoplifting provisions rather than accept another plate of casserole ladled out by another kindly smiling church volunteer. Some drift into outlaw gangs or bottle gangs or party gangs. They may ride the rails city to city, lay over for a few days of temporary or seasonal work, perhaps an easy welfare check. The money is spent on a two- or three-day party before moving on. Positive self-esteem and identity are derived from predation and nose-thumbing nonconformity. In Snow and Anderson's (1987) study, the identity talk of these persons was characterized by fictive storytelling and showy embraces of a street culture identity.

> On the coldest night (−32 degrees Fahrenheit) of the winter of 1989, a Minneapolis TV news crew went under a freeway bridge for a human interest angle on the weather. A couple was camping out there. The two were bundled in thermal clothing and seemed to delight in the opportunity to dance and hoot for the mini-cam with upraised bottles of red sloe gin. As they caroused, the man swore, "No f***ing way!" to the reporter's question as to how they had decided against going to a shelter for the night.

There are also fight solutions during this second stage. Some employ a psychological variant of tunnel vision to work long days and weeks at low paying jobs in the spot labor pool to pay their own ways out of homelessness. Some neglect their health and other nonmonetary needs to the point that such single-mindedness seems pathological. Others become political or religious activists and proselytize among their peers. Some in this stage move through food queues rudely, bumping and jostling, taking as much as they can get and damning anyone who dares to raise a voice of protest or objection. Such disarming behavior evokes indignation from many who observe it. However, to conclude from such displays of ingratitude that these are "lowlifes" is to commit the fundamental attribution error of emphasizing trait explanations to behavior and minimizing situational factors (Nisbett, Caputo, Legant, & Maracek, 1973; Storms, 1973). To be sure, there are numbers of homeless people who would be diagnosed as antisocial personalities or seen as having entitlement mentalities. However, both of these adaptations are found in the higher socioeconomic status (SES) classes as well. Neither the antisocial personality nor the welfare mentality is prototypical of street people. Indeed, there is no one prototypical personality or type.

There are many homeless persons whose hostility and ingratitude to benefactors proves that it can be easier to give a handout than to receive one. Precise therapeutic skill and high "flak tolerance" are required to penetrate such a person's defenses and interfere with the many "loser" messages that he or she is receiving. Such messages typically originate from self-talk as well as from the outside world.

It is sometimes a bad outcome when a homeless person ceases to act in a hostile and ungrateful fashion. This may mean that he or she has acquiesced to the "loser" messages and ceased fighting them. This signals arrival at the third stage (the Exhaustion Stage according to Selye). "Street person" is now accepted as one's identity. The emotional reactivity that characterizes the first two stages is blunted among these persons, emotions having become superfluous distractions from the numbing routine of survival tasks to be practiced every day. Such persons go through handout lines nondescriptly and convey gratitude with automatic smiles and minimalist words to meet the bare requirements for such a transaction. They no longer seem troubled by conflicts over self-esteem or pride. Their primary motivation is to maintain themselves in survival conditions that expose them to the fewest dangers while requiring the least expenditures of energy and money. There-and-then thinking is jettisoned along with emotional reactivity.

This third stage corresponds with the phenomenon known as shelterization (Gounis & Susser, 1990; Grunberg & Eagle, 1990; Rivlin & Imbimbo, 1989). First identitified in the shelters and street cultures of New York City, shelterization refers to an institutionalization syndrome of passivity, dependence, apathy, and neglect of personal hygiene which befalls even nonpsychotic people if they languish in shelter life for months and years. "The adaptation to shelter life includes the development of a shelter vocabulary, the assimilation of shelter themes, the acceptance of shelter ideas and beliefs, and an eroding will" (Grunberg & Eagle, 1990, p. 522). Ungerleider, Andrysiak, Siegel, Tidwell, and Flynn (1992) observed similar phenomena among street people in Los Angeles. They described it as a "restructuring of reality" which takes place as homelessness becomes a way of life. "It would seem to follow that earlier intervention (with an individual's episode of homelessness) would be more effective before the ego reorganization occurs and before secondary gains become highly valued" (p. 113). Research also indicates that being raised outside of a parental home and enduring multiple placements as a child is predictive of homelessness as an adult (Susser, Struening, & Conover, 1987).

Many features of shelterization among nonpsychotic persons would be classified as negative symptoms or behavioral deficits when displayed by people who have schizophrenia. And thus it is not only by economic coincidence that so many psychotic persons are found amidst the street culture. The professional and popular literature highlights the plight of psychotic persons who are severely disorganized and seemingly abandoned to the elements and street predators. But it is also true that many psychotic persons on the streets are something less than disorganized and prefer to sit alone at drop-in centers rather than attend community support programs or activities where they will be forced to interact with others. The socialization level that they seek is more like parallel play than interaction, and it can be achieved by mere physical co-presence with others.

> From middle to late morning, four of five days in any week, Diane and Linda sat next to each other near a front window in the lobby of a public library for several years. Despite this daily physical proximity, they were seldom observed speaking to each other. Both suffered from schizophrenia and neither would consent to treatment. Diane, the older and more educated of the two, typically wore a grimy blue stocking cap pulled down to cover up missing eyebrows. She chanted frequently and aimlessly into the air space above Linda's head. In the afternoons, she left her spot to indulge what was perhaps the last vestige of her previous social class: she played shuffle-board with passers-by in a nearby park. Linda seldom offered eye contact or sensible speech to anyone. After years of coaxing and cajoling, one library staff member formed a relationship with Linda that resembled that of animal trainer to seal. Linda walked up to say good morning to the woman in exchange for a cigarette that she took back to her seat next to Diane and smoked.

One cannot glibly dismiss the thesis that these two women preferred such a lifestyle to any that effective mental health treatment might have provided for them. Many such persons have already experienced and rejected trials of hospitalization, anti-psychotic drugs, supportive housing, and aftercare treatment. The street practitioner is advised to first take a stance of tolerance toward such people and shift to a treatment stance only in gradual and careful approximations. These people are usually reluctant to acknowledge any dissatisfactions with their street lifestyles.

Grunberg and Eagle (1990) ventured that a subsample of their shelterized residents who never left the confines of the Fort Washington Shelter were content there because they had mastered that environment better than any previous one of their experience. These are the secondary gains referred to by Ungerleider et al. (1992). The idea that positive self-esteem and identity can be derived from creating a safe niche for oneself within a wretched and dangerous environment cannot be overlooked.

> Mark was a well-spoken black male in his forties who moved back and forth among various shelters and camp sites during a period of years. He frequently became embroiled in verbal altercations with site staff and other street people due to a haughty, imperious manner. Whenever he was beaten up or robbed or otherwise victimized—usually at the hands of his acquaintances rather than those of strangers—Mark would seek out "my psychologist" within the next day or two. The psychologist would then serve as a captive audience to whom Mark would recount (in exquisite and self-righteous detail) his latest episode of having been outnumbered and preyed upon.
>
> What underlay this pattern? Mark described his living on the streets as an extended pilgrimage for purposes which he preferred to keep to himself. At various times, he alluded to a bitter divorce, DWIs, and a brief trial on the anti-psychotic drug halperidol. His ready response to every empathic statement uttered by the psychologist was to deflect it by saying, "I don't mind *that* so much as . . ." He would then trail off into a cynically humorous perspective on the incident, after which he would slap the psychologist on the shoulder and laugh as he departed.

Most practitioners would view such a recurrent script of help-rejecting complaints as a manifestation of personality disorder. In street work, it is better to frame it as a manifestation of personal pride. By being willing to acquiesce to the role of Mark's "foil," the psychologist accomplished something akin to supportive psychotherapy, which is preferable to dismissing the man as intractable and untreatable. Nothing beyond this scripted alliance was ever achieved with Mark, but he did refer several mentally impaired persons to the psychologist. Mark once explained such referrals as reciprocation for the free counseling sessions described above, "even though none of 'em ever did me any good!" The fact that he felt a need to reciprocate at all signals some value of the sessions to him. Perhaps such reciprocation helped him to maintain his denial/pride in functioning as an outreach arm of his psychologist as often as he was a recipient of treatment sessions.

PRACTITIONER-OF-LAST-RESORT

Just as people who experience homelessness are changed by the process of adapting to it, so too must mental health practitioners change their response styles to accommodate homeless persons. Such adjustments are critical when working with people who are encountered in the latter two stages of homelessness.

They are less important when working with those in the first stage. The Alarm Stage person is receptive to the practitioner's input and willing to do the foot work, the paper work, and the waiting work necessary to take advantage of available resources. A battered woman who has left her abuser for the first time is a good example. Psychotic persons in this stage are willing to try new medications, new placements, and so on. The more positive expectations of people in this stage are dramatized by the privileged treatment offered to them by one San Diego shelter (Dahl, 1992). Newly homeless persons at "Father Joe's Country Club" are given manicures, swordfish for dinner, and comfortable sleeping quarters, while the long-term homeless people at this shelter receive the more traditional bowl of soup and a cot.

But while many persons met in the first stage can provide a positive intervention experience for the practitioner, they are also likely to benefit from traditional office culture practices. It is recommended that the street practitioner link these persons up with traditional service providers whenever possible so as to be free for the more numerous and difficult people who are encountered in the second and third stages of homelessness. Susser, Goldfinger, and White (1990) have advocated a similar position, "We believe that the emphasis . . . for the homeless must be on accommodating our techniques to the needs of people who refuse to be treated elsewhere, rather than on selecting those who are easier to work with and who, therefore, may be able to make use of other mental health agencies. The outreach clinician then becomes the 'clinician of last resort' rather than a substitute for other accessible resources" (p. 466). Practitioner-of-last-resort is an apt label for one who practices amidst the street culture. Such a label connotes that there are serious obstacles inherent in the work. It also confers license to change standard methods in order to address those obstacles.

Before examining various "last resort" methods in some detail, it is important to note that they do not call for any new theoretical approaches to abnormal behavior. A wide range of approaches already exists, and the pragmatic practitioner who can draw from all of them will have the best possible preparation for street work. Thus, biologic models are applicable to psychotic and otherwise seriously impaired persons and for those whose physical health problems complicate mental health status. Psychoanalytic formulations are relevant for understanding the complexities of resistance and transference that are encountered among street people, as well as the varied countertransference reactions that street persons evoke from practitioners. Paradoxical techniques offer innovative ways to approach the problems of resistance and noncompliance. Cognitive-behavioral concepts such as learned helplessness and locus of control help to explain the demoralization and depression that are virulent among these people (Goodman, Saxe, & Harvey, 1991). Many of the lowest functioning individuals require the quasi-parental methods associated with case management (Swayze, 1992).

Each of the above perspectives will be altered to some degree by the contextual variable of street culture. Even so, it is not one's theoretical perspective that requires adjustment so much as a basic assumption about the nature of the working alliance in mental health work. That basic assumption is the pretext of an empowered, sympathetic expert delivering service to a needy, suffering recipient. The terms "patient," "client," and "case," reverberate this assumption. Their emphases may vary, but each of these terms connotes a reciprocal role relationship wherein each of the two parties to an intervention share certain perceptions, expectations, and a limited range of interaction patterns in concert with the other. One such expectation is that the interaction take place at the recipient's behest but on the provider's territory.

No such assumptions or implications may be taken for granted in street work. Often their opposites are true: outreach interventions typically begin at the expert's behest but in the recipient's territory rather than vice versa. As a semantic concession to these changed assumptions, the terms "patient," "client," "case," and "consumer" have been dispensed with in the present work. The words "person," "individual," and "people" will be used instead. These are less presumptuous, more liberating descriptors that are consistent with the ecologist-practitioner model advocated here. It is better when entering a new culture to refrain from the use of preassigned roles and identities. Instead, observe what roles and identities arise from the culture itself. In addition, one mental set of the ecologist-practitioner is to empower the person for whom the intervention is intended rather than treat that person as a passive recipient (Toro et al., 1991). To achieve this, it is necessary to use a collaborative style and strive to understand homelessness through the eyes of those who live it. A generic referent like "person" discourages stigmatization and encourages flexible boundaries.

The syntactic convention whereby the adjective "homeless" is transformed into a noun is another practice that is avoided here. The use of "homeless," "schizophrenic," and "alcoholic" as nouns tends to center a person's identity in the malady that afflicts him or her. Given the pervasive impacts of schizophrenia and homelessness upon their victims, one can argue that such conventions are not entirely inappropriate. Nevertheless, they are in no way empowering of a person and they focus attention upon a person's deficits. Minkoff (1987) has taken a similar position and suggested that homogeneous attitudes and treatment plans are discouraged by keeping the person and the malady separate. Thus, "homeless person" and "homeless people" is used in this book, acknowledging the tiresome repetition that this entails.

There are many parallels between the ecologist-practitioner model and the client-centered psychotherapy approach associated with Carl Rogers and humanistic psychology. However, the ecologist-practitioner model endorses the philosophical tenets and underpinnings of Rogers' work much more than it does his nondirective methods. A practitioner-of-last-resort must always remain free to step out of an empowering role and into a power-wielding one because he or she works among psychotic persons who may lack or lose behavioral controls. Occasionally, this occurs with nonpsychotic persons as well.

Samuel was a strapping, fifty-three-year-old white male from Memphis whose right hand had been amputated at the wrist. He prevailed upon a psychologist to help him resolve problems with his partner. As his history unfolded over several contacts at a drop-in center, this presenting problem proved to be only the most recent example in a life pattern of svengali-style relationships with younger men. He saw himself as having a mission to rescue young gay men from prostitution and cruising, and he was good at it. However, in time he would grow dependent on the younger man's dependence upon him; when his partner grew stronger and sought equal status or (more commonly) attempted to leave him, Samuel would become enraged and threaten violence. On one occasion he had held such a partner at gunpoint to prevent him from leaving. The weapon had been shot out of his hands by a Memphis SWAT team. He lost his hand in this incident and subsequently spent several years in a forensic hospital. Upon discharge, he departed the Memphis area because of his notoriety there and drifted north.

One day he appeared at the drop-in center in an agitated and vigilant state. He did not approach the psychologist; as the psychologist approached Samuel he was observed to be muttering angrily to himself about the partner. Samuel's controls were tenuous and he grumbled that he would "mete some justice" when he met up with the partner at the shelter that night. The psychologist suggested that they walk to the emergency room to get him calmed down. Samuel declined and immediately walked away from him.

The psychologist arranged for back-up support with the drop-in staff before returning to insist to Samuel that they go to the emergency room

> immediately for possible admission to the hospital. Samuel glared back at first, but then he dropped his head slowly and nodded. When he looked up again, he insisted upon time to arrange for the safe transfer of his things from the shelter to a storage locker at the Greyhound depot so that these wouldn't be lost or stolen in case he was hospitalized. The psychologist gave him two hours to do so, during which time Samuel was to call the drop-in after an hour and give a progress report. Samuel was told that if he did not call in after an hour or meet the psychologist at the emergency room in two hours, then the psychologist would have the police issue an "all points bulletin" on him. Samuel's jaw tightened as he listened to this threat, but ultimately he agreed to the conditions, made the call, and appeared at the emergency room on time. He was admitted to the hospital for a week. After discharge, the relationship with the psychologist was strained. They met less frequently, for shorter periods of time, and to less depth. Samuel spoke little about his partner problems except to say that they were "alright, I guess."

Prior to the hospitalization, all of the contacts had occurred at Samuel's behest in terms of timing, length, and level of privacy requested (back room privacy versus a table on the fringe of the drop-in center's socializing area). The psychologist had applied his skills to the issue that Samuel wanted to focus on. After it was determined in the first visit that Samuel's partners were neither underage nor runaways, the psychologist declined to advise or direct Samuel's behavior in any direction. Clearly the shift to "strong-arming" Samuel's voluntary hospitalization had lasting negative effect on their relationship, but if there is a threat of physical violence toward self or others, relationship maintenance becomes a secondary concern.

Still, such interventions are the exception rather than the rule in street work. In office culture work, the practitioner seldom leaves the authority role with the person who is receiving treatment. In street work, the practitioner steps into the authority role as little as possible. Such a reversal is made necessary by the many and varied resistances of these people in the early stages of contact. One reason that members of the clergy enjoy a better reception among street people than do professionals is because of their readiness to step out of role and adopt more of a peer perspective, in other words, "there but for the grace of God go I." Few of them proselytize on the streets (and those who do are usually ignored or scorned by the street culture). Yet many clergy report that they are eventually sought out for spiritual guidance by street persons who had initially met them in some less formal context.

Thus one's credibility as a street practitioner may hinge on establishing one's credibility as a person first, or "there but for good family background, socioeconomic circumstance, and few psychosocial stressors go I." The practitioner projects credibility as he or she sees and affirms the personal pride that lies beneath resistances and other noncompliant behaviors. In Samuel's case, this pride was stroked by allowing him time to secure his possessions before hospitalization. This concession to his pride was made at an expense of two hour's anxiety to the psychologist who was involved. At times, this level of anxiety is not so readily allayed.

Rona was a gaunt, white female who claimed to be thirty-two but looked much older. She said that she was a carnival worker who had been inadvertently left behind after a stopover. With several fits-and-starts of irritation, she made cryptic mention of a failed marriage, a lost farm, and two "nuthouse" admissions for suicide attempts that had occurred in the months after she had been gang-raped and thrown off of a boxcar by a "bunch of thieves." The fate of the man she had been traveling with was never known but "probably a lot worse."

All these events had occurred more than a decade prior to the contact, and she could not or would not account for the intervening years. What she'd come to the psychologist for was help with committing suicide because she reckoned a psychologist would have a lot of experience with suicide. She wanted to know what the best suicide method was for someone who wanted to make it look like natural causes.

At first, the psychologist made the standard assumption that the request constituted a "cry for help," however muted. He set about inquiring as to "why now?" But Rona would have none of that. As the questions moved beyond her specific request, Rona bristled, stomped her foot once on the ground, said, "You don't need to know all that cock 'n bull. Are you going to answer my question or not?" As an afterthought, she added that she didn't care about pain. She reckoned that she could handle that as long as it looked like natural causes. When the psychologist still hesitated, she threw up her hands in disgust and moaned, "You just don't know your shit now, do you?"

Thirteen years earlier she had taken out a $5000 life insurance policy on herself, and she had named the granddaughter of a now-deceased aunt as beneficiary. She had done this to repay the kind words that the aunt had said of her at a "nuthouse" (commitment?) hearing after one of her suicide attempts. Rona had had no contact with this beneficiary since but had kept abreast of her whereabouts. Despite her "carny" lifestyle, she had never missed a premium payment, but she was frustrated to have recently learned from the insurance company that her death benefit would be forfeited in the event that she committed suicide. In fact, in addition to wanting advice as to a suicide method, she wanted the psychologist to write down "in a certified way" that she was of sound mind and not from a nuthouse so she could not possibly be suspected of suicide.

She continued to press for a yes-or-no answer until the psychologist finally answered in the negative. She left, scowling about the waste of her time and was not encountered on the streets again.

American society has just concluded an era of conspicuous consumption, an era in which the acquisition and multiplication of speedy wealth was linked with goodness. Street persons have amassed little wealth or have lost what they had amassed previously. Given the harsh publicness of their not measuring up in material ways to mainstream society or to the generations of their families that preceded them, many homeless persons are led to consider suicide.

Should this request still have been interpreted as an unconscious "cry for help" that merits a "last resort" intervention from the psychologist? Psychiatrists who prescribe anti-depressant medications to homeless persons can seldom be certain whether they are treating target symptoms of depression—low energy, sleep disturbance, anhedonia, helplessness/hopelessness, paranoid thinking—or naturally occurring adaptations to living on the streets. The unique challenge of street work is that one must interpret "clinical" data through the prism of a culture that is both very similar to and very different from one's own. As Koegel (1992) observed, the weighting of cultural factors in mental health interventions is much easier when the cultural differences in question are salient, for example, racial or ethnic versus socioeconomic.

It is heartening for the practitioner when people with difficult first contacts return months later with a positive recollection of that first encounter. Usually, casual observations of the practitioner in street sites, or trusted references from other people, or hearsay among the street culture itself paves the way for these surprise return visits.

CHAPTER 2

The New Homelessness

Bachrach (1992) defined modern day homelessness as an absence of stable housing in a context of disaffiliation from social supports and resources that are normally available through the mainstream culture. The ecological perspective of street work takes account of two additional facets of homelessness. First, homelessness occurs not in a vacuum but against the backdrop of a street culture with its own resources and supports, however limited these may be. Second, there are individual differences among homeless persons in the extent to which each affiliates and identifies with street culture.

For these and other reasons, the street practitioner acquires a different familiarity with homelessness than that of most scholars and researchers. Researchers have typically used methods that involve one or several lengthy and formal contacts with numerous members of a cross-section of homeless people. These approaches have yielded an informative, aerial perspective on the forest of the homelessness problem that is not otherwise available to practitioners who work beneath the canopy.

HISTORY AND DEMOGRAPHICS

Homelessness is no recent phenomenon in the United States. During this century alone, there have been several distinct sociological waves of homelessness. Migrant workers who follow the harvests have always been a key source of labor for the food-producing sector of the economy. Their ranks have been filled by Latin Americans, Hispanics, and other immigrant groups. The psychological stressors associated with homelessness among these groups are mitigated by the preservation of nuclear and extended family units during their migrations. Such groups demonstrate that a stable support system can persist without geographical stability.

During the first half of this century, much of this migratory labor was performed by white males. These men indulged their penchants for solitude and their disdain for society by hopping freight trains for a life on the road. This wave of homelessness grew large and varied enough to spawn its own social strata. Terms like "hobo," "tramp," and "bum" took on distinct status meanings (Snow & Anderson, 1987). At the top of the ladder were the hoboes, migratory workers whose lifestyles and exploits have sometimes been romanticized. An outdoor hobo convention is held annually in rural Iowa to celebrate this subculture and to preserve some of its folklore. In their heyday, hoboes looked down scornfully upon their other homeless brethren, the tramps (migratory nonworkers) and the bums (nonmigratory nonworkers). Although many hoboes preferred a solitary life, the evolution of distinctive customs, strata distinctions, and oral mythology provided them with some measure of group membership and identity whether or not they chose to camp with others of their ilk. They could rely upon a support group of the road, an elusive but ever-present network of assistance for when times got rough. In-group status was reinforced by spurning the tramps and bums as inferiors, that is, elevation of the in-group through consensual disparagement of out-groups.

Estimates as to the number of homeless people produced by the Great Depression range between 200,000 and 1.5 million (Rossi, 1990). There were sizable components of both local and transient homeless persons in this wave, and the former generally fared better than the latter. After showing proof of city or state residence, a local would either be permitted to reside in an urban shantytown ("Hooverville") or assigned to one of many dormitory rooms that local authorities partitioned out of abandoned warehouses. Many homeless persons doubled and tripled up with their extended families. This wave of homelessness is best conjured in visual images of grainy black-and-white photographs or filmstrips of grim faces hunkered down in large overcoats while vending apples from makeshift street corner stands. Many transients found their way to rural work camps operated by the alphabet agencies of the federal government during the New Deal era. The rural component is epitomized by the Dust Bowl Okies of John Steinbeck's *The Grapes of Wrath.* These were homeless families who traveled west seeking the promised land of California. They traveled as intact social units with all of their possessions lashed to their Model Ts. Again, the preservation of family ties and other social supports and networks among these people served to mitigate the stressors associated with poverty, unemployment, and residential instability.

In the 1950s and 1960s, the prototypical homeless person in the United States was the skid row alcoholic. He was generally a middle-aged white male, and groups of such men were often portrayed as huddling around oil drum fires in alleyways, speaking little or not at all to each other as they tried to keep the circulation going in their rag-wrapped hands. Their beverage of choice was a "fortified" (i.e., high alcohol content) wine that could be stashed in an overcoat pocket and drunk from the bottle with a brown bag twisted around it. These men slept in boarding house rooms or single-room-occupancy (SRO) hotels when they did not pass out elsewhere. Some of them subsisted on modest pensions. Others eked out a way of life on the spot labor market that would pay cash enough for a day's work to keep one supplied with alcohol and minimal provisions for the night. Hard times or flashes of inspiration would sometimes drive a man to the gospel mission or soup kitchen where some clergyman or altruist would direct him to a place where he could "take the cure." These men were alienated from family and loved ones. Police and public officials sighed over many of their corpses before delivering them to medical school laboratories where they would serve as cadavers.

A distinct skid row subculture evolved to support these men with a set of informal institutions: flophouses, pawn shops, "greasy spoon" restaurants, as well as bars and liquor stores. Moral judgments about alcoholism prevailed over medical ones in the days before the disease concept of alcoholism took hold. These men did not organize nor raise voices of protest to their stigmatization. They did not dispute the "loser" label assigned to them by the mainstream culture, but its impact was mollified somewhat by a code of norms that evolved within the confines of their institutions and created status differentiations among them (Rooney, 1976). Thus, on skid row the statuses associated with the words "drunk" and "alcoholic" were quite different (Wallace, 1968). While both drunk and alcoholic drank frequently and to excess, the drunk may or may not have been an alcoholic. The drunk was understood (or misunderstood) to be one who drank in order to conform to a group norm that viewed drinking as a celebratory act rather than an addictive necessity. The drunk would typically drink as a member of a "bottle gang" rather than alone, and bottle gangs abided by a code of sharing. Members of the group would pool the yields of their panhandling and petty crime, their liquor, their identities. A sense of belongingness and in-group insulation from the mainstream culture afforded the skid row drunk some measure of stability and affiliation. By contrast, the alcoholic was a solitary drinker whose closest relationship was with his alcohol. He interacted little with others and did not experience group identity or the ego insulation that in-groups provide. His status in the skid row subculture was lower than that of the drunk.

This portrait of the skid row culture of the 1950s reflects sources like Bogue (1963) who conducted a sociological study of skid row

Chicago in 1955. Bogue's work was followed by parallel portraits depicting skid row Philadelphia (Blumberg, Shipley, & Shandler, 1973) and the Bowery of New York (Bahr & Caplow, 1974). The only hopeful note sounded by these works was the prognosis that skid row as a social institution appeared to be in an advanced stage of decline in the 1970s. In fact, Lee (1980) reported a 50 percent decline in the skid row populations of 41 U.S. cities between 1950 and 1970. Prevailing academic wisdom held that this decline reflected changing economic trends (Rossi, 1990). That is, the mechanization and automization of many unskilled jobs caused spot labor markets to evaporate and, in time, the central city skid rows that supplied that labor force diminished also.

The precipitous rise of homelessness in the 1980s was a different sociological phenomenon than the other waves of homelessness just described. Rossi (1990) has called the affected people "The New Homeless." No prototypical image or generalizations fit them as well as the other portraits above fit previous waves of U.S. homelessness. Instead, the New Homelessness must be viewed as a heterogenous stratum of society. In-group cohesion, insulation, and identity processes have evolved slowly and less completely among these people because of their great numbers and diversity.

It is a disturbing paradox that the numbers of the New Homelessness have approached those of the Great Depression during a decade of sustained economic growth. The incidence and prevalence of homelessness is ever-changing, and its multidimensional aspects sustain an ongoing controversy as to how homeless persons are to be counted (Burnam & Koegel, 1988; Fischer & Breakey, 1991; Rossi, 1989; Wallace, 1968). Should there be a durational requirement that a person must meet to qualify as homeless? Does one count only those who sleep outdoors in camps, beneath bridges, over sidewalk grates, and so on, or include those who sleep in shelters at night? Does one count only those who lack a permanent address or include the large number who are episodically homeless? What about those whose housing is so marginal that they live at chronic risk of becoming homeless?

With operational definitions of homelessness changing from study-to-study and writer-to-writer, it is no surprise that prevalence estimates of homeless individuals vary also. At times, it appears that this methodological uncertainty has been exploited to serve varying political ends. For example, the lowest recent estimate of numbers of homeless individuals in the United States is 300,000 by HUD and the highest, 1.5 to 3 million by the National Coalition for the Homeless.

Rossi (1990) has endorsed a 1987 prevalence estimate of U.S. homelessness at 500,000 individuals as reported by the Urban Institute (Burt & Cohen, 1988). Since experts from opposite ends of the political spectrum (Foscarinis, 1991; Kondratas, 1991) have continued to endorse this number, and because the federal government has not issued an official count of homeless persons since 1984 (Bachrach, 1992), the Urban Institute number will be adopted here as valid for discussion purposes. Such an estimate means that in 1987, the number of homeless individuals in the United States approached the populations of the states of Vermont and Alaska and exceeded the population of Wyoming (U.S. Bureau of the Census, 1992). Moreover, the annual growth rate of homelessness has been estimated by the federal government to fall between 10 and 38 percent (U.S. General Accounting Office, 1985 and 1988, as cited by Rossi, 1990). If one adopts the 25 percent midpoint of this range (which also corresponds to the growth rate of homelessness projected by Reyes and Waxman in 1989) and applies it in compounded fashion to the six years between 1987 and 1993, one arrives at a current estimate of 1.02 million homeless persons. Such growth would mean that the numbers of the New Homelessness now approach the current population of Idaho and exceed the populations of not only Wyoming, Vermont, and Alaska, but also Rhode Island, North Dakota, South Dakota, Delaware, and Montana.

Another dimension of the increasing numbers of homeless persons (and one that is grounded in actual counts) is the increase in shelter beds over the past decade. During the early 1980s, the number of public shelter beds in New York City doubled from 3,000 to 6,000 (Bach & Steinhagen, 1987; Struening, 1987); by 1991, that shelter system was serving 24,000 people a day (Bearak, 1991). During the same time period, Minneapolis witnessed a 300 percent increase in shelter usage (Bauerlein & Farley, 1990).

After its size, the most confounding aspect of the New Homelessness is its heterogeneity. This is conveyed well by Rossi's 1985–86 survey of homeless people in Chicago (Rossi, 1989, 1990). Rossi's work was conducted 30 years after Bogue's original study of skid row Chicago, thus making a comparison of homelessness in the 1950s and the 1980s possible. In addition, Rossi collected control group data that enabled him to compare his mid-1980s sample of homeless persons to domiciled poor persons from the same city and time period.

Compared to their 1958 counterparts, New Homeless Chicagoans are heavily over-represented by minorities, women, and families. The number with pensioner status has decreased dramatically: whereas Bogue's 1958 subjects had a median age of 50, Rossi found a median age of 37 for his sample. He further calculated that this median age had been declining at a rate of six months per year during the previous decade. If this trend has continued, the median age of homeless individuals is approaching the early thirties at the time of this writing. Another contrast between the 1958 and 1985 samples is in their respective levels of employment. Twenty-eight percent of Bogue's group were employed on a full-time basis compared to a mere 3 percent of Rossi's sample. More than half of Bogue's subjects were employed full or part-time during any given week whereas only 39 percent of Rossi's respondents had worked at all during the previous month. The homeless Chicagoans of 1985 did not show any significant educational deficiencies when compared to 1985 Chicagoans as a whole.

The degree of social alienation associated with homelessness has mental health implications. As discussed previously, other waves of homelessness in this century have permitted the maintenance of the family unit (the Dust Bowl Okies; migrant farm workers) or led to the formation of in-groups and subcultures (the hobo camp; skid row bottle gangs). Even the vast numbers of homeless people created by the Great Depression found solace and solidarity in the fact that the rest of the country was suffering along with them. Such a state of affairs did not exist during the 1980s.

Rossi found modern day homeless Chicagoans to be an alienated and isolated lot as conveyed by a number of social indices. Ninety-two to 95 percent were not married at a time when the nonmarried rate among Chicagoans as a whole was 57 percent. The proportion of homeless persons who had had no contact with their biological families (parents) or orientation families (marriage) during the previous year was 33 percent. Fifty-two percent of the homeless Chicagoans claimed to have no good friends, and 30 to 40 percent could name no one who could provide them with help during a major crisis. One out of four reported no contact with their families during the previous year and claimed to have no good friends. Rossi (1989) concluded "whatever the process, the outcome is that many homeless are completely isolated, and most have only very superficial ties to others" (p. 177). This isolation could not be explained as a function of transiency since 89 percent of Rossi's homeless persons had lived continuously in Chicago for more than a year. Such a finding is counter to prevailing stereotypes of homeless people as "transients." It also indicates that disaffiliation occurs despite temporal and spatial opportunities to maintain established ties.

Rossi's 1985–86 sample was comparable to Bogue's 1958 sample on several indices. Twenty percent of both samples reported having serious criminal records. The prevalence of chemical dependency in Rossi's sample was equivalent to Bogue's in that one out of three homeless individuals could be classified as drug or alcohol dependent. The 1985–86 cohort showed fewer of the debilitating medical conditions that were common among Bogue's sample. This difference can be attributed in part to the relative youth of Rossi's homeless sample and to significant advances that have taken place in the health sciences and technologies. Such a change is hardly cause for optimism, however. One-fourth to one-third of Rossi's sample reported chronic medical ailments. Physical health problems induced by street life include peripheral vascular disease, infectious and parasitic diseases, respiratory diseases, and skin and joint problems (Breakey, 1992). As of 1991, mortality rates for homeless individuals were reported to be three times greater than those of the general population across all age groups (Williams, 1992). This same report gauged the life expectancy of homeless people to be 20 years lower than that of the general population.

Mental impairments are more prevalent in the New Homelessness than was true in 1958. Rossi administered symptom scales to his homeless subjects and found evidence of clinical depression or psychotic thinking in 20 to 30 percent of them. Moreover, Rossi's homeless group proved to be significantly more impaired on these scales than was his control group of domiciled poor persons. Other investigators report that histories of prior psychiatric hospitalization are admitted to by 25 to 40 percent of samples of homeless persons (Dennis, Buckner, Lipton, & Levine, 1991). Many people have coexisting problems of mental impairment and chemical dependency, the so-called "dual diagnosis" population (Drake, Osher, & Wallach, 1991). This was a rare phenomenon 30 years ago, but now at least 10 to 20 percent of homeless persons present with it (Tessler & Dennis, 1989). Farr, Koegel, and Burnam (1986) reported that 46 percent of their mentally impaired homeless persons from Los Angeles had problems with alcohol or drugs.

When a broad range of studies employing a broad range of impairment indices are taken as a group, the extent of mental impairments among people of the New Homelessness is usually condensed to a prevalence rate of one in three (Bachrach, 1992). In contrast, Bogue "estimated" that 9 percent of his Chicago skid row sample were severely disturbed and another 11 percent showed milder signs of mental impairment. This greater prevalence of mental impairment in the New Homelessness has been its most publicized aspect (Koegel & Burnam, 1992; Rossi; 1990, Snow, Baker, Anderson, & Martin, 1986). The bizarre and pitiable behaviors of psychotic persons provide good video copy and attract more attention than drab, mundane poverty. Thus, mentally impaired persons are good theater at a time and place in which the mainstream culture derives much of its information from television. A less apparent reason for media exaggeration of prevalence is the fact that many psychotic persons are too socially or cognitively alienated to be self-conscious about their selection as part of a media story. Their cooperation for a videotaped interview can be purchased for a package of cigarettes or less. Homeless persons who are not so impaired often shun media attention unless it promises a more significant advantage. While journalists may view their work as consciousness-raising, many street people view it as a tool of stigmatization. The net effect is that many of the non- and less-impaired persons among the street culture avoid the media spotlight while those who are more apathetic and disorganized do not oppose it. To be fair, the media has rightfully called attention to the plight of the most impaired segment of street culture and moved many to question the issues and policies surrounding public sector psychiatric care. Nevertheless, it has done so at expense to consciousness-raising among the mainstream culture as to the more fundamental dynamics of the New Homelessness that affect mentally impaired and non-impaired alike.

One in three homeless persons can be diagnosed with a mental impairment (Rossi, 1990). This is three times more prevalent than was true 30 years ago. Why the increased prevalence? To some extent, the increase reflects changes in the diagnostic nomenclature itself. The entries in DSM I and II were fewer in number and scope than those of DSM IV. Controversial categories like personality disorder are now assigned more liberally, and studies have shown prevalence rates of personality disorder ranging from 21 percent (Bassuk, Rubin, & Lauriat, 1984) to 42 percent (Breakey et al., 1989) among samples of street persons. Another reason is that while societal taboos against acknowledging such impairments exist today, these taboos are not as pervasive nor as extreme as they were during the days of Bogue's study. As recently as the 1950s, some communities still offered the equivalent of bounty payments to anyone whose actions led to the hospital commitment of a mentally impaired person. Bogue believed that many of the mentally impaired whom he encountered were AWOL from institutions. Certainly there was more cause to conceal mental impairment in the 1950s than in the 1980s.

Another critical factor in the increased prevalence of mental impairments is the positive correlation between poverty and mental impairment (Dohrenwend & Dohrenwend, 1969). Rossi's data showed the relative poverty of the New Homelessness to be greater than that of Bogue's sample, "Correcting for the intervening inflation, the current average annual income of the Chicago homeless is equivalent to only $383 in 1958 dollars, less than one third of the actual 1958 median. Thus, *the new homeless suffer a much more profound degree of economic destitution,* often surviving on 40 percent or less of a poverty-level income" (italics by Rossi, 1990, p. 957).

The question remains to what extent this higher prevalence is primarily a cause or an effect of homelessness. One side of such a debate is the social selection position that maintains that mental impairments, chemical dependency, medical conditions, and so on, are pathways to homelessness. From this microcosmic vantage point, an individual's earning capacity is limited or disrupted by disability, thus necessitating a lifestyle drift down to the lower social classes and reliance upon "safety net" resources that were designed to provide for subsistence living only. Wright and Weber (1987) estimated poor physical health to be a causative factor in one out of eight incidences of homelessness. They further reported that a third of the persons served by the Robert Wood Johnson Health Care for the Homeless Project identified alcohol and drug abuse as the single most important factor in their becoming homeless.

On the other side of the spectrum are proponents of social causation models, which represent more macrocosmic viewpoints (Lorion & Felner, 1986). Such scholars argue that it is the stressors that cause homelessness followed by the stressors that accompany homelessness which create and account for the high prevalence of mental impairments among homeless persons.

Put succinctly, social selection models emphasize homelessness as an effect of mental impairment while social causation models view homelessness as a cause of mental impairment. Lorion and Felner (1986) offer a literature review of the current status of this debate. Not surprisingly, most authorities view the relationship between homelessness and mental impairment as a complex interplay of social selection and social causation forces. That is, homelessness and mental impairment interact upon and within the individual in ways that defy reduction to simple cause-and-effect notions.

Although it may seem unnecessary to belabor this beyond its academic aspects, the chicken-egg question is also a psychodynamic theme for many homeless persons with whom the street practitioner comes into contact. Most homeless individuals do aspire to cause-and-effect reductionism as part of the process of moving through the stages of acculturation to street life. Therefore, the attribution(s) of a street person as to whether mental health problems were caused by homelessness or vice versa is a key theme for the practitioner to surface and appreciate, particularly in the early stages of outreach. It matters little whether these subjective beliefs match more objective realities, or whether the practitioner necessarily agrees with them. The practitioner who responds to a homeless person's premise of "normal-guy-who-got-chewed-up-and-spit-out-by-The-System" by inquiring as to a family history of mental impairment is challenging the person's social causation attributions with social selection ones of the practitioner's own. Such a turn in a first interview threatens the working alliance no matter how usual, customary, and reasonable that practitioner's inquiry might be. Many a street person who admits to having a psychological problem is also adamant in the belief that street life is the cause of the problem and not the effect. In early contacts, that individual may prefer that the conversation revolve around the external stressors of street life that created the mental health problem rather than upon inner, psychological pain. Empathy is the appropriate response from the practitioner.

Another distinct group of street persons are the chronically psychotic individuals. Most of these people show signs of schizophrenia or some variant of another psychotic disorder. The presentations of these people will steer the practitioner's thinking in the direction of social selection attributions. But few of them will ever admit to having a mental impairment in the present, and a large number will deny ever having had such an impairment in the past. The fallacy of such denials and the presence of severe symptoms and deficits will tempt the practitioner to discount such attributions outright as "lack of insight." However, suspending one's own attributions in order to indulge the psychotic person's denial is recommended in outreach. Again, empathy is the proper response, even if it is difficult to accomplish with persons who display disordered thought or (more commonly) "poverty of content" in their speech.

SOCIAL SELECTION PROCESSES

People with schizophrenia were typically committed to state mental hospitals during the first half of this century. For all of their dehumanizing evils, state institutions provided these people with low-demand environments to which they could adapt, albeit an adaptation which few others would aspire to. Cloistered confinement prevented social selection drifts of severely impaired persons into poverty and worse. It spared their families pain and the mainstream culture many inconveniences.

Was this not a better outcome than to allow them to be culled from the mainstream by predators, or to be shunned and crowded out to the barren margins because of inability to conform to the mainstream's direction and pace? Wistful looks back to the state hospital era are less rare now than they were during the past three decades. These are "lesser-of-evils" looks to be sure, but they have been elicited by the many psychotic people who are either directly encountered on the streets or are encountered indirectly via periodic segments of television news coverage. A number of these psychotic people do sleep in cardboard boxes, do dive into dumpsters for food, and do fall prey to predators.

Deinstitutionalization is commonly blamed. It began in the 1960s with the systematic discharge of long-term residents from state institutions to the community. This had been made possible by the discovery and development of psychoactive drugs in the 1950s. These drugs do not cure schizophrenia or bipolar disorder but continue to be the best available treatment for the positive symptoms of these conditions, that is, aberrant cognition, bizarre/dangerous behavior, and other such deviations from the norm. The removal or reduction of positive symptoms renders a person less frightening, less alienating, and more socially acceptable to family, significant others, and the mainstream culture as a whole. Thus these drugs made many seriously and persistently impaired persons passably acceptable for return to their home communities. Unfortunately, such drugs have little effect on negative symptoms, such as poverty of speech content, social withdrawal, apathy, and other behavioral deficits. The elimination of deviations does not compensate for the deficits. What was worse, years of institutionalization had not only failed to remedy negative symptoms/behavioral deficits but had also eroded what adaptive skills these people had possessed when first hospitalized. Many people experienced a return of positive symptoms/behavioral deviations once they discontinued their medications. Such noncompliance was (and continues to be) common among those who experience medical side effects. Noncompliance is also common among those who resent daily dosages as so many reminders of a condition for which they feel ashamed.

It was recognized at the outset of deinstitutionalization that these people would require ongoing social treatments and supports as well as medications if they were to make successful transitions from institutional to community living. The 1963 Community Mental Health Centers Act was passed by the federal government to facilitate the change in treatment philosophies. It provided both direct start-up funds and indirect financial incentives to support community-based mental health treatment. It also presaged a relaxation in federal disability requirements through which mentally impaired individuals would qualify for federal entitlement programs for the first time.

In response to these initiatives, the states collectively reduced the patient censuses of their centralized institutions from more than 550,000 in 1955 to 103,000 in 1992 (Bachrach, 1992). This five-fold reduction is all the more remarkable when one considers that it was accomplished over a period of steady population growth and no apparent decrease in the incidence of severe mental disorders. What is often overlooked in the rush to condemn deinstitutionalization and community mental health is that thousands of formerly institutionalized psychotic persons have been successfully discharged to the care of their families or to supportive residences over the past thirty years. Many have adapted to this change with a measure of success reflected only by the fact that they have been reintegrated into the mainstream culture and not been heard from again.

Interestingly, a majority of "first-institutionalized, then de-institutionalized" persons are in their fifties and sixties today. Psychotic individuals of this age are not frequently encountered on the streets; in this literal sense, then, the preoccupation of the academic and popular literature with linking deinstitutionalization and homelessness appears misplaced. However, deinstitutionalization has evolved into a catch-all term for a series of complex and interlocking forces. These forces have conspired to permit a large number of severely impaired people to drift down to the street culture.

The list begins with levels of government and their monies (Torrey, 1992). Passage of the Community Mental Health Centers Act (CMHC) effectively shifted the burden of fiscal and treatment responsibility for severely impaired persons from the states to the federal government. The heady beginnings of the community mental health movement followed on the heels of Erving Goffman's (1961) *Asylum,* Thomas Szasz' (1961) *The Myth of Mental Illness,* and Ken Kesey's (1962) *One Flew Over the Cuckoo's Nest.* These works reflected and shaped a culture-wide revulsion for large state institutions. It was in such an atmosphere that the federal government elected to bypass state authorities and award community mental health funds directly to citizen's boards of local communities.

Regrettably, many of these communities were disillusioned to find that deinstitutionalized psychotic persons were difficult to manage and unrewarding to treat as outpatients. CMHC resources were gradually shifted away from these intended beneficiaries and channeled to putative prevention programs which in some cases included outlays for swimming pools and tennis courts (Torrey, 1992). Many psychotic persons went unserved or underserved at CMHCs because practitioners preferred to work with less disturbed persons who were more like themselves. Even now, Torrey (1988, 1992) finds cause to upbraid the mental health professions for ongoing reluctance to treat severely impaired persons in favor of more lucrative work with those whom he has called the "worried well." Marcos (1990) observed that the worried well and the practitioners who served them evolved into a political constituency over the years, a constituency that influenced mental health policies and resource allocations in its own best interests. The needs of the severely impaired were poorly represented until the Alliance for the Mentally Ill coalesced much later.

As former patrons of the severely impaired, the various state authorities might well have applied valuable oversight and corrective action to these developments. Instead, the states moved to extricate themselves from fiscal and treatment responsibilities for severely impaired people. Money that was saved by closing state hospital beds was not earmarked for the newly discharged people now living in communities. They were perceived as the federal government's charges now, what with federal monies sponsoring most CMHC startups and mentally impaired persons' new eligibility for entitlement programs. With state monies channeled away from mental health and federal CMHC funds increasingly shifted to care of the "worried well," the supportive housing, aftercare services, and day treatment centers required to support psychotic people in their transitional adjustments went underfunded and underdeveloped. Moreover, as states' centralized responsibilities for these people dissolved, fragmentation and structural disorganization filled the vacuum left behind (Shore & Cohen, 1992). Bureaucratic obstacles and service coordination problems now made getting help a confusing prospect of delays and paperwork for psychotic persons, many of whom suffered from significant cognitive impairments to begin with. This development has since become the raison d'etre for the emergence of mental health case management as a subspecialty (Schutt & Garrett, 1992).

This benign neglect of the severely impaired gradually acquired philosophical and legal rationales to support it. The works of Szasz, R.D. Laing (1960), and others ushered in an anti-psychiatry era that supported psychological denial of mental impairment (Marcos, 1990). People would no longer be forced into mental health treatment as before, and commitment to a state hospital came to be viewed first and foremost as a potential infringement upon one's civil rights. Armat and Peele (1992) have offered a sardonic history of the expansion of civil liberties for the mentally impaired. Encouraged by some early successes of deinstitutionalization, legal advocates and sympathetic courts authored legislation that made it as difficult to get a mentally impaired person committed into a hospital as it had formerly been to get the person out of such a hospital. This legislation tightened civil statutes to the point that commitment to a hospital hinged almost entirely on the state's proving that a person was imminently dangerous to self or others. Because predicting dangerousness is not something that mental health practitioners have ever done in a reliable fashion (Monohan, 1981), it was a legal standard that proved eminently arguable and difficult to satisfy. Evidence of mental impairment per se was relegated to a secondary concern, except when it served a court's purposes that it be otherwise.

> Repeated assaults outside a homeless shelter were attributed to a white female of 53 named Maggie. She smiled sheepishly when confronted with these assaults, neither admitting to nor denying them. If anything, she glowed within the notoriety which this behavior brought to her, even as she refused to cooperate with a psychological evaluation or acknowledge the possibility that she might be mentally impaired. In one of the assaults, she had kicked a small child in the stomach after this child had accidentally stepped on her foot while running about in a supermarket. Maggie's explanation was that the child and its mother should have known the consequences would be "my terrible, swift sword" before stepping on her foot.
>
> Because of Maggie's lack of cooperation, no history or diagnosis could be established. A court commissioner elected to dismiss a petition for the civil commitment of Maggie before the proceedings were even begun because no definitive DSM III-R Axis I diagnosis had been offered. Such a diagnosis was required to satisfy "the prevailing interpretive stance as to meeting the statutory requirement that a substantial mental disorder be present."
>
> Two days after this dismissal, Maggie shoved a passer-by down a flight of escalator steps. As she explained later, he had "dared to step past *me!*" when she herself had chosen to stand still while riding the conveyance.

Torrey (1988) offered other anecdotes in which mentally impaired persons were legally but inappropriately released by courts or their agents. There are few who would argue against the objectives of minimizing hospitalizations and implementing less restrictive treatment alternatives whenever possible. However, these objectives have congealed over the years into a reflexive ideology which acts as a distractor variable in treatment decisions (Kuhlman, 1992). Adherents to this ideology include advocacy and consumer groups, CMHC authorities and supporters, civil libertarians, and even political conservatives (who deplore the fiscal outlays associated with hospital treatment). An ironic achievement of the civil liberties forces is that some states have enacted laws which expand a psychotic person's right to refuse medication even after that person has been involuntarily committed (Armat & Peele, 1992). In effect, the treatment innovation which made the expansion of civil liberties to mentally impaired persons possible can now be withheld from those persons as an exercise of those very liberties. Such practices have given rise to the cynical refrain that severely impaired people have been left on the streets to "die with their rights on."

A fact which lurks behind this ideology is that there are 450,000 fewer psychiatric beds in the United States than there were thirty years ago (Torrey, 1988). The effects of this are also felt by those people who have voluntarily sought hospital care and become caught up in the revolving door syndrome. Public sector hospital admissions have become brief and oriented toward stabilizing a person or restarting/adjusting the person's medications. Because so many others are in competition for scarce hospital beds, rapid discharges are effected that do not always take account of follow-up care arrangements. Limited or poorly coordinated follow-up services then set the stage for another psychotic episode, which in turn necessitates another brief admission as the cycle repeats itself.

A related legacy of deinstitutionalization (and the one which befell Maggie after her escalator incident) is the laundering of mentally impaired persons through the criminal justice system. There they are subjected to over-crowding, jailhouse ethics and mores, and maladaptive behavior models such as seldom existed in the mental institutions of the 1940s and 1950s.

> A maximum security forensic psychiatric ward received a most unusual admission for such a danger-laden setting: a quiet, compliant, nondangerous man with schizophrenia who showed no positive symptoms. He was so out of place on a maximum security ward that the circumstances of his commitment were investigated. It was learned that he had never shown dangerous behavior at any time in his recorded life, but he regularly urinated in the street when sober and in the presence of police. In the first few of these encounters, the officers had taken him to the local psychiatric hospital, thus initiating a series of "revolving door" admissions after which the man discontinued his medications. Finally, mental health officials blocked an additional effort by police to hospitalize him after yet another episode. The police were left with no recourse but to press criminal charges to get him off the streets as merchants demanded. After a brief stay in jail, he appeared in court under a charge of lewd and lascivious behavior. When the judge recognized his mental impairment, she ordered a competency-to-stand-trial evaluation, which in turn necessitated the man's commitment to a maximum security forensic ward.

The majority of those who are criminalized by such a process languish in jails (Fischer, 1992; Lamb & Grant, 1982, 1983). A recent survey of U.S. jails concluded that one in fourteen of all jail inmates suffers from a serious mental impairment (Torrey, 1993). Mental health treatment units attached to jails and prisons are now the rule rather than the exception in large cities and institutions. This state of affairs is succinctly captured by the title of a recent conference paper, "Service Stress in the Largest Mental Institution in the World: The Los Angeles County Jail."

So pervasive has been criminalization and reliance upon other supervised, congregate residences (e.g., skilled nursing homes) for the severely mentally impaired that one authority wrote of "transinstitutionalization" as a common outcome of deinstitutionalization (Talbott, 1981). Marcos (1990) took such a conclusion even further, "Unfortunately, the proportion of mentally ill individuals institutionalized in different settings has remained relatively constant in the past decades" (p. 7).

Advocates for community-based mental health have argued that such outcomes could have been minimized if adequate funding for community mental health programs had been forthcoming from the beginning. There is evidence to support this in the performance of some of the model community systems, for example, the Madison/Dane County, Wisconsin, program referenced earlier. Still, the previous story of the maximum security patient occurred in conjunction with such a system, and it was by no means an isolated incident.

The problems of CMHCs extend beyond ideological biases, limited resources, and the worried well. Many have shaped their programs to serve the literally deinstitutionalized person, that is, a docile, compliant, skill-deficient individual who readily defers to an assertive authority. Halfway houses, board-and-care homes, foster homes, and so on, often resemble institutions in their social milieus. They impose curfews, prohibitions against alcohol and the opposite sex in one's room, mandatory meetings, roommates not of one's own choosing, medication compliance as a condition of stay, and so on. Persons who do not conform to such rules or treatment plans may be deemed "inappropriate" for the setting. Others who are sensitive to stigma and role aspects of residing or congregating exclusively with people who are mentally impaired may withdraw from such settings. People who self-select out of traditional treatment systems are common in the street culture; they value the greater freedom and increased leeway to deny their impairments which the street culture offers.

The majority of the severely impaired persons of the New Homelessness are too young to have been alive when institutionalization was still in vogue. They came of age at a time of civil liberties expansion for the mentally impaired, and this is reflected in their presentations. A clinical prototype which fits many of these people is the "young adult chronic patient," an oxymoron first coined by Pepper, Kirschner, and Ryglewicz (1981). These are individuals in their late twenties to late thirties who have used or continue to use drugs and alcohol to an extent which camouflages their serious symptoms and adaptive deficits from themselves as well as others. The young adult chronic person is not distinguished by symptoms so much as by long-standing functional impairments and social deficits. Pepper et al. (1981) described them as "chronically young" and observed that they represent the first generation of mentally impaired persons who have not been protected by institutions. The problems that this group have in common are "acute vulnerability to stress, difficulty in making stable and supportive relationships, inability to get and keep something good in their lives, and repeated failures of judgment that can be seen as an inability or refusal to learn from their experiences" (p. 464). Lamb (1982) described them as stuck in Erik Eriksen's adolescent stage of identity versus role diffusion. In his view, they reject mental health treatment because it is tantamount to admitting failure, "Even today, many patients fail to take their psychotropic medications in order to avoid dysphoric feelings of depression and anxiety that result when they see reality too clearly; they prefer grandiosity and blurring of reality to a relative drug-induced normality" (p. 466). Bachrach (1982) emphasized the stress that young adult chronic persons induce upon their support systems, "Young adult chronic patients generally alienate family, friends, and other crisis resources, and the psychiatric service system must assume a major support role during the recurrent crises in their lives" (p. 192). According to Bachrach, paperwork and formal treatment settings may prove to be barriers to meeting the mental health needs of such persons. She recommended an understanding of street culture to those who would serve them.

A more current profile of young adult chronic persons from McLaughlin and Pepper (1990) is as follows: they are crisis-ridden, physiologically and psychologically oversensitive, pervasively immature. As a group, they have a lower incidence of schizophrenia and bipolar disorder than do older chronic groups, but personality disorders, violence, alcohol and drug use—these latter being implicated in many of their psychotic episodes—are more common. And yet despite their major deficits, they have normal aspirations.

Perhaps a better descriptor for this group is the "stably unstable." Bachrach (1982) observed that most of them would have been permanently hospitalized if they had lived 25 to 30 years ago. Just as automaton-like passivity was the product of excessive institutionalization in the 1950s, so is stable instability a product of insufficient institutionalization in the 1970s and 1980s. As such, many of the severely impaired persons of the street culture reflect shortcomings of the least restrictive treatment era rather than those of the deinstitutionalization era (in the literal sense of that term).

The American Psychiatric Association Task Force (Lamb et al., 1992) recommendation that treatment programs for homeless mentally impaired persons be tailored to an individual's unique needs seems to be a truism at first glance. Upon reflection, however, it can be seen as a subtle rebuke of community-based programs that continue to offer "one-size-fits-all" programs for illusory schizophrenic persons who have just emerged from years of institutionalization. Young adult chronic persons who do not fit into such programs have drifted (or been driven) away from them. Their encounters with mental health practitioners in the 1990s are increasingly likely to take place in street culture sites.

SOCIAL CAUSATION PROCESSES

The list of stressors and combinations of stressors that can lead to an incidence of homelessness is unlimited. Street practitioners soon learn that each individual's story of decline has unique twists and turns, and that some of these turns have therapeutic import. Precipitating stressors of homelessness include loss of employment, underemployment, catastrophic medical (or other) expenses, divorce and family dissolution, physical/sexual/chemical abuse by one's partner, termination of workers' compensation or disability benefits, and so on.

Poverty is a great leveler. Although there are different entry points for "hitting the skids," and different speeds and pathways down them, all converge on the same end point. A vast majority of homeless persons do not become homeless because of severe psychological deviations or deficits. Nor do they appear to be mentally impaired when encountered in the first, "denial" stage of acculturation. However, at some indeterminate point in the second or third stage of acculturation to the streets, the precipitating stressor(s) act in concert with the ongoing stressors of homelessness per se to produce mental impairment. Most commonly it is a form of depression, although Rossi (1989) saw the term "demoralization" as more descriptive. Goodman, Saxe, and Harvey (1991) wrote of homelessness as a psychological trauma in that it produces social disaffiliation and learned helplessness. "Among those who are not psychologically traumatized by becoming homeless, the ongoing condition of homelessness—living in shelters with such attendant stressors as the possible loss of safety, predictability, and control—may undermine and fatally erode coping capabilities" (Goodman et al., 1991, p. 1219). Winkleby and White (1992) found that homeless adults who claimed to have had no mental impairments when first made homeless were likely to develop such impairments over time.

Depressed, demoralized, and/or traumatized persons make up the largest component of a street practice. The practitioner must take stock of the social forces and stressors that act upon these people as part of life in a street culture. Such forces both underwrite homelessness and set obstacles that hinder a person's escape from it.

It bears repeating that the relative poverty of the New Homelessness is significantly greater than that which existed on skid row during the 1950s. Few of Bogue's subjects were so destitute as to be forced to sleep outdoors, a common phenomenon now. As previously observed, Rossi found that the annual incomes of modern day homeless Chicagoans amounted to less than one-third of the incomes of their 1958 counterparts after correction for inflation. He further noted that the spending power of General Assistance and Aid for Dependent Children payments has been allowed to erode with inflation over the years. In contrast, Social Security retirement benefits were substantially increased in 1972 and indexed to inflation rates thereafter (Rossi, 1989). As a result, the number and proportion of welfare recipients and single parents in the New Homelessness are relatively high, while the number and proportion of elderly are relatively low.

Those who are willing and able to work their way out of homelessness in the 1990s find a difficult labor market for doing so. At the time of Bogue's study, the U.S. economy was production-oriented, such that unskilled and semi-skilled laborers were able to make a livable wage. The present economy is increasingly service-based and many of the high wage, production-based jobs that require a modest level of education and work skills have been lost to automation or exported to countries with lower labor costs. The fast-food restaurant has replaced the auto assembly line as a prototypical job of the less-than-skilled labor force.

Other economic developments have breathed new life into day labor contractors and temporary agencies. The rising costs of health care insurance and other employee benefit programs have induced many employers to trim their permanent work forces as much as possible. In times of greater demand, these employers contract for short-term help through temporary agencies, thus minimizing personnel costs associated with employee benefit packages, unemployment compensation, and so on. Labor contractors and temporary agencies in turn recruit and deliver street people to perform the types of unskilled labor that do not entail contact with the public. For homeless persons, such employment poses enough drawbacks to merit the label "slave labor." A portion of the wage is taken to support the contractor. There is no health insurance and no other employee benefits. Most job sites do not permit ready access to a telephone, and little consideration is given to the needs of temporary workers anyway. The "temp" lacks control over his or her transportation and cannot drive to an interview for a permanent job during lunch hour. Such lifestyle costs put the street person at a decided disadvantage in the job market.

But perhaps the most demoralizing of the many facets of the New Homelessness is the lack of affordable housing. On the demand side of the housing equation, consider that the youngest of the post-World War II baby-boomer generation have now entered their late twenties and early thirties. Virtually all of this birth cohort who seek to establish independent households are now in the housing market. Next, consider the supply side of the affordable housing equation: during the 1970s, one-half of the nation's supply of single room occupancy (SRO) units were destroyed (U.S. Department of Housing and Urban Development, 1984 as cited by Dennis et al., 1991). Wittman (1992) cited one estimate of low-income housing needs to be five million units currently. Hartman (1986) had earlier reported that there were times when as many as half of the housing voucher recipients of Boston and New York City returned their vouchers to housing authorities. These went unused because there were no units available for renting.

The policies of the Reagan-Bush administrations are most often blamed for the affordable housing shortage. Such charges are a call to arms for political football with each side dashing down the field with selected government statistics to score its points. For example, *Time* magazine stated that in the decade beginning with 1980, federal outlays for rent subsidies and home building programs for the poor dropped more that 400 percent from $41 million to $10 million (Church, 1990). Conservative critics impugned these figures for having confused authorizations with actual outlays (Anderson, 1992; Kondratas, 1991). In her *National Review* article, Anderson offered other government figures which purported to show that federal outlays to low income housing programs actually increased during the 1980s.

Although conservative writers dispute prevalence estimates of homelessness and defend Reagan-Bush administration housing policies (e.g., Horowitz, 1992), they do not deny the existence of the New Homelessness. Both Horowitz and Anderson assign blame for the New Homelessness to the Supreme Court for decisions which have upheld citizens' constitutional rights to loiter and live as vagrants. After juxtaposing this affirmation of vagrancy rights with yet other government statistics which show high rental vacancy rates during the 1980s, these writers imply that people are homeless because they choose to be homeless.

A more compelling defense of government housing policy during the past decade was offered by Anna Kondratas, a HUD official of the Bush administration. After having conceded that there is less housing available for the poor in 1990 than ten years previously, she attributes this to a list of private sector forces: "The poor have lost more affordable housing to urban renewal, inflation-driven housing speculation, gentrification, rent control, exclusionary zoning, tax policy, and other such phenomena than to any putative budget cuts" (Kondratas, 1991, p. 1228).

As was the case with prevalence estimates of homelessness, the best approximation of truth concerning government policy and homelessness is to be found in statements and numbers that are not challenged by either side. The following is such a set of statements and numbers:

1. Only 80,000 new units of low income housing were to be built in 1990, in contrast to 187,000 in 1980 (Church, 1990).
2. Budget authorizations for subsidized housing did decrease from $26.9 billion in 1981 to an average of $10 to $11 billion in the years 1982–1988 (Anderson, 1992; Foscarinis, 1991; Horowitz, 1992).
3. During the 1980s, the consumer price index for rental housing increased faster than the overall consumer price index (Anderson, 1992).

This last fact merits amplification for the benefit of street practitioners. The fact that rental vacancy rates increased in the 1980s does not mean that these vacancies were affordable to the poor. To the contrary, between 1973 and 1983 the increase in median apartment rent rose 137 percent while the median family income rose 79 percent (U.S. Bureau of the Census, 1983). It is worth considering how shelter costs (rents) are different from other costs of living: an indivisible lump sum payment is required at the beginning of the month before shelter is consumed. It cannot be cut back upon or rationed by the consumer like other costs. "One cannot pay less rent for the next few months by not using the living room" (Hartman, 1986, p. 73). The act of moving into rental housing requires payment of a first month's rent and at least one additional month's rent to be escrowed as a deposit against damages. In some regions, an advance payment of utility costs is also required. Thus, renting a studio or efficiency apartment in Minneapolis in 1991 at $313 per month required an outlay in the first month of $700. A person who works full-time at the minimum wage and who sleeps in a shelter and eats in soup kitchens would have to be able to save 100 percent of his or her income (gross pay) for more than two months just to enter the rental market. Retaining the apartment after that first month requires more than half of one's gross pay; to afford that, one must live a Spartan existence with the enduring threat that a layoff or medical hardship or transportation loss would be sufficient to send one out into the streets again. The demoralizing arithmetic of the New Homelessness was summarized by Rossi (1989), "In twelve large cities surveyed between 1979 and 1983, the amount of inexpensive rental housing available to poor families dropped precipitously, averaging 30 percent. At the same time, the number of households living at or below the poverty level in the same cities increased by 36 percent . . . If we restrict our attention to that portion of the housing stock that is ordinarily occupied by poor, unattached single persons, then the decline is even more precipitous" (p. 182).

Gentrification of the cities is generally conceded to be a significant factor in the affordable housing problem. The majority of the real estate which was used to revitalize the central cities and urban skylines of the 1980s had previously been occupied by SRO hotels and other inexpensive rental units. Despite their eyesore qualities, these units did house people and were affordable to the poor. Those who were dislodged from these residences lacked the financial and political clout to challenge their displacements. They encountered higher housing costs elsewhere due to rampant investment and speculation in real estate during the 1970s and 1980s. They also endured over-crowding, a higher incidence of substandard housing, and other social and psychological costs associated with the loss of an affordable residence (Hartman, 1986).

Most housing units lost to gentrification have not been replaced. In Minneapolis, the gentrification of the 1980s resulted in the destruction of 1,831 units of low-cost housing, of which only 255 had been replaced by 1990 (Bauerlein & Farley, 1990). It is a source of bitterness among many advocates for homeless persons that so many SRO units were sacrificed for commercial real estate and office towers. Now, due to overdevelopment of that sector, such office buildings contribute substantially to the vacancy rates of the 1990s.

In the summer of 1989, the author met a woman at a wedding reception in Washington, D.C. She described her occupation as "commercial development" and went on to explain that her firm scouted cheap or deteriorating apartment buildings for their proximity to the Capitol, developed a buyout package for the landlord, and then connected the landlord with a firm or organization desirous of locating its headquarters closer to the Capitol. When asked what became of the people who were displaced by such transactions, the woman replied, "Oh, in D.C. we have shelters."

The New Homelessness is no longer so new. Complacency toward shelter life has probably spread in direct proportion to media coverage of shelter life. Yet shelter conditions vary widely across the country. The Twin Cities area has received national exposure for its (relatively) enlightened and hospitable treatment of street persons. Many of its mainstream citizens have volunteered at least a night of service to a soup kitchen or a shelter through affiliations with charitable, religious, or service organizations. Usually they have encountered homeless men and women whose basic physical needs appear to have been well met. In the Twin Cities, there are so many free meals available on a daily basis at different sites and times that it is difficult to go hungry without a conscious effort to do so. When overnight temperatures fall below 32 degrees Fahrenheit, the local Red Cross ensures that all unsheltered individuals have access to a bed somewhere. Free clothing is both abundant and available. Free health care is available at different street sites on different days. And so is entertainment: many shelters have purchased VCRs or subscribed to cable TV.

By no means are these the grim conditions of New York City's notorious Fort Washington shelter (Bearak, 1991; Grunberg & Eagle, 1990). Twin Cities' shelter volunteers have commented on this, and a few have even ventured to say that they could tolerate such conditions on a temporary basis. But shelter life is not conducive to a temporary stay (Rivlin & Imbimbo, 1989). It is one thing to join the street culture and quite a different thing to leave it. The demoralizing arithmetic has already been discussed; beyond the numbers are concrete, day-to-day problems that keep one tethered to street institutions like the shelter and the labor pool.

Confronted with large numbers of comparably dressed, high-turnover patrons, the staffs of shelters, drop-in centers, and other sites have trouble getting to know and keeping track of the people. Individualized attention and support are in limited supply. Many shelters impose time limits on length of stay in order to discourage shelterization. Many are closed during the daytime; if a street person applies for a job, there is no daytime telephone number to leave with a potential employer. If one is fortunate enough to reside in a shelter that is staffed during the daytime, one must still worry whether giving that number to a potential employer will evoke doubt or discrimination when the telephone is answered by someone who identifies the place as a shelter. Labor pools and temporary agencies have few incentives to help a street person. The productive temporary worker with a good attitude is their bread-and-butter. In fact, unless day labor contractors have a placement contract with the companies which they supply—a rare occurrence when the work involved is unskilled or semi-skilled—they have a vested interest in their best workers *not* obtaining full-time jobs. Some street persons have reported that they were blacklisted by labor pools after having taken a day off to look for a full-time job.

Another lifestyle expense to a street person who wishes to work is the problem of going to and from the job site on a regular basis. Labor pools generally provide transportation to job sites; left to his or her own devices, the street person faces significant logistical problems. Shelters and other street culture sites tend to be concentrated in the central cities at a time when most jobs are being created in the suburbs and exurbs. Public transportation systems also tend to be oriented to central cities. Bus service to industrial parks and other work sites along circle freeways is often expensive and infrequent—perhaps nonexistent for second and third shift workers. It may also entail significant distances to walk. It is also difficult to look presentable for a job interview when one must carry all of one's possessions around in a backpack. This presupposes that the homeless job applicant had already competed successfully on the previous night for the limited showering and laundry facilities available at the shelter.

A life in the street culture that is fashioned from welfare or workfare may be no less difficult. Koegel, Burnam, and Farr (1990) were surprised to find that only 5 percent of their inner city sample of homeless persons from Los Angeles were receiving welfare benefits at the time of their survey. A much larger number of their sample had received such benefits in the past, but had lost these by breaching requirements that they keep various appointments, acquire signatures, attend job classes, do projects, and so on. The study's authors also encountered a blatant admission of discriminatory practices against homeless persons, "A high-level official in the Department of Public Social Services has acknowledged that the procedures governing application for and maintenance of general relief are purposely designed to cut off and/or alienate as many people as possible" (Koegel et al., 1990, p. 103). Blasi and Preis (1992) of the Los Angeles Homeless Litigation Team found that a quota system had been established for the number of daily applicants who could be provided with general relief. One of the ways that this program was manipulated was through selective seasonal enforcement of legal identification requirements (driver's license or certified birth certificate). Such credentials are difficult to obtain when one lacks money for fees and a permanent mailing address; once obtained, such qualifications are readily stolen or lost as part of day-to-day life on the streets.

There seems little reason to assume that these practices are confined to Los Angeles County. Such discrimination touches upon the social stigma of homelessness and the negative self-statements which this stigma engenders. In response to many and sundry negations from the mainstream culture, it is natural for the long-term homeless person to affirm all that is left to affirm: acceptance of a street identity and the full acculturation that goes with it. Such a person joins that segment of the street culture that conservative writers like Horowitz and Anderson accuse of choosing to be homeless.

Mental health practitioners (and other interveners) must reach a person before full third-stage acculturation has taken place. It is at such a stage that chronic depression shades into character disorder.

The following essay was written by a street person and published anonymously in a shelter newsletter.

Tough Enough

You can call us "bums," "winos," alcoholics, or lazy, but the one thing we have in common with the rest of society is that we are all human beings and therefore deserve respect.

Life is "tough enough" when you have a good job, a home, and family—just trying to make payments, facing the everyday trials of getting by. But if you think that's hard, then try being one who wants a home, family, and job, one who wants to be loved and to give love, one who is so far down, but is trying harder than he's ever tried in his life to pick himself up and become something again in life. Now that's "tough enough."

Starting with the basics, okay, like a job—that doesn't sound too hard, right? Well, first of all, I'll need some clean and decent clothes to wear, and a shower, haircut, and shave. Oops, there's no money for a haircut, but could probably manage a shower and shave Now I'll have to find some want ads in a restaurant or someplace and pick out a few jobs I can do. Without any quarters, I'll have to walk across town to a place where I can use the phone for free. Well, one job is already gone, but the other—way out in the suburbs—is interested in hiring me. How do I get there to fill out the application? Maybe I can get a bus token. Got one. Been hired too. Only problem is, it's a second shift, and I don't know where I can sleep when I get off work. Hell, I don't even know how I can get to and from work until I get a paycheck. Oh well, can't take that job; have to keep looking for a day job, I guess.

Nine days later, after a bout with a day labor place to make a few bucks to help pay for "cigs" and bus fare, I've found a day job, working from 7 A.M. to 3:30 P.M. in a factory for $4.25 an hour. Not much, but better than nothing. I have to leave by 6 A.M., so miss out on breakfast where I'm staying, and don't have money for lunch yet, so I get dinner, and that's it. Oh well.

Three weeks later, and there's money in my pocket, though it's hard being paid every two weeks; at least it's something. Have to leave the shelter in two days, as my time is up, and I still don't have enough money to rent a place. Don't think my job would appreciate me bringing my clothes and stuff to work every day. Guess I'll just have to do it, and hope I can get some one-nighters at the shelter.

If I can do all these things, I just might make it, but if anything goes wrong anywhere along the way, the whole thing collapses and I have to start over again. But how many times can you pick yourself up and try again? After so many times of failing, you become that bum, wino, alcoholic, or lazy good-for-nothing. Now that's "tough enough."

CHAPTER 3

Resistance

It is pointless to try to categorize impaired street persons into those who are products of social selection versus those who are products of social causation. Certainly the stressors of homelessness take their toll on people who are already impaired by schizophrenia or bipolar disorder, probably more than on nonpsychotic persons. As for those who have been demoralized by homelessness, many of their life histories reveal Axis II conditions and maladaptive coping styles—particularly substance abuse—that contributed to their membership in a street culture.

Psychotic and nonpsychotic street persons differ in ways other than symptoms versus lack of symptoms. One area of divergence is their characteristic modes of resistance. The first line of resistance by psychotic individuals is typically forthright denial of or "lack of insight" into their conditions. Some express this nonverbally by avoiding eye contact or maintaining silence around mental health practitioners. Others walk around, away from, and sometimes through a practitioner at the first threat of such a contact.

By contrast, the first line of defense for demoralized people is often some variation of the "chip on the shoulder" theme, for example, "if it weren't for all the hassles and hoops that The System makes me deal with, I'd be able to get off the streets all by myself." These people may seek to engage (and corner) practitioners with politicized discussions. Or a practitioner may be asked whether or not his or her proper role is confined to serving psychotic persons. Such questions are usually posed by people who are ambivalent about the practitioner's availability to themselves. Many demoralized persons are also concerned that they not be lumped together with psychotic people in anyone else's mind. This in itself is an encouraging sign because it indicates that self-concept and personal pride persist in some positive ways which can be built upon.

Some authorities have charged that resistance to accepting help among homeless persons is not widespread, and that perpetuating such a myth serves to justify inaction. In the first report by the American

Psychiatric Association's Task Force on the Homeless Mentally Ill, Baxter and Hopper (1984) wrote that "policies for the mentally ill homeless should be framed to meet the predominant needs of the bulk of this population. To focus on the exceptions—those who allegedly refuse assistance—will . . . leave the majority unaided" (p. 132).

The spirit of this statement can be endorsed even as its content is disputed. Resistance toward mental health practitioners is widespread among homeless persons and it is offered in manifold and complex forms (Bachrach, 1992; Dennis et al., 1991). The fact that Baxter and Hopper were not mental health practitioners themselves may explain why they were not so impressed by it. No other profession elicits the ominous misconceptions (or bad memories) associated with commitment hearings, locked wards, electroconvulsive treatments, and so on. One psychiatrist recalled that in the early days of his involvement with an outreach project, he was advised to stay out of a drop-in center while meals were being served. It was thought that his presence on the premises would be sufficient to frighten some street people away from their only free meal site.

Some severely impaired individuals reject not just mental health care but basic supports as well. They defy logic and are too numerous to be dismissed as exceptions.

> Jerry was a psychotic man whose crazed, robotic appearance rendered his age and national origin difficult to identify (this also served as protection from predators). Over several years of observation, he scarcely spoke when others were present. He ignored all outreach overtures with the same robotic indifference. People cleared a path whenever he entered a drop-in center because of his odor and appearance. He came only to collect day-old doughnuts and loaves of bread which were regularly donated in large quantities by area bakeries. No one knew where he spent his nights.
>
> Just before the onset of winter, the heavy coat that Jerry wore all year round had progressed to a state of severe disrepair. Most of its lining and insulation material dangled outside of the coat and remained attached to it by mere threads. Drop-in staff feared for Jerry's survival in the cold but he refused to acknowledge their offers of a replacement coat. Subsequently he was offered a plastic bag with holes cut into it for his arms and head. It was hoped that he would use this to keep the coat's lining against his body. He would not acknowledge this offer either. Other street persons suggested that a replacement coat and plastic bag be left next to the doughnut tray for Jerry and perhaps he would take them along with his doughnuts. This did not work either. Eventually he dropped out of sight; later it was learned that he had been committed to the state hospital after being

found on the night of the winter's first freeze. A police sweep of abandoned buildings had discovered him still wearing the favored coat with its dangling lining.

A psychologist had previously declined to initiate civil commitment proceedings on Jerry's behalf because he had been doubtful whether clothing inappropriate to the weather would meet prevailing legal standards of dangerousness to self due to mental impairment. His previous experience had been that the wearing of multiple layers of clothes by street persons on hot summer days had never been viewed as dangerousness to self, and thus Jerry's winter behavior seemed likely to be viewed in the same legal light.

There is some merit to Baxter and Hopper's (1984) charge that the resistant, hard-to-engage traits of homeless people have been used against them. It echoes the position of the conservative columnists, and at times it echoes street persons themselves, particularly those in the third stage of the acculturation process. But it is one thing to resign oneself to a fate that one feels powerless to change and another to embrace street culture as a desirable life style. Frequently, a person's intent to express the first attitude comes out in words that endorse the second one. Street cultures are heterogeneous and any characterization of street people that aspires to universality does not do them justice. Mental health practitioners should be skeptical of street persons who would volunteer their love of the street life. Those who are content amidst the street culture have little cause to celebrate this in public, much less consort with a mental health practitioner for that purpose. The person who trumpets street culture to a practitioner is likely "whistling" as a way to master the "dark." The practitioner should not be quick to hum along.

This discussion leads into one of the basic postulates of outreach work: When a street person initiates a contact with a mental health practitioner or permits him or herself to be engaged by a practitioner, the manifest content of such a contact is less important than the fact that the contact took place at all. If the practitioner works in street culture sites, he or she will have many interactions which, on the surface, seem destined to keep him or her at a psychological arm's length. The manifest content may be "I like it out here on the streets, I wouldn't have it any other way." The practitioner does well to accept such proclamations at face value for the moment. But over time, most of these will prove to have been trial balloons, reaction formations, assertions of personal pride, or some other form of posturing with subtle meanings that could not have been plumbed in that first moment.

A shelter director introduced a psychiatric social worker to a gathering of 35 guests during a nightly community meeting. As the meeting was breaking up, the social worker was approached by George, a black man of about 60 who had close-cropped salt-and-pepper hair and horn-rimmed glasses through which he frequently squinted. George spoke loudly enough that the other guests who were milling around could hear him. He first made it clear that he was not contacting the social worker about mental health problems of his own but rather for help in dealing with the crazy decisions of the shelter staff in various realms that affected the guests' lives. He saw her as someone who might be drafted into an advocacy role, and his next sentence was an affirmation that he had become homeless by choice. He claimed to be on a multi-year odyssey to research and write a book about being black and homeless in America.

The loud voice was meant to convey to the other shelter guests that they need not infer that George was mentally impaired and in need of a social worker just because he was seen talking to one. And yet over subsequent months, an informal therapeutic alliance developed between these two. Whenever the social worker would broach the issue directly, George would negate it by characterizing her as "a breath of fresh air" on the streets, or as a fellow intellectual with whom he felt free to share his "deepening *angst* for the huddling masses around us." George did not attempt to date the social worker nor otherwise behave in ways to suggest he was seeking a personal relationship. And at no time did he ever show her his book or allude to it again. Perhaps the book was a fictional device to preserve "face" and respect in a culture that provides little of either. However, this remains a conjecture because the social worker never inquired about the book. As she saw it, to have done so without a clear invitation from George would have risked what working alliance they had. She believed that their alliance prospered because key aspects of George's resistance went unaddressed.

In contrast, leaving Jerry's resistances unaddressed almost contributed to his death. Typically street practitioners encounter the shades of gray between these two extremes of resistance problems. Dealing with resistance is the realm of practitioner skill that is most often tested by street work. It is different than in an office culture setting where the respective motivations and roles of practitioner and recipient are well-defined from the outset. In office culture contexts, resistance to treatment tends to be more delayed in its onset and more easily interpreted or negotiated away. In a street culture where less-than-motivated recipients interact with less-than-invited practitioners, resistances to treatment are present from the outset. These are more often fudged or finessed by the street practitioner than interpreted.

THEORIES OF RESISTANCE

As compound adjectives, the phrases "treatment resistant" and "hard-to-treat" typically modify nouns such as "client," "patient," "sample," and "population." Such usage tends to confer upon them the trait-like qualities of endurance and consistency across time and situation. When the descriptor is then applied to an individual, it subtly lowers its user's expectations for that person to change. And because an array of people and their myriad ways of resisting become grouped under this single descriptor, significant differences among them tend to become leveled rather than sharpened. Labeling a person as treatment resistant also enables a practitioner to avoid confronting possible deficiencies in the treatment itself or in the practitioner who is offering the treatment (Hartman & Reynolds, 1987).

This trait conception of resistance began with Sigmund Freud (1933) who assigned responsibility for its emergence in psychoanalysis to the analysand. Examples include coming late to or forgetting appointments, blocking during the free association process, and rejecting the analyst's interpretations. Such behaviors were seen as unconsciously motivated and they occurred despite the analysand's significant investments of time, money, and motivation. At various times, Freud wrote about treatment resistance as a manifestation of the death instinct, as a masochistic and regressive striving against growth and enlightenment, and as a function that served the bidding of the superego (Freud, 1933). But even as his thinking about the sources of resistance changed over the years, Freud always viewed it as a natural phenomenon that was consistent with his philosophy of man (Singer, 1970). That is, once a person has been rendered conflicted and neurotic, he or she will attempt to maintain that equilibrium and resist efforts to destabilize it, however painful and maladaptive that prevailing equilibrium may be. Freud's psychology stressed intrapsychic events over interpersonal ones, and he preferred to think of the psychoanalyst as a neutral and non-involved observer. Thus, he viewed the essence of treatment resistance as residing in the analysand rather than as a function of the interaction or relationship between analyst and analysand.

Psychoanalysts since Freud have viewed treatment resistance as arising from the anxiety provoked by the analyst's interpretive work (e.g., Greenson, 1967). Other views of treatment resistance have emphasized that change of any kind is inherently aversive and that resistance to change is a natural response to these aversive qualities (Dowd & Seibel, 1990). The following excerpt from Singer (1970) offers an existentialist's view of treatment resistance, "In rejecting insights and in avoiding self-understanding—in resisting—the patient expresses his preference for the despair implicit in the statement 'I have no choice' over the despair inherent in the recognition 'I have all choices'" (p. 246). Cognitive therapists have echoed this theme by citing the inherently noxious aspects of altering one's world view to a more functional and adaptive appraisal of reality (Liotti, 1987; Meichenbaum & Gilmore, 1972).

During the past two decades, the phenomenon of resistance to treatment has been elevated to center stage by proponents of paradoxical techniques (Weeks & L'Abate, 1982). From their perspective, the interpersonal dialectics of power, influence, and control underlie many psychological symptoms and failed treatments. In order to bring about change, the paradoxical therapist construes symptoms and resistances as allies rather than opponents. Practitioners who prescribe symptoms (e.g., Frankl, 1967) or reinforce resistant behaviors (e.g., Kuhlman, Sincaban, & Green, 1988) act out logical extensions of this thesis. Finally, treatment resistance has been framed as normal behavior through the postulates of psychological reactance theory (Brehm & Brehm, 1981). Reactance theory posits a fundamental human motivation to act freely and without restriction upon one's environment. Any encounter or interaction that imposes restrictions upon one's freedom of choice (e.g., a practitioner's prescription for change) will elicit a tendency to oppose that restriction. Whether one acts in accordance with or in opposition to the prescription depends on extant situational forces, including the relationship between the parties involved.

At this juncture, it is worth noting that the prevalence of treatment resistance among nonhomeless people is significant as well (Meichenbaum & Turk, 1987). In one study of general medical patients, DiMatteo and DiNicola (1982) found that 50 to 60 percent of patients failed to keep appointments for preventative interventions and 30 to 40 percent failed to keep appointments for corrective (symptom relief) interventions. Haynes, Taylor, and Sackett (1979) reported that 30 to 40 percent of general medical patients failed to follow preventative regimens and 20 to 30 percent failed to follow curative regimens. Compliance with mental health treatments is typically lower than it is for general medical treatments (Meichenbaum & Turk, 1987). And perhaps no evidence of treatment resistance is more striking than Ley's (1986) research on noncompliance with health care recommendations on the part of patients who were themselves practitioners. Ley's patient sample included psychologists, physicians, pharmacists, nurses, and dentists; their noncompliance rates ranged from 12 to 100 percent with a median rate of 80 percent.

Meichenbaum and Turk (1987) provide a comprehensive literature review and analysis/synthesis of the research concerning treatment resistance (their term is "non-adherence to treatment"). Their work does not address putative unconscious or natural tendencies to resist treatment, but it does focus on what can be gleaned from surveys and studies of thousands of compliant and noncompliant subjects as to their expressed reasons for adhering or not adhering to treatment regimens. The gist of Meichenbaum's conclusions is that practitioners overestimate the importance of their ministrations and underestimate the importance of their interactions and relationships with recipients. Their recommendations for reducing non-adherence emphasize more time and care devoted to the practitioner-recipient relationship and the specific communications that take place within this.

Thus in an outreach context, the street practitioner should attend to communication and relationship variables first, diagnosis and treatment second. It has become fashionable of late for workshop leaders to assert that there is no such thing as treatment resistance, only a failure of the practitioner to negotiate and insure treatment compliance. While this is a provocative outlook for office culture practice, it loses relevance when applied to street work. After all, voluntary collaboration must be established before it can be resisted.

Many of the barriers that preclude a voluntary collaboration between practitioner and street person reside in different cultural perceptions. The "appointment" is a good example. Mental health practitioners are accustomed to structuring their work lives around appointments. Appointments provide a measure of temporal control over the parameters of distress that one is exposed to. In most office culture contexts, one is paid when an appointment is kept and not paid when it is not kept. The appointment has given rise to certain idiomatic expressions, e.g. "I have a four o'clock, and then a five-thirty," and so on. It is not overstatement to consider the appointment as a key organizing principle of a practitioner's life.

For street people, appointments pose many difficulties, and failures to keep them must be understood accordingly. They are inconsistent with a life style that is jobless, transportationless, telephoneless, and moneyless. Still, homeless persons are perceived as having limitless time at their disposal; also, as nonpaying recipients of goods and services, they tend to acquiesce to subordinate roles and quietly accept any appointments that are dictated to them. If multiple or conflicting appointments must later be prioritized or juggled, most street persons will assign a lower value to a mental health appointment than to one with a financial worker, Legal Aid attorney, or personnel department. And because they live in a cash-and-carry culture that lacks convenient and permanent storage facilities, street persons are more susceptible to losing money or to being victimized by extortion or assault.

After such occurrences, they must immediately jettison their non-emergency appointments to seek the essentials of food and shelter. There are yet other times when the cost or inconvenience of taking public transportation—or of making a telephone call to cancel an appointment—is prohibitive. Moreover, public sector mental health appointments must often be scheduled far in advance. Life on the streets is subject to considerable day-to-day and week-to-week instability. By the time such appointments come around, they may seem irrelevant because the street person's original concerns have changed.

The office practitioner who is on the receiving end of a failed appointment is naturally chagrined by it. However, it is not warranted that he or she conclude from a failed appointment that a street person was insufficiently motivated for treatment. Limited resources and volatile shifts in needs and priorities must be understood as part and parcel of life in a street culture. The only way to minimize appointment problems in office settings is for the practitioner to adjust his or her expectations to accommodate cancellations and no-shows from homeless people. Back-up activities like paperwork can be at the ready but not the returning of telephone calls if only one line is available. The practitioner who returns calls may tie up the line so that a street person is unable to get through from a payphone. The practitioner must take responsibility for maximizing the telephone access of someone who lacks a permanent residence, telephone number, and predictable whereabouts.

In summary, a walk-in format whereby a practitioner is always available to see whomever comes in without an appointment is the best office-culture model for serving the needs of homeless people. However, outreach visits to street culture sites repesent a much more desirable venue of engagement.

CULTURE-SPECIFIC RESISTANCES

There are a number of culture-specific resistance themes like "appointments" that the street practitioner encounters on a regular basis. The framework offered by Meichenbaum and Turk (1987) has been adopted to organize these themes into subgroups. What all themes have in common is the potential for modification through the outreach process.

Past Experiences with/Future Expectations of Treatment

This source of resistance is particularly relevant to outreach work with psychotic street people (Caton, 1990; Dennis et al., 1991). Thirty years ago—before deinstitutionalization had begun in earnest—Bogue (1963) reported that a sizable percentage of his skid row sample were A.W.O.L. and hiding out from mental institutions. Those scholars and researchers who have since referred to deinstitutionalization as a "dumping" process usually fail to address many psychotic persons' preferences for being so dumped. As Baxter and Hopper (1984) wrote, "the regularity with which mentally disabled homeless people express a strong preference for getting by as they do rather than submitting to hospitalization, where a bed and three meals are assured, says much about human resistance to institutionalization" (p. 120).

It also says much about resistance to the treatments associated with inpatient care. Often those same treatments—most notably psychotropic medications—are declined in outpatient and community-based treatment settings. Refusers typically cite past experiences with dystonic reactions, extrapyramidal symptoms, and other side effects of taking such medicines. They also have reason to fear long-term consequences from such treatments, especially the neurological condition known as tardive dyskinesia. Chronic headaches, episodes of confusion, and memory loss are frequently attributed to past regimens of electoconvulsive therapy. Many psychotic people experienced episodes of seclusion, restraint, and perhaps worse as part of inpatient stays in their pasts. They recall victimizations and betrayals by practitioners, courts, and families. Many have learned the hard way that while medications may render them more acceptable to others, chemical agents do not remedy adaptive deficits or damage already done to family and support system relationships. Psychotic symptoms are easier to reconcile with one's pride than are a doctor's pills.

So many horror stories about the evils of involuntary commitments and electroconvulsive therapy are out there that street practitioners risk developing an undue prejudice against these interventions themselves. Those people who have benefited from these treatments (or who have benefited from any mental health treatments, for that matter) seldom appear in the street culture. The psychotic persons who do appear there represent the less responsive end of the treatment spectrum and are not representative of the spectrum as a whole. Practitioners may also permit themselves some skepticism upon hearing from different people accounts which bear a striking resemblance to each other and to the plot of the film, *One Flew Over the Cuckoo's Nest.* The mental health professions have probably underestimated the impact of this film upon the proliferation of figurative memories of past hospitalizations among former inpatients.

It is important for a street practitioner to assertively inquire about past treatment episodes and to bring to the surface of discussion any negative treatment experiences from the person's past. The practitioner must anticipate that past treatment experiences shape expectations of future treatments even before these new treatments have been conceived. If the street practitioner can learn what went wrong in the past before it is recreated in the present, he or she can deprive the resistant party of some protest themes. The practitioner can inquire whether or not the person has seen *Cuckoo's Nest* and how the street person's own past experiences were alike and different from those depicted in the film. Such a request calls upon the street person to separate reality from drama, perhaps to find some positive aspect(s) of the prior inpatient experience.

Compliance Violates Lifelong Belief Systems and World Views.

A more recent movie, *What About Bob?,* has also tapped and shaped resistance to mental health practitioners. Its plot has been related to this author on several different occasions by different street persons, each of whom grinned broadly at the telling. The story involved tables being turned on an arrogant, condescending mental health practitioner by a nerdish and needy person. It was the proverbial downfall of elitism and the uplifting of the underdog.

There are many among the street culture who view mental health practitioners as part of the social and economic elite. The practitioner's alliance with The System is presumed to be greater than her or his alliance with the street culture. Those who volunteer their services are less culpable than salaried practitioners, but the motives of volunteers are also viewed with cynicism. At times the naked expression of such negative sentiments can be appalling for the practioner.

> One woman with whom a group of practitioners had never had direct contact spent a period of weeks tracking their whereabouts and activities. She used a stopwatch to record exactly how late each practitioner was for each scheduled visit to a street site. The group's outreach approach was informal and they would typically spend time chatting with people at open tables; this woman recorded such times as "loafing at taxpayer's expense" because street people were not being escorted to an office for a private session. She maintained an air of righteousness throughout her project and never revealed the source of her motivation. When approached, she would refuse to talk about her purpose. This was ultimately made clear when she took her data to a local alderperson.

> A paranoid man had resisted outreach efforts by various intellectualizing maneuvers, for example, "Freud used cocaine, no different than those rock stars (crack users) over on the corner there!" Yet across a

series of contacts he seemed to be searching for a face-saving way to open up to a psychologist without acknowledging that he needed to do so. To facilitate this, the psychologist would search for a neutral topic that would highlight what the two of them had in common.

Once the psychologist approached the man in a drop-in center while he was leafing through an article in a weekly news magazine. The cover highlighted the controversy involving the logging industry versus the preservation of the habitat of the spotted owl. Without looking up, the man asked if the psychologist had seen this article and what he thought about it. The psychologist responded that he could appreciate the positions of both sides on the matter and hadn't made up his mind one way or the other. Despite this noncommittal answer, the man exploded, "Well, I think it's a disgrace, all you yuppies getting worked up over some goddamnn little bird losing its home, but you don't give a goddamnn about species of your own kind sleeping out on the streets!"

This man's preemptive attack reflected resistance themes that had little to do with the spotted owl controversy. Such persons seldom (if ever) appear in office culture practices, so one has no guidance from prior training and experience to fall back on. The paradigm that most closely resembles this kind of situation is mandated treatment wherein a person is ordered into treatment by a judge or a parole board. The practitioner in such circumstances inherits a negativism that would be more appropriately directed elsewhere. Storch and Lane (1989) have referred to this as external resistance to change. They stressed that it is important for a practitioner "to step away from the patient's designation (of him or her) as 'the enemy and available scapegoat' . . . Only by the therapist's acknowledging the legitimacy of the patient's negativism towards the mandate, and dissociating both therapist and therapy from this external resistance can the internal resistance to change be successfully addressed" (p. 25). According to this view, the psychologist must acknowledge the legitimacy of this person's anger about all of the sentiment and effort expended on behalf of owls.

But what of the psychologist's dissociating himself from "you yuppies?" This dilemma is brought into greater relief when one substitutes the phrase "mainstream culture" for "you yuppies." It comes more naturally for practitioners to distance themselves and dissociate from such "treatment resistant" people rather than from their own identifications with the mainstream culture.

Salaried practitioners must be prepared for point blank inquiries about what they earn. If the person who asks it is new, such a question undoubtedly represents a litmus test that should neither be sidestepped nor redirected. The author's response to this question has been to say,

"I am doing well enough and living comfortably in the suburbs with a house, a wife, 2.4 children, and a Weber Grill." The last two items are meant to inject levity and self-mockery into an interaction that had been shaped by the street person to stir class conflicts between us. Humor has the power to dilute conflict with its fleeting moment of emotional intimacy.

> Once this response was overheard by a grim, tense-looking activist who was not as amused as the person to whom the humor had been directed. The activist guessed aloud that my salary was forty thousand, and then he excused himself to borrow a pocket calculator from one of the drop-in center staff. When he came back, he interrupted the conversation and announced that if my salary had been directed toward the subsidy of affordable housing units, the rents on seven such units could be paid for every month. He then turned to me and suggested that I introduce myself as "Dr. Seven."

Encounters with this magnitude of effrontery are rare. They are usually conducted for the benefit of an audience of other street persons. Fortunately (for the practitioner, anyway), many homeless persons have not thought deeply enough about such issues to have an opinion about them. Others who have considered and even endorsed the activist's position are equally sympathetic to the fact that practitioners contribute to the well-being of street people. Still others see such incidents as reflecting negatively upon the activist.

But regardless of their opinions, all street persons who witness (or hear about) such a confrontation are keenly interested in how the practitioner responds to it. In the above instance, I nodded acquiescently in the direction of the activist but said nothing and merely waited for him to leave before resuming the prior conversation. Working uninvited within such a culture calls for high levels of tolerance and civility under all circumstances.

Clothing is a visual symbol of the socioeconomic gap between practitioner and street person. In a street culture site, it may serve as a lightning rod for resistance based on class consciousness. Formerly the author taught college courses in the mornings prior to visits to drop-in centers. Over time I grew inured to crossing between socioeconomic zones, and there were a number of occasions when I would forget to remove my tie before entering a drop-in center. It would seldom take long before a street person would comment "nice tie;" once a man took hold of my tie between his thumb and forefinger and complimented me on its material.

> Another tie interaction took place during my ninth contact with a proud but demoralized Native American man in his mid-sixties. This man regularly took hostile delight in maligning the legal team's work by making public proclamations of their incompetence. He was also fond of making double-edged suicide threats which he would hedge or retract when someone responded to them. None of my prior contacts with him had lasted more than three minutes. Once he had interrupted my conversation with someone else in order to try to sell me a broom. On another occasion, he had laughingly handed me a brown paper bag which he said had a bomb in it. Another time he informed me that he had just punched out a psychologist and was on the run from the police. He further suggested that if I really wanted to help the homeless I would let him move into the basement of my home.
>
> On this ninth contact, he walked up and jeered that since I was already a rich doctor I had no excuse for wearing the same tie every day. On this occasion, I responded in kind by telling him that if he didn't like my ties he could very well write to his congressperson and request a government stipend for me so that the sorry state of affairs with my ties could end. He seemed genuinely tickled by this and even lingered a while to chat. On the next day, he again mocked my ties (although I wasn't wearing one) and then asked for some private time "in back." For a first time, he talked seriously and at some length about the depression and desperation that lay beneath all of the hostile pranks.

It is difficult to imagine such occurrences in an office culture setting. Yet here it occurred as a public display because I was on a foreign turf to which I had gone uninvited. Under these conditions, one responds with tolerance and the occasional like-minded rebuttal. This man's proactive initiation of all of our previous contacts made tolerance of him easier to justify. The "thou doth provoke too much" theme suggested that he was fighting against his own urges to open up with his pain to someone trained to listen and help him with it. It is not uncommon to encounter street persons who adhere to "the best defense is a good offense" as a principle of resistance. Such a modus operandi probably damaged their relationships with family, friends, and employers in the past.

It may seem an easy solution to the clothing dilemma to simply wear t-shirts (sweatshirts in winter), sneakers, and jeans and be done with it. However, this would deprive many practitioners of important affirmations of their own identities. Moreover, there are people in the street culture who would see this as pandering, that is, invoking the false pretense that the practitioner is as much of a street person as they are. Some psychotic street people react with paranoia to extreme out-of-role behavior. Still, if one can weaken the display of socioeconomic contrast without calling attention to it, some barriers to productive outreach are also weakened. Dressing down to the extent that one blends into the surroundings but does not conceal one's practitioner status represents a good compromise. If one decides to dress toward a complete blend with the street culture surroundings, a nameplate is advised so that no street person need feel deceived by appearances.

There are other ways to respond to socioeconomic gap resistances. Tobacco use remains prominent in street cultures and so the practitioner should refrain from asking for "no smoking" courtesies that he or she can live without. Sharing in the meals served at homeless sites is not difficult (although one Twin Cities' drop-in center that is popular with Native Americans offers oatmeal thinned with bacon grease for breakfast). The cross-cultural respect shown by partaking of such meals is appreciated by street people. Being willing to help people but not to share in their meals is sometimes seen as condescension.

Embarrassment, Skepticism, or Fatalism about Treatment

All mental health practitioners are aware of the stigma attached to being diagnosed or labeled as mentally impaired. However, in the office culture one obtains little first-hand experience in dealing with stigmatization as a source of resistance. This is because most people who feel shamed by the stigma either never present themselves for help or have already worked through most of that resistance on their own prior to being seen for a first time. Practitioners who work with persons mandated to treatment by judges, and so on, tend to have more exposure to the power of stigmatization. Not infrequently it becomes the dominant issue of such treatments and assumes precedence over whatever criminal act had given rise to the mandate.

> A psychiatrist often took note of a middle-aged white man with a cane at the different street culture sites that he toured. This man invariably offered eye contact and a wan smile to the psychiatrist. The look on his face was worn and beleaguered in a way that seemed to beckon to the psychiatrist to approach him. However, if the psychiatrist sustained the eye contact too long or took a few steps in the man's direction, he was quick to raise his hand and wave the psychiatrist off. Whenever he did so he would smile while calling out the same phrase in the same tone, like a mantra: "I ain't so bad off yet that I need to start messing with you, doc!"

> A twenty-fivish black man was known to have a serious problem with alcohol abuse but continued to deny it. He had a wide-eyed innocence

about him that belied a hulking frame that stood out in any street culture site. This man drew considerable attention from female providers who soon recognized the severity of his alcohol problem and tried to guide him to a psychologist for assistance with it. After months of resisting such referrals, he was finally persuaded to approach one, which he did in a nervous, deferential fashion, appending "doctor" to the end of every statement he made. His talk with the psychologist lasted all of 15 minutes during which he volunteered little and thanked her often. He never approached her again; when she next saw him and walked up to chat, he quickly worked into the conversation that he considered himself to be one of her most grateful "ex-patients."

It is important to address a street person's attitude toward the stigmatization of mental impairment as part of proceeding toward diagnosis and treatment. If the city is one with a wide range of accessible community-based programs, the street practitioner may assume that prospective outreach candidates have probably rejected these programs because of stigmatization and/or negative treatment experiences there. Communities that offer little in the way of such programming will have more "dumped" individuals whose presence on the streets more likely reflects the unavailablity of services rather than their unacceptability due to stigmatization.

A woman in her late twenties had been living alone for a summer in a cave along the Mississippi river. She was seen as having paranoid schizophrenia because of her constricted affect and steely interaction style. She was also convinced of a delusional belief that she was being followed by the FBI because she had served as an unwitting guinea pig in a navy experiment that had infected her with "submarine germ warfare." She resisted offers of help if someone mentioned psychiatry or mental health because she took this to mean that she was not being believed. An astute outreach worker finally linked her with a psychiatrist by portraying him as an expert on her strain of "germ sicknesses." Suitably forewarned, the psychiatrist introduced himself as such; in subsequent conversations, the psychiatrist would substitute the phrase "germ sickness" every time he might normally have thought or said "paranoid schizophrenia." When he encountered little resistance from the woman, he proceeded to prescribe anti-psychotic medications and arrange for her placement in a board-and-care facility.

Resolving this resistance proved to be a matter of persuading all concerned to talk to this woman in her own idiom for her condition. It is not deception to set aside one's professional terminology for another person's private metaphor, particularly when this leads to moving someone off of the streets. The woman accepted the board-and-care placement because that staff also saw fit to accommodate her private metaphor.

There are times when a street practitioner will be tempted to set aside her or his own identity in the interest of minimizing resistance. Merely introducing oneself as a mental health practitioner is often sufficient to induce nervous smiles, joking accusations that one is out to psychoanalyze everyone, and the like. Over months and years it becomes a repetitive drudgery of street work to grin and bear the humorous (and not so humorous) asides, and to occasionally observe people in retreat of one's approach. Such episodes are best taken as a practitioner's experiential education in what bearing a stigma means. Moreover, in the process of handling such rebukes—and being observed doing so—the practitioner has opportunities to model coping behaviors that street people would not see otherwise.

> This vignette concerns a boisterous, devil-may-care "regular" who had reached stage three of the acculturation process. He liked to tease and provoke staff and touring practitioners upon their arrival at a shelter, apparently to violate the numbing routines which make up street life. Upon spying the psychologist, he would loudly announce "here comes that guy from the looney bin!" The psychologist soon learned that ignoring such comments only increased the volume of the subsequent laughter. The smiles on the faces of those who had been listening convinced the psychologist that some comeback was in order to maintain a viable presence.
>
> At the psychologist's next visit, the man called out, "Lookie there! There's that doctor that's humming those looney tunes again. Hey, doc! These guys don't believe me that you told me I was crazy last week!" To this the psychologist replied, "They shouldn't believe you because I never said that. You must have been hearing those voices again."

Thus began a ritualized, two-lined joking relationship. Whenever the psychologist arrived at places which this man frequented, the eyes in the room would turn toward them in anticipation of the coming repartee. In time it became clear that this was all to the benefit of the outreach work. A member of the audience would approach the psychologist later and refer to this jesting as an "ice-breaker" for getting started in talking about more serious matters. A playful frame had been cast around the endemic resentment and resistance felt toward mental health practitioners on the streets. This jesting also showed the psychologist's willingness to interact with street people in their language rather insist upon preservation of the sober, respectful distance which characterizes most professional interchanges. The psychologist had stepped out of role and it had rendered him more socially acceptable.

Motivation to Maintain Self-Control

This source of resistance among the street culture is more subtle and difficult to detect than the others. It revolves around the pride inherent in enduring high levels of misery and distress and not asking for others' help while doing so. Some draw dignity from the act of opposing those who would help them—one street corner evangelist likened a psychologist's presence amidst the culture as akin to that of the tax collector of biblical times. Many street people tacitly endorse the theme of the man with the cane cited above, "I may be down, but I'm not so far down yet that I need your help!"

This is a difficult resistance to deal with because it is also a manifestation of a person's ego strength. Given that there are few other sources of dignity and pride available to these people, the street practitioner should be willing to accommodate it whenever possible.

> Charles was a forty-five-year-old Native American man with chronic schizophrenia. He was also a twenty-year veteran of the local street culture. He had been a violent man in his youth and had earned a reputation around town such that no treatment-based residence would consider him anymore. He was also evicted regularly from shelters and apartments due to his angry posturing, hoarding behaviors, poor upkeep of his residence, and/or the fact that he was so huge and "pumped" looking that landlords sought to be rid of him at the first sign of trouble. He also had a mentally impaired girlfriend who went in and out of the state hospital 30 miles away on an irregular basis.
>
> On one occasion, Charles asked a psychiatric nurse to lend him two dollars so that he could put gasoline into a friend's car and drive up to visit his girlfriend. He asked this begrudgingly, even angrily, as if the nurse were his last resort. After the nurse had given him the money Charles swore that he would pay it back with interest. When the nurse tried to assure him that this wouldn't be necessary, Charles stormed off. He never mentioned the loan again, but repayment was made to the nurse more than a year later. For reasons that were never made clear, this repayment took place through a third party. It came in the form of two silver dollars and a meandering note to the effect that this was the same thing as paying the nurse back with interest on the money because the nurse's children would love to have the silver dollars and could save them until they were worth something, as Charles himself had done as a kid.

Most practitioners would be moved to attempt a return of the silver dollars to this man. But because of the way that Charles had defined the situation, the nurse never did so. All signs suggested that Charles would have taken such behavior as condescension or insult.

To some street people, a mental health practitioner in their midst is an egregious affront to what little pride they have left. It is seen as blaming the victim, a veiled message from mainstream society to the effect that "you are homeless because you are defective and need to be fixed" (not because of a lack of affordable housing, etc.). A mental health intervention is then seen as an implicit certification of failure.

In this respect, mental health practitioners are set apart from all other practitioners on the streets. They are targeted for more shunning, more gamesmanship, more overt and covert hostility than are their fellow practitioners. At times street persons may go to considerable lengths to set a mental health practitioner up or to prove her or him wrong in some way. In the following instance, a street person's success in doing so led to a psychological lift that is difficult to fathom otherwise.

> Joseph was a hippie-styled man of 36 who suffered from chronic schizophrenia and/or chronic brain syndrome due to extensive drug and alcohol use (he never offered enough historical information for an accurate diagnosis). He safeguarded his self-illusions and pride, declining to apply for SSI despite meeting the criteria for it. He did not believe himself to be disabled, but would accept general assistance payments as long as a doctor such as the author would sign a form every three months to keep him off of the work readiness program. He resolved this apparent incongruity by framing it as if I were doing it for him as a favor rather than on the basis of my clinical conclusions that he was disabled. After I would sign his form, he would grin and put his arm around my shoulder and say, "thanks buddy." Our alliance was never strong enough to address this charade; after my signing, he would leave immediately, ignore my presence at the sites for the next three months, and then show up at the last possible instant, needing his form to be signed and mailed in a hurry. He would say that he had been confused about my whereabouts until the last minute despite the fact that I had given him several copies of my tour schedule which included telephone numbers for reaching me at any time. Gradually I came to attribute some of this behavior to cognitive deficits associated with his chronic condition.
>
> On one such occasion—the Friday before a holiday weekend—he found me at a drop-in center at 4 P.M. with his certification papers being due that day. He was his usual breathless and desperate self, but happy to have found "my buddy" to sign for him. It was his plan to run them down to the welfare office himself before 4:30. I balked at this

because it was standard practice for me to mail such forms, and because he had always been so easily confused and disoriented that I did not trust him to get the papers to where they needed to go before the deadline. Thus as I was signing the form I told him that I didn't think he could make it in time, but that I would put the form in Tuesday morning's mail and would make a call to emergency social services if he needed a voucher to get through the long weekend.

Upon hearing this, he uttered a short curse, snatched the certification paper from my hand and headed for the door, shouting back at me that he didn't have any time to argue further about it. I saw him again on the following Tuesday in the same drop-in center. I learned that he had made it in time and had delivered it to the right person. Moreover, all weekend he had been telling the story of my opposition to him "taking care of his business." In fact, he was telling of it at that moment to the drop-in center staff who were standing around him. Although I was tempted to upbraid him for his behavior, I half-bowed and half-nodded through his rendition of the story. His face first relaxed, then lit up later as he realized I was validating his story as he was telling it.

I believe it significant that this man never showed any confusion or disorientation again when he needed his papers signed. Moreover, drop-in staff later commented that a noticeable and enduring improvement in his mood and mental status seemed to have been triggered by the incident. There are undoubtedly other explanations for this, including the fact that such perceptions and attributions by drop-in staff probably include an element of their own attitudes toward mental health practitioners. Nevertheless, because of "last ditch" personal pride and the other culture-specific resistance themes just reviewed, the street practitioner will likely encounter (if not trigger) more instances of defiance-based change in street work than in other treatment contexts.

RESPONDING TO RESISTANCE

The basic functions of resistance are to safeguard a person's self-concept and protect the person from the destabilizing effects of change. Responding to resistance should minimize threats to self-esteem but still destabilize the other's world view to some modest extent. What follows should not be viewed as a list of specific techniques that dissolve or bypass resistances, thereby facilitating outreach work and rendering street people more receptive to the practitioner's offerings. Rather, they are attitudes that the practitioner can cultivate in the spirit of respectful curiosity that is consistent with the ecologist-practitioner model. These attitudes do not so much dissolve or bypass resistances as render them less necessary. Most of them have already been touched upon in the previous vignettes.

Empathy

The ability to engage difficult persons who may say or do noxious things hinges upon an empathic appreciation for the motives and meanings behind such behavior. It is unfortunate that the attitude of empathy championed by Carl Rogers has so often been trivialized as an echo-like response by a psychotherapist who invokes the very words that the other person had just uttered.

It is also unfortunate when mental health practitioners confuse empathy with sympathy. Sympathy conveys a note of condescension that is not always well received. At times it may elicit resistance behaviors by itself despite the sympathizing person's best intentions. In contrast, empathy has been conceived as essentially a cognitive exercise that is relatively unfettered by the feelings and values of the empathizing person (Wexler, 1974). It is the stance or attitude of placing oneself in someone else's shoes and striving to view the world as close as possible to the way in which that other person is viewing it—and subsequently permitting one's interventions to be guided by that world view. One can upbraid Joseph for having snatched and run away with the certification form, but holding my tongue and nodding along to his self-righteous explanation of the incident supported his own sense of mastery. Along similar lines, one does not rise to debate the "Doctor Seven" charges, and if a woman wishes to perceive her impairment as "submarine germ warfare," there is little to be gained by correcting her.

On the other hand, the empathic attitude is not the same thing as limitless tolerance. The woman who tracked and timed the mental health team and took her findings to an alderperson once claimed that she knew many who needed help but were afraid to ask for it. When it was suggested that she could help remedy this by introducing practitioners to these people, she smiled and said, "No, that's your job, this is mine." The empathic conclusion about her stance was that she needed to show practitioners up for reasons that had little to do with the mental health needs of homeless persons. It was therefore appropriate to rebuke her by saying that she was contributing more to the problem than to its solution.

Set a High Intolerance Threshold for Rejection

In the first chapter it was recounted how karate chops were pantomimed around a practitioner's head as he walked through a small group of strangers (p. 7). After passing through this gauntlet, he turned and asked if there were anything else he could do for them that night. The alternative responses of ignoring the behavior or asking security guards to intervene would bring nothing of value. And while the "choppers" themselves were not impaired and unlikely to seek the practitioner's help later, the payoff for such tolerance comes in what they tell others about it.

Steeling oneself to the discordant notes of sarcasm, cynicism, and "cheap shots" is desirable. But there are also situations—typically ones that repeat themselves in ritualistic fashion—which call for a reaction to some symbolic challenge. Hence one sometimes banters back, is confrontational, and so forth. Whatever the response, the street practitioner must not be easily discouraged by rejections. What Lamb (1982) wrote about young adult chronic patients holds for street persons in general, "It is important that we try to minimize our disappointment if our offers of help are rejected: we need to accept that our powers of persuasion are limited. Otherwise our feelings of disappointment are communicated to the patient, who experiences them as a sign that he has failed to measure up again" (p. 468).

Support Self-Help Efforts/Activism

Many of the themes that underly resistant behavior (e.g., "the spotted owl") attest to attitudes, energies, and personal resources which would be of use to organizations who represent homeless persons. Thus, resistance behaviors can be reframed as skills and directed to better uses. It is mildly amusing for the practitioner to observe how a heretofore recalcitrant person begins to beam when his or her oppositional views are afforded some respect. Besides serving as a recruitment vehicle for self-help organizations, such framings are inherently uplifting for a demoralized person and may prove to be the start of a therapeutic alliance. Those street persons who actually follow up on such referrals will avail themselves of opportunities to experience the empowerment, comraderie, and self-affirmation that comes with joining like-minded people in a rightful crusade.

Sense of Humor

In this context, humor is considered to be an attitude rather than a technique. It is a language of play that is invoked to tenderize things which are too harsh or conflictual to accept in their unadulterated forms. Culture-wide fears about secret psychoanalyses and being labeled were aired in banter by the wisecracking adversary at the shelter. Bantering back in front of the shelter guests signals that these (non) issues are not so dire or weighty that they cannot be played with. Humor is often chosen as a vehicle for expressing negative sentiment because it offers its generator a fallback position. One can decommit from the negative sentiment by claiming that, after all, one was only joking. Responding to humor in humor preserves this escape route. In this sense, it is not far removed from the consultation situation in which an ambivalent person seeks mental health advice under the guise that it is to benefit the proverbial unnamed "friend."

Sometimes a street person will indulge humor that targets the self along the lines of gallows humor (Kuhlman, 1988). If such humor is started proactively by the street person, it may be considered an invitation for the practitioner to inquire into underlying pain and desperation which the person has trouble bringing up more directly.

There are no firm guidelines for deciding whether one should interact within this language of play or nudge the street person into another dialect. Cues like the social situation (public versus private) and the strength of the alliance (first-time versus multiple contacts) help to guide such a decision. The practitioner can also draw on prior humor experiences from other contexts.

Stepping Out of Role

This general term best encompasses all that has been discussed thus far. It is particularly effective among those street people who hold to rigid, stereotyped expectations about practitioners and their behavior. Showing that one is not locked into a practitioner's role may be reciprocated by a street person electing not to stay locked into a resister's role.

For example, if the practitioner's title is "Dr.," introducing oneself by one's first name—"Dr. Tom Kuhlman" instead of "Dr. Kuhlman"—offers an invitation to informality and relaxes role-related expectations. People who wish to address a doctor will address me as "Dr;" those who wish to do otherwise can address "Tom."

When no one is requesting to be seen, it is productive to "hang out" and socialize rather than retreat to a quiet place to read or do paperwork. Informal equivalents of diagnostic and therapeutic interviews sometimes materialize in the middle of a crowded, smoke-filled room of cardplayers at a drop-in center. Some street people actually prefer the camouflage of a public conversation to a noticeable retreat to a private room in back in the company of a mental health practitioner.

Sometimes it is wise for the practitioner to perform small favors, such as provide short rides or small loans. Susser et al. (1992) have endorsed gift-giving and newspaper delivery as valid outreach methods under certain conditions. A first hour with one churlish bipolar person was spent playing pick-up sticks with coffee stirrers in the center of a drop-in center; later that winter, the same psychologist helped the man to jump the battery of his car. A social worker once accompanied a woman with schizophrenia on a long walk to an ex-boyfriend's house, even though the purpose was to ask him to return a long-stemmed rose that she had given to him five years earlier. It is in this spirit that Susser et al. (1990) described the introduction of a psychiatrist into a shelter for mentally impaired women by having him run the weekly game of bingo.

Self-Disclosure

This is another way for the street practitioner to step out of role. This interaction stance is often viewed critically outside of humanistic circles, but it is particularly called for when the practitioner must negotiate resistant attitudes which are grounded in socioeconomic gaps or in the practitioner's presumed alliance with The System. Self-disclosure has been shown to generate its own reciprocity effects (Jourard, 1971). Thus, a street person may feel compelled to self-disclose something at the same level of intimacy as that which he or she had received. For those practitioners who object to self-disclosure under all circumstances, street work offers the compelling argument that its people have either not responded to or become alienated from treatment approaches that are grounded in detached objectivity. One must try something else.

But the fact that all else has failed does not confer license to engage in freelance methods—particularly not those which prioritize the practitioner's sociopolitical positions over homeless persons' needs. Practitioner-of-last-resort is a liberating role but it is not one that is divorced from the traditional motives and objectives guiding all mental health philosophies. There is a danger that the practitioner will lose sight of these in the context of daily bouts with resistant and rejecting street people. Such bouts serve to remind the practitioner of the uninvited guest that he or she is. They also stir difficult emotions that must be self-monitored and sometimes reined in.

CHAPTER 4

Coping with Countertransference

The other side of the resistance coin—that of mental health practitioners toward treating street people and poor persons generally—has been discussed at length by Lorion and Felner (1986) and by Chafetz (1992). Something of a nadir was achieved in recent years when a psychologist—a member of the American Psychological Association's Division of Public Service, no less—ventured to say in a public forum that inferior practitioners and public service work went hand-in-hand. Practitioner resistance is so financially entrenched that Torrey (1992) has called for a mandatory tenure of public service for all mental health practitioners whose educational expenses are underwritten by government loan programs.

For a street practitioner to negotiate the resistance within the mental health professions is a minor achievement; to negotiate those of the street culture effectively and over time is a major one. The pervasive resistance of street cultures may be conceived as a transactional process whereby the collective demoralization of the street culture is passed on to the practitioner. This chapter focuses on the maintenance of a healthy outlook in the street practitioner. It is by design that such a consideration precedes indepth discussion of the mental health problems of street people. This prioritization of the practitioner's needs is neither an indulgence nor an indictment. Instead, it is an assertion that the street practitioner as change agent must take extraordinary steps to minimize or manage countertransference reactions that would otherwise impede effective functioning. As discussed in previous chapters, countertransference problems are likely to be greater on the streets than they are in office culture settings.

All of the mental health professions have shed illusions of practitioner immunity to the problems that practitioners treat. "Stress management" and "burnout" have become part of modern day jargon, a consensual acknowledgment of the ongoing toll of human service work upon those who practice it. The term "coping style" has been used to refer to a person's characteristic ways of handling the stressors that are encountered as part of day-to-day life.

The subtle foreignness of the street culture to middle class practitioners who enter it calls for variations in coping styles that are difficult to anticipate. The author's preferred coping style is to engage a sense of humor whenever possible. There is research evidence that documents the stress management properties of humor (Lefcourt & Martin, 1984). But some kinds of humor do not translate well into street work. For example, nothing-is-sacred, gallows humor (à la *M*A*S*H* and *Hill Street Blues*) is appropriate for settings that elicit autonomic arousal, existential paradox, and group cohesion based on mutual dependence (Kuhlman, 1993). Street culture is different: the stress of poverty is unremitting and tedious but only seldom leads to autonomic arousal. Moreover, there are few paradoxes to appreciate in poverty, and the street practitioner typically works alone amidst a group who view him or her as an outsider rather than as a comrade. Most of the copacetic humor that arises in street work refrains from targeting homeless persons and thus does preserve them as "sacred."

> Carl was a regular weekly volunteer to a drop-in center that served difficult people. His demeanor was pious, undemanding, and soft-spoken. He had a soothing effect on most people and, as a result, he was often assigned to monitor the waiting line that extended out of the drop-in and into the street during lunch hour. His job was to maintain order and fairness there without creating tension and resentment. He was good at it.
>
> One day Carl calmly advised a young hispanic man not to get back into line for seconds until everyone else had been served their firsts. The man exploded into a verbal rage of Spanish and smeared his used paper plate on Carl's shirt before storming off. Carl stood there speechless until another volunteer came forward with a wet towel and wiped him off, saying with obvious sarcasm, "he took the words right out of our mouths, Carl. We've been meaning to tell you that for months!" A couple of street people in line who knew Carl well picked up on this and jeered at him facetiously about his having displayed such bad manners.

The street person's behavior was inexcusable. If Carl had become outraged neither the street people who had witnessed the incident nor Carl's fellow volunteers would have blamed him. However, the ventilation of emotions was not the coping style of this pious volunteer. Humor materialized instead, but note that it was not the kind that would reinforce "us-versus-them" scripts. Those practitioners who cannot detach themselves in some fashion, and those practitioners who can detach themselves only in us-versus-them scripts that target homeless people need to seek debriefing from their colleagues and/or find other avenues for their volunteer work.

Coping styles other than humor are also altered by street work. It is common for social workers to come to identify more with street people than with their own supervisors; astute supervisors know not to challenge this. The line between service provision and advocacy becomes comfortably blurred. Few office culture practitioners would offer a ride home to a recipient without some hesitation, but this is common practice—and sometimes a *sine qua non*—in street work. Susser et al. (1990) wrote about practitioners teaching street clients "constructive sociopathy" to help them pressure and manipulate the very service systems which employed the practitioners. Most clergy do not bring up spiritual or religious issues with a street person unless the street person raises them first. One local exception to this rule is a charismatic woman who is renowned for washing the feet of street people in imitation of Christ in the New Testament. By virtue of such dedication, she has license to call street people to prayer.

One can always cope with the stressors and negativism of the street culture without resort to the washing of feet. And yet reflexive deference to office culture standards is not in order either. Instead, a street practitioner's freedom to meet his or her own stress management needs is limited mainly by the extent to which such actions occur at real or symbolic cost to those whom they serve. This is a standard that revolves around issues of countertransference.

VIEWS OF COUNTERTRANSFERENCE

Unfortunately, the widespread confusion and mystery surrounding countertransference make it a difficult standard to apply. The classical view of countertransference defined it as unconscious feelings, conflicts, and neurotic symptoms originating from the psychoanalyst's life that distort or otherwise interfere with the psychoanalyst's ability to understand the analysand. Freud (1910) was hardly enamored of this discovery, ". . . we are almost inclined to insist that he shall recognize this counter-transference in himself and overcome it . . . we have noticed that no psycho-analyst goes further than his own complexes and internal resistances permit" (pp. 144–145). Thus countertransference was a hindrance to treatment. The need for its remediation came to serve as a rationale for the directive that all psychoanalysts undergo a personal analysis as part of their training. It acquired connotations of error and became something of a bugaboo that encouraged defensiveness among psychoanalysts themselves, thus sometimes augmenting the very problem which its identification was meant to minimize.

In time, new conceptions of countertransference emerged that deviated from the classical view. A distinction was drawn between acute and chronic countertransference reactions, the former referring to situational lapses and the latter to ongoing habitual blindspots of the psychoanalyst (Singer & Luborsky, 1977). Springmann's (1986) differentiation of "client-induced" from "therapist-induced" countertransference corresponds to the acute versus chronic model. Both dichotomies retain the classical implications that countertransference is error but "connotations of sin and shame" (Abend, 1989) are confined to chronic/therapist-induced countertransference.

The normalization of countertransference began with a revised definition offered by Heimann (1950): countertransference encompasses all conscious and unconscious feelings which the practitioner feels toward the recipient. Later versions proposed that the practitioner's emotional reactions are an important therapeutic tool: Otto Kernberg (1965) is best known for championing this viewpoint in the treatment of borderline personality disorder. Wolstein (1959) viewed countertransference as operative in all treatment situations and as changing from session-to-session and person-to-person. Grossman (1965) expanded the concept further, deeming it a "universal human psychological reaction which occurs in one person towards another as a result of exposure to the transference feelings of that other person" (p. 252).

In concluding, a recent essay on the historical and cultural roots of countertransference, Abend (1989) observed that some version of the revisionist view is now accepted by all but the most orthodox of psychoanalysts, ". . . countertransference and analytic empathy are no longer seen in many quarters as denotations of easily and comfortably distinguishable classes of mental activity . . . It makes even less sense to suggest that analysts' emotional reactions to patients are ever simply realistic, or for that matter, merely accurate responses to the patient's material, wholly unaffected by the analyst's own past and particular psychic makeup" (Abend, 1989, pp. 386–387).

As newer psychoanalytic views of countertransference broadened and normalized it, cognitive theorists like Jerome Singer framed countertransference as a special set of cognitive biasing operations (Singer, Sincoff, & Kolligan, 1989). According to this view, countertransference is a normal consequence of a practitioner's information-processing style. It arises whenever session material fails to assimilate with/accommodate to operative scripts, schemas, and prototypes of the practitioner's prior experience or the "current concerns" of the practitioner's personal life. Of particular relevance in the present context is the fact that the model of Singer et al. (1989) addressed countertransference distortions based on the socioeconomic gap between recipient and practitioner. "Given that the sociocultural context in which the analyst grows up shapes his or her schemas and scripts, psychotherapy with *foreign* patients may pose special countertransference problems. Such interactions may lead to a surge in countertransferential reactions because the patient's associations and experiences may appear highly novel to the therapist" (Singer et al., 1989, p. 350). Substitution of the phrase "low socioeconomic status" for "foreign" does not alter the validity of the statement.

> Joan was a white female in her thirties with either paranoid schizophrenia or paranoid personality disorder. She enlisted the aid of a social worker solely to obtain subsidized housing on the basis of psychiatric disability. At that time, the local administrators of the Section Eight housing authority required a statement from a physician to establish disability. This posed a problem for Joan because she refused to go for an evaluation to the only medical clinic that was contracted with her particular managed care/medical assistance program. The social worker pressed Joan for several weeks until she finally provided an explanation for her refusal to go to that clinic. Twenty years earlier, Joan had been taken there as an adolescent after she and her father had returned to the Twin Cites following a harrowing six months of riding the rails together. At that time she had told the general practitioner about having found a decomposed human head in a train yard, and the general practitioner had snapped, "you watch too much TV!"
>
> After relating this story in a grudging fashion, Joan added, "I bet he grew up in a nice house and don't know nothing. All doctors want to do is push pills . . ."

A SAMPLE OF THEMES

Most conceptions of countertransference have originated from office culture practices where well-to-do people with conditions in the mild-to-moderate range of the severity spectrum voluntarily seek the services of mental health practitioners. Street work addresses those in the moderate-to-severe range of the spectrum, and many of these people are less than voluntary about it. Some have had negative experiences with mental health practitioners in the past, and there is also the foreignness factor of socioeconomic status differences between practitioner and street person, plus multiple sources of support for resistance and noncompliance.

All of the above factors combine to render countertransference and its management a different sort of challenge on the streets. Countertransference is used here in the revisionist sense of the term and refers to all subjective reactions evoked in the practitioner by the people and situations he or she encounters in the street culture. Such reactions are to be considered a normal part of street work, but two extreme positions are to be avoided or remedied. One extreme is the "connotation of sin and shame" which professional traditions have attached to less-than-complete objectivity. The other extreme is that of unbridled subjectivity and thoughtless deference to "gut feelings" or sociopolitical righteousness.

What follows is a range of expectable countertransference reactions that occur when the typical resistances of street people interact with the typical motivations of practitioners who serve them in either a volunteer or salaried capacity.

Altruism and Its Expectations

Seldom (if ever) do financial incentives bring practitioners to street work. Those who do it for a public sector salary can often find less stressful ways to make the same money. Most other public sector mental health positions are comfortably grounded in the office culture of appointments, support staff, and other institutional trappings that prioritize the conveniences of scarce practitioners over those of the people whom they are to serve.

Street work is not famous for its intellectual stimulation either. While there are many intriguing life stories to be heard, the intellectual challenges which do arise are confined to negotiating resistance and intervening effectively in situations that did not fare well in past treatment attempts. These challenges lose novelty value over time. In addition, street work is performed against an unstable backdrop in which regularly scheduled (practitioner controlled) sessions must be deferred to the exigencies of people who often live off the land.

With none of the common reward systems fully operative, it follows that many middle class practitioners are motivated to do street work by social conscience, spirituality, and/or altruism. When such is the case, does the practitioner expect that street people will validate the inherent goodness of volunteer work (or, for a salaried practitioner, the inherent goodness of declining the easier office culture life)? More to the point, does the street practitioner of any capacity anticipate expressions of gratitude from street people for his or her altruistic endeavors? Gratitude is certainly a reasonable expectation, but many street people in stages two and three of the acculturation process will not fulfill it. Some of the prouder ones choose not to openly admit to any gains that they may have realized; others (such as Mark, p. 17) are prone to express an opposite reaction. Yet others may have hidden agendas: a request from a street person for information about SSI may camouflage a tentative request that the practitioner endorse the person for SSI. Not infrequently those who have such agendas are individuals whom the practitioner deems to be least qualified for such benefits. The ultimate outcome of such an interaction thus has potential to become decidedly negative for all concerned, even though the practitioner has served the person well. Female practitioners who work with males are chagrined to be asked out on dates rather than thanked. It is bad enough when a woman is made to wonder if her intervention efforts had been misinterpreted all along. In addition, any disappointment or anger expressed by the man who is rejected for such a date will (at best) leave a bad aftertaste for all concerned. At worst, violence or threats of same are possible.

Other street persons seem to have no manners, or they are poorly socialized, or they are so preoccupied with their own needs that they pay scant attention to the interpersonal needs of the practitioners who serve them. Still others are disappointed when the practitioner proves unable to say or do something that will make their pains go away now. Signs of the "Is that all there is?" reaction range from furtive glances toward the clock to looking around the room and even inviting someone else to join the interview so as to "ditch" the practitioner on that other person. Isolated instances of ingratitude are not so difficult to tolerate, but these can accumulate over weeks and months. In time, these may coalesce into the practitioner's own demoralization syndrome, a condition that is aggravated by random encounters with individuals who are on "Doctor Seven" and "I'm-reporting-you-to-my-alderperson" missions.

It is heartening to observe practitioners who come to the work motivated by an altruism that insulates them from such trials and tribulations. Such a person would make a good role model if not for the fact that the ability to operate in such a selfless manner often represents only one facet of a deep philosophical, spiritual, or religious commitment to the work. The availability of such a person as a role model is limited to the appeal which others find in adopting that same world view for their own. Still, transcendence is a solution to countertransference problems.

A black female attorney who had devoted one night of volunteer service a week for several years was raped by a street client during a private consultation that took place in the furnace room of a shelter. She returned to that same shelter on her regular night after a layoff of one month, during which time the perpetrator had been caught and jailed. Her return seemed to cause more anxiety for her many street clients and fellow service providers than it did for her. She was grateful for their expressions of concern, but also assured them that she had begun personal therapy and expected to fully recover. As for her prompt return to street work, she offered a behaviorist's logic that the longer she stayed away from it, the more power her fear of it would wield over her. Implicit in this statement was an assertion that her street work was not something to be compromised. Thus, she resumed her work as before, albeit with more vigilance and security precautions. As weeks and months went by she displayed a disarming candor in raising the subject among groups of fellow providers whenever security concerns or coping with stress were being discussed. Her contributions at such times were typically brief and to the point but deeply valued by all.

This extraordinary response reflects an extraordinary person, but one who was as solidly grounded in her particular spirituality before her victimization as she was afterward. This is the sort of altruism that is lived, and it cannot be taught or acquired through imitation or reading. Those who live and work in harmony with their world views are invaluable as sounding boards for others because they are less prone to countertransference distortions. Unfortunately, transcendence cannot be taught to others as if it were a mere coping skill.

A more manageable adaptation is to simply lower one's expectations of gratitude. The practitioner should try to look at his or her interventions from a street person's perspective: the physiological relief imparted by medications, a flash of insight, the reassurance that comes with accurate empathy or finally finding someone with answers to questions that no one had been able to answer before—all of these benefits pale in comparison with the deprivation levels to which the street person returns after an intervention ends. It also follows from this that those sincere expressions of gratitude which the practitioner does receive may be taken to heart and savored.

Rides and Loans and Cigarettes

Some practitioners hesitate upon being asked to perform small favors. Traditionally, this issue has been viewed in terms of maintaining optimal relationship boundaries. Such considerations lose relevance amidst a culture that operates in the lower reaches of Maslow's (1970) hierarchy of needs. It is also possible that the small favors dilemma troubles street practitioners because such assistance could be as readily provided by less-trained others (Cohen & Marcos, 1992). Providing a ride or a small loan does not call upon the expert knowledge or human relations skills that mental health practitioners possess. Some practitioners perceive (project?) a subtle note of disrespect in such requests. There are the more general concerns about enabling or reinforcing beggary, and concerns about loaned money being spent on alcohol or drugs.

These are all understandable reactions. Perhaps they do not reflect condescension and cynicism so much as they reflect the dearth of traditional reward mechanisms available to street practitioners. It may help for the practitioner to view the provision of rides or loans or cigarettes as an outreach method. As such, it may have an impact not only upon the immediate beneficiary but also upon others to whom "the word gets out" from the immediate beneficiary.

Mitchell was a proud, young black man who had moved to the Twin Cities in search of a "geographic cure" for his past involvements with gangs and cocaine. He found the legitimate job market difficult to pierce because he lacked a high school diploma and local references. However, he was bright, had an infectious personality, and prevailed upon people to "pull the strings of the system for me." He assured all whose help he enlisted that he would wait patiently to be connected to a full-time, "livable wage" job and that he would work odd jobs and sleep in shelters in the meantime. He declined to apply for general assistance, ostensibly because he was certain that one of "my benefactors" (shelter providers, practitioners, and the like) would eventually deliver for him. These benefactors tried instead to persuade him of the value of returning to school for his G.E.D. (high school equivalency diploma) so that he would not have to rely on others. He would usually respond to this smilingly, saying that he was too old to return to school and that he was sure someone would deliver any day now, and in the meantime were there any odd jobs he could do?

Mitchell sought a psychiatric resident for counseling when he learned that his father had died suddenly in Albuquerque. Most of this counseling revolved around whether or not to return home to the family and his not wanting to call them for help in purchasing an airline ticket for this purpose. Ultimately he decided to go; to obtain money for the trip, he approached the black proprietor of a dry cleaning store. This proprietor was willing to provide him with a loan or gift, but Mitchell would accept neither. Instead, he proposed to sell the dry cleaner's clothes hangers as advertisements (the tissue covering their frames had the establishment's name on it). After the proprietor consented to this, Mitchell made the rounds of his benefactors with the story of how he had been able to refuse the proprietor's charity because he knew that they would all need to buy hangers to put their white, middle class winter clothes on for the summer. Although the resident had no such need for the hangers and told Mitchell so, she agreed to buy ten dollars worth.

It was in the winter after Mitchell had left town that the extent of his salesmanship skills were finally appreciated. Whenever the resident visited a street culture site and had to hang up her coat, she was invariably offered one of Mitchell's hangers (no one who had bought any of these had bothered to take them home). In fact, in the first part of that winter, Mitchell's various benefactors would exchange a greeting of "nice hangers" when visiting each other's sites upon being offered such a hanger. By doing so, each person reinforced a group cohesion around a favorite person whom each had served at one time or another. It is doubtful whether Mitchell could have earned his airplane ticket in any better way.

Unless one chooses to promote and advertise small favors, a practitioner's concerns about being deluged with requests for rides, loans, and so on are not warranted. The reason for this is that the distrust of mental health practitioners on the streets serves to hold down demand for such favors. Even so, the practitioner's public relations are served by the spread of knowledge that he or she has provided such favors to someone at some time.

Offering such favors to a difficult person is a different matter than merely responding to requests for same. The vexing problem is to decide when such favors ought to be offered and whether this necessarily involves the practitioner making implicit judgments as to a potential recipient's worthiness. The practitioner is advised against reliance upon subjective feelings about a particular person at a particular time. Instead, he or she should consider to what extent an assessment or treatment issue is likely to be served by offering favors in a given situation. Such a standard also provides an unbiased rationale for declining to assist other persons who solicit such favors only because "the word has gotten out." Confining one's largesse to people with whom outreach is desired or a working relationship already established keeps the practitioner away from making value judgments. It is also a comfortable position from which to say no to people with whom the practitioner is not working.

Dislikable/Dangerous Persons

Not rendering value judgments about homeless people does not mean that the mental health practitioner need strive to maintain unconditional positive regard for all. There are dislikable and dangerous people in the street culture, as there are in all other strata.

Groves (1978) offered a fourfold classification scheme of dislikable clients and the countertransference reactions that they elicit from caregivers: "dependent clingers," for example, elicit aversion and avoidance behaviors. "Entitled demanders" elicit fear, "manipulative help-rejecters" elicit guilt and a sense of inadequacy, and "self-destructive deniers" elicit malice (Bachrach, Talbott, & Meyerson,

1987). All four types are present on the streets, along with career criminals, some of whom evade authorities by blending into this anonymous culture. One also meets perpetrators of taxpayer fraud (the Leona Helmsleys of this strata) as well as predatory types who prey upon vulnerable street persons.

The street practitioner cannot expect to be entirely safe from physical danger. Becoming known within a street culture brings with it some degree of immunity from predation, but this is neither comprehensive nor guaranteed. The female practitioner should consider possible advantages in not looking or dressing her best. Some women have been advised against wearing jewelry pieces by friendly street persons. Generally, discretion and common sense will enable the practitioner to minimize safety risks, but one sometimes encounters trouble when it is least expected.

> The author had just parked his car behind a drop-in center for a customary Monday morning stop. The lot seemed deserted as I proceeded toward the building except for a small huddle of three men 30 yards away who were bent over something in the midst of them. One man looked up and saw me, after which he and a second man ran off in the opposite direction. The third, a large man who wore mirror-lensed sunglasses, walked deliberately in a direction that was seemingly chosen to intercept my path. I concluded that I had stumbled upon some sort of drug or contraband transaction involving the two other men, and that this third one who approached me was a bodyguard or filled some other "muscle" role. Still, the man's slow, deliberate manner of approach implied that the situation had not yet been defined as emergent. As my path was about to cross in front of his, I offered him a smile and a nod, as if to say "good morning." The man stopped, nodded back, and withdrew in a continuous motion which suggested that up to that moment his entire attention had been keyed to my own movements.

Once I was safely inside, I resisted an urge to call the police. Such actions are best reserved for emergencies of imminent or ongoing physical danger to self or others. With the danger having elapsed in this situation, there was no evidence of any crime and hence little that the police could do. Meanwhile, it is a decided disadvantage for street people to observe a practitioner in consultation with the police. Many street people have concrete reasons (both real and imagined) to fear the police. Others view police as convenient symbols of The System, and still others are angered by the double standard whereby police respond better to a practitioner's call for assistance than to a call from a low status homeless person. The police officers themselves may view such calls as more nuisances than emergencies. The more often such perceptions are reinforced, the more slowly they are likely to respond to that caller and site in the future.

Countering all of these practical considerations is one compelling argument for calling the police. It exerts some personal control over the situation (whether real or imagined) and thus provides some sense of mastery. If meeting such a need is critical, the street practitioner should not hesitate to make the call provided that this decision has been made on the basis of a cost/benefit analysis rather than the heat of emotion. The street practitioner must also keep in mind that his or her role is one of practitioner-of-last-resort. Law enforcement and street safety is the province of others and should be left to those others.

Beyond the countertransference issues raised by specific situations are the cumulative effects of encountering larger numbers of dangerous and dislikable people than one commonly meets in office culture practices. Periodically it is important to pause and reflect on the private attributions that one makes about these people. It is true that the same social selection processes responsible for the drift of many psychotic people into the street culture also operates upon people with severe personality disorders of either the inadequate ("loser") or antisocial ("asshole") variety. But it is also true that their seeming disproportionate numbers are artifacts of the outreach process itself. The engagement rules of outreach eliminate barriers to contact between strangers. Wearing a nameplate and seeing people on their turf rather than on one's own invites harassment to some extent. And with the obstacles of client registration, fee accountability, and the lag time before an appointment removed, the street practitioner is available to a greater number of impulsive and frivolous contacts than in the office culture. In the absence of comparable data from middle class sites (e.g., suburban shopping malls), it is not valid to conclude that dislikable persons are any more prevalent in or characteristic of street culture. Dislikability may sometimes reflect the perceiver's own cultural biases.

Moreover, some disliked people make legitimate requests for service. Restless boredom and aimless provocations sometimes belie a growing self-awareness that one has authored many of the miseries and failures that had previously been attributed to situations or to other people. A disliked person's motivation for help may be as genuine and optimal as anyone else's.

> The author was once engaged by a thirtyish white male as he waited in line for a shower at a shelter. He wanted help with his depression. As it turned out, he was depressed because he had again bitten hands which had fed him, a recurring theme of his life which he explained

> as, "I've just never been able to say 'no' to a good time." He was chemically dependent but insisted that his lapses in judgment were not confined to or controlled by alcohol and drugs. Sometimes he would leave a town because it suited him to do so ("I get claustrophobia when things get too familiar") or because he wanted to evade gambling debts or bar tabs so as to begin again elsewhere with a fresh start. He would always do well for a while until a good time would present itself and "lead me astray." When I asked about times in his life when he had thought himself successful, a boyish animation came to his face and he said, "you probably won't believe this but I was in Hell's Angels once! I got tattooed on my initiation!" Without further ado he rolled up his sleeve and proudly showed off his tattoo. "Hell's Angels" was spelled "Hell's Angles."
>
> This man showed no recognition or concern about the misspelling. I was seized by an impulse to laugh which was so strong that I excused myself so I could indulge it in the confines of the bathroom. While composing myself there, I imagined that the misspelling had been done on purpose and that the man had been initiated purely to serve as a laughing stock for the gang.

Such a strong reaction is rare but unnerving for the practitioner. It is to be understood as a signal that the practitioner has lost empathic contact through the shift of a seemingly hopeless encounter into the realm of play. Episodic lapses into condescension, cynicism, and burnout are other occupational hazards of street work. No one can claim immunity to them or find solace in the illusion that such reactions "can't happen to me." It is under such illusions that a practitioner's distaste for a particular person's lifestyle, values, and/or belief systems will bring to mind such phrases as "refractory to treatment" or "severe character pathology." Such thinking masks value judgments being rendered as to who is worthy of a practitioner's attention and who is not.

In this particular instance, the man was referred to a different street practitioner for a second opinion. In the office culture, second opinion referrals are typically made of people who present with clinical complexities or specialized needs. Most second opinion referrals in street work are prompted by countertransference reactions. I informed my colleague that the man had elicited a strong personal reaction from me such that I believed I could not do justice to his request for counseling. The person on the receiving end of such a referral prepares him or herself for the possibility of a similar reaction and is thereby less prone to be impaired by it.

Sometimes countertransference signals will be faint to nonexistent when a practitioner arrives at conclusion of "untreatable." Such a conclusion may well be accurate and the street person should be given this opinion directly, preferably with an explanation as to how it was arrived at and what it means. This may serve as a spur to defiance-based change in some other venue. And in light of the unfathomable margin of error in arriving at such conclusions, the street practitioner may also refer the person on to an office culture facility. The rationale for this is that such a person is unlikely to benefit from treatment unless the motivation for treatment is a deep and driving one. The bureaucratic obstacles, time delays, and inadvertent snubs of the office culture represent a test of that inner motivation to change. Those in lesser states of readiness will become dropouts, but those who endure the barriers of the office culture are clearly more promising candidates for change than the street practitioner had initially thought. If contacted by the new practitioner for information, the referring one should emphasize the street person's surmounting of these barriers as much as any Axis II problems that exist. Referrals to office culture sites should not be made when a person shows clear Axis I problems or appears to be in the throes of a significant psychosocial crisis. Under such circumstances, the delays imposed by office culture barriers are likely to make matters worse, the street person more desperate—and perhaps also evoke more behavior for middle class practitioners to dislike.

Lies

Recall Joan (p. 79) who had found a decomposed human head in a train yard as an adolescent. This information was introduced as reality, but what if the twenty-years-ago physician had been correct about Joan's having watched too much television. Perhaps there had been no decomposed head, no train yard. For that matter, perhaps there had been no such physician and no prior visit to that clinic by Joan as an adolescent. Perhaps the whole story had been concocted on the spur of the moment to conceal other reasons for not wanting to see a physician. Perhaps the social worker allowed a vivid, compelling image of an adolescent finding a decomposed head on railroad tracks to overpower her knowledge of the statistical infrequency of such events. In fact, her suspicions to that effect had been raised after she viewed a similar scene in the then-current feature film, *Stand by Me*.

What is truth and what is fiction? Many mental health practitioners would respond that such a question is of minor relevance when compared to the interpersonal dynamics that have arisen between the social worker and Joan concerning the former's efforts to persuade the latter to see a physician. While this is an astute consideration, it is also one that is steeped in office culture standards. In street work, entitlement program benefits derived from tax dollars are often assigned on the basis of clinical judgments and guesstimations of truth by mental health practitioners. The practitioner may have only one clinical contact and no treatment records or history available other than what is provided by the street person. Moreover, those who fabricate such stories and succeed with them are likely to share this later at the drop-in centers and thus incite other street persons to attempt the same thing.

All of this imposes additional countertransference freight on the street practitioner to determine whether or not he or she is receiving "the truth." Another incentive to settling for "the-truth-and-nothing-but-the-truth" originates among street practitioners themselves. Those who work with difficult or unresponsive people under conditions over which they have little control tend to develop their own in-group standards of success (Kuhlman, 1993). This is done to recognize and justify the group's collective effort. In street work, it becomes a badge of skill and savvy not to have been fooled or taken advantage of.

The street practitioner may be assured from the outset that there will be no shortage of lies, stories, and other manipulations directed in his or her way. The levels of deprivation that prevail upon the streets and the dismal prospects that street people perceive to be their futures enable them to rationalize all manner of deceptions in the service of underwriting their own survival. They can also point to the Boeskys, Milkens, and Keatings of the national news to justify their actions.

The mental health practitioner who is not willing to be deceived or "made a fool of" at least some of the time is not well prepared for street work. Vigilance to the truth-versus-manipulation dichotomy will mean that one's "third ear" is occupied in ways other than helping a person master pain and solve problems. In light of the street culture's alienation from the mainstream culture, practitioner mistakes that occur from suspending one's disbelief are preferred over ones that occur from suspending one's belief. This is not to say that gullibility is acceptable, or that one may adopt a cavalier attitude toward the responsibility for making accurate judgments about eligibility for entitlement programs. It is to recommend that the street practitioner be more generous with the benefit of the doubt than with the doubt of the benefit. One needs to resist pressure from peers, supervisors, and systems to define good street skills in terms of not being manipulated or fooled. There are many worse things that a practitioner-of-last-resort can do.

The train yard instance was one in which it was not so critical whether or not Joan had been telling the truth. However, she was being clear about a need for special assistance if she were ever to proceed to an examination by a physician. Her message was to "Stand by Me" through this process and not expect her to go and see the physician alone.

The social worker decided to physically accompany Joan to her examination. She waited in the waiting room for Joan and had every opportunity to inquire of the support staff as to the existence of medical records dating back to the time of Joan's adolescence when the contact with the first physician had purportedly taken place. The social worker chose not to make such an inquiry. She decided that the information which this would have given her about Joan was not as important as sparing herself the possibility of acquiring fuel for prejudice and cynicism toward the next street person who would tell her a story that was difficult to believe.

Advocacy

Few mental health practitioners have ever received training or support for advocacy interventions. Advocacy straddles and blurs the boundary which separates studious objectivity from countertransference and over-involvement. Advocacy does not tap one's intellectual acumen or specialized training either. It touches on many of the same countertransference issues as do the provision of rides and loans.

Advocacy has been legitimized and encouraged by authorities who champion the cause of the severely mentally impaired (e.g., Lamb, 1992; Torrey, 1988). In street work, it may also weaken resistances to treatment as an individual or collective intervention. Susser et al. (1990) reported on a women's shelter in New York City where enrollment in a mental health program was initially spurred by the fact that the program provided easy access to free hygiene supplies. The impaired recipients of this program next sought and received advocacy efforts on their behalf in dealing with various aspects of the shelter bureaucracy. Only after the program had achieved some successes in this realm did its staff deem it wise to promote mental health treatment *per se*. While some women remained resistant to such treatment, many others displayed a new openness to it. Susser et al. concluded that the staff's advocacy activities had served to change the connotation of mental health treatment from one of punishment to one of benefit.

A psychologist was summoned to the bus depot on a Friday afternoon by an emergency social service agency. She was to intervene with a mentally impaired itinerant who had called emergency social services in order to request financial assistance for the weekend. The itinerant proved to be an eccentric man in cowboy dress who smiled easily, referred to himself as "plumb" good-natured, and insisted upon addressing the psychologist as "little lady." He was not notably symptomatic but admitted to psychiatric hospitalizations in his past and being on SSI for his "nerves." His suitcase had CROCODILE DUNDEE and FROM THE LAND DOWN UNDER printed in large, bold letters on its two sides.

The man explained that he had come to Minneapolis because his SSI check originated there. It hadn't come to him in the mail that month and so he had come north to fetch it himself at the post office. Being out of money and realizing he would have to stay at least one night and maybe two depending on the post office, he had been directed by Traveler's Aid to call emergency social services for a voucher. They had insisted that he furnish them with proof that he had not received his check that month before they would consider giving him a voucher.

Upon learning this, the psychologist telephoned emergency social services who verified the man's version of what had been said to him. The psychologist proceeded to dispute the agency's actions, alluding several times to her doctoral status for persuasive effect. She labeled it an "epistemological paradox" to ask someone to submit definitive proof of something that could only be defined in terms of its non-occurrence. The emergency social services person responded that she hadn't really looked at it that way before and subsequently faxed a voucher to cover the man's room and board expenses for the weekend.

Advocacy is not always an unidirectional process of street person versus System. Just as many middle class people perceive and respond to street people according to stereotypes, so too do street people perceive and respond to middle class persons. The danger of advocacy is for it to shade into over-identification. The street practitioner operates best by being able to shift empathic reference points between the middle and lower classes. At times, this means that he or she must show the street person how the latter's own biases and stereotypes often contribute to adjustment problems.

Mary was a hispanic women in her late forties, a de facto neighborhood leader despite being disabled by bipolar disorder. At one point, she broke up with a male partner who subsequently put the word out on the street that he was going to kill her. Mary began to carry a small firearm for protection and confided this fact to her favorite staff person of the drop-in center that she frequented. When this staff person learned that Mary had the weapon on her at the time of this revelation, she escorted Mary out of the building and banished her for a month because of Mary's knowing violation of that center's rules against firearm possession on the premises.

Mary flagged down the psychiatric nurse a few days later outside the center and complained bitterly about this banishment. After telling him the story, she pulled the gun out of her halter top and waved it in front of the nurse, saying "you gonna lock me out too, nurse?" (Since they were outside of the building at that time, he was able to shake his head, "no.") Mary went on to charge that "you middle class people who work nine-to-five then sleep in the suburbs" had no idea what the streets were like or of a woman's need to defend herself.

Time spent in a street culture teaches empathic acceptance of the need to carry a weapon. In fact, there was more validity to Mary's possession of the weapon than there was to her attributions about her banishment. Street sites invariably forbid weapons, but their reasons have nothing to do with class consciousness.

When the nurse was given an opening to speak, he suggested to Mary that she had misread staff's determination to preserve a safe environment as class bias. Her face tightened as he said this and he decided not to dwell on her attribution error or explore the rejection message of the banishment. Instead he told her what regular carriers of firearms had told him that they did, which was to bury or hide their weapons when they went into a drop-in center or shelter and retrieve them when they left. She indignantly responded that she knew plenty of people who carried weapons and concealed them when inside these places and just didn't tell anyone. The nurse countered that the shelter staff were not in the detective business and preferred not to install metal detectors and sacrifice what humaneness they could maintain in their sites to guard against such concealed weapons. But by Mary's acknowledging her weapon, she placed her favorite staff in a quandary over whether to honor their special relationship versus the handgun ban. The nurse then told her that he supported the staff member's action and would have done same thing.

Mary dropped her class-consciousness diatribe and seemed somewhat pacified by his suggestion that she take this up with her favorite staff after the banishment was over. Such a recommendation implied that the nurse would not advocate on her behalf to have the banishment lifted, which is what he believed had been Mary's agenda in the first place. Weeks later, he again encountered her inside the drop-in center. She returned his eye contact and greeting at that time but immediately looked away from him afterward. He interpreted this as discouraging any follow-up about the incident and thus he never learned whether she had taken his advice or not.

KEEPING PERSPECTIVE

The street practitioner must endure closer proximity to sexual intimidation, drug deals, and firearms—plus less protection from these—

than office culture settings normally impose. Nevertheless, direct encounters are exceptions rather than the rule, and common sense precautions reduce a mild risk of victimization to a minimal one.

There are no such common sense precautions that will eliminate a wide array of countertransference and stress reactions. Periods of burnout are inevitable. The quandaries associated with being both uninvited guest and practitioner-of-last-resort extend beyond those faced by ethnographers and other such participant observers. Yet one more stressor: street people disappear and die more frequently and unpredictably than do office culture people.

> Six months after his return to Albuquerque, Mitchell wrote to the dry cleaning proprietor who had subsidized his ticket. The letter included a check for the full amount of the airfare and the news that Mitchell had earned this money at a full-time job. He added that he had been staying clear of his old haunts, vices, and crowds, and more heartening still was the news that he was enrolled in a night school and pursuing his G.E.D. finally.
>
> Three months after this first letter, the dry cleaner received a letter from Mitchell's mother thanking him for all he had done for her son. She revealed that Mitchell had been shot to death, presumably by old gang acquaintances who were settling old scores with him.

An untimely death of a well-liked person is difficult enough, but among some providers who knew Mitchell, this was also taken as a metaphor for their work. There is no prophylactic or antidote for such reactions, only the minor consolation that the demoralization thus visited upon providers keeps them in empathic resonance with the people whom they serve. After a short time of wincing and mourning, one must shrug and turn one's attention to the next person.

There are proactive and reactive steps that the practitioner can take to manage and minimize the effects of stress. These include the stress management techniques that have been popularized by various workshops and publications. Strategies that are more esoteric to street work have been described in the previous chapter as well as this one. A final step involves keeping variety in the social spheres of one's work. It is desirable for the street practitioner to work with traditional, office culture people at the same time he or she is working on the streets. A practice that includes people who are less disturbed, better motivated, and more respectful of the practitioner's expertise and authority will neutralize or balance some of the rejection and discouragement which characterizes outreach work.

Those who must work exclusively as practitioners-of-last-resort have been forewarned that such work entails greater degrees of freedom and discretion, looser boundaries, and much more resistance and rejection than are customarily encountered in mental health work. These conditions also predispose a street "specialist" to over-identify with the street culture. Identifying with one's recipients is a key stage in the process of empathy, but it is only one stage. The empathic practitioner maintains a distinction between the recipient's world view and the practitioner's own. It is continuous vacillation between these two perspectives that generates effective mental health interventions. The over-identified practitioner vacillates less frequently or perhaps not at all. He or she accepts the perspectives, beliefs, and enemies of the street person as objectively valid rather than subjectively valid. This compromises the practitioner's ability to effectively mediate between the street culture and the mainstream culture (which sponsors entitlement programs, treatment and support services, and other assistance mechanisms). The overidentified practitioner comes to see The System as the enemy. Perhaps he or she sits down at a drop-in center table and takes part in the ongoing raillery at the expense of certain System workers, programs, or paperwork. Such joining-in is likely to spillover later into the practitioner's interactions with those very facets of The System. Just as a practitioner's development of an "us versus them" schema against street people must be avoided, so too must an "us versus them" schema against The System be avoided. Indulging a street person's resentment of the mainstream serves no better purpose than indulging a mainstream person's contempt for the street culture.

Keeping one foot planted on each side of the line separating social classes is difficult. But it is submitted here that such bridges must multiply if the problem of homelessness in America is to be substantially reduced. There is no shortage of culprits upon whom to blame the homelessness problem, and there are voting booths and "private life" activities through which one can address these. Financial workers, intake clerks, application takers, and other System representatives with whom the street practitioner must interact on a street person's behalf are not appropriate targets just because they are more concretely available and have names and faces. The street practitioner accomplishes more for the people he or she works with by preserving an ability to empathize with System workers as well. "Constructive sociopathy"—casually dropping one's "Doctor" title at every opportunity, or appealing to the other's sense of "epistemological paradox"—will accomplish more than displays of righteous indignation. In fact, the practitioner is likely to meet a number of System workers with divided loyalties to street persons and System. Many of these are willing to be "sociopathized" on behalf of homeless persons if conditions seem to warrant this.

The importance of collegial input for identifying and controlling countertransference reactions is well-recognized. It will not be belabored here except to note that the street practitioner should avail her/himself of consultation opportunities with colleagues from both inside and outside of street work. Insiders offer the advantage of contextual empathy for the practitioner's dilemmas, but also the biases generated by "groupthink" cohesion (Janis, 1982). Outsiders offer a more detached perspective which is valuable for practitioners in a field where the standards of practice are not yet well established, and where the pitfalls associated with countertransference reactions are so numerous.

CHAPTER 5

Schizophrenia, Street Types

The street practitioner's grounding in the literature on schizophrenia should include the writings of Thomas Szasz and R.D. Laing, each of whom espoused the view that mental impairment exists primarily in the eyes of its beholder. The main function of mental impairment diagnoses according to Szasz (1970) is to justify imposing controls upon those who would deviate from mainstream norms of behavior. Laing (1967) viewed schizophrenia as a sane response to an insane world.

Mental health practitioners are usually quick to dismiss these anti-psychiatry views. But it does not take long before one senses that such ideas are very much alive within street cultures. They are certainly more alive than are deinstitutionalization, the revolving door syndrome, and other prisms through which academics and professionals usually view the problems of homelessness. The creation of a working alliance with a psychotic street person often means that the practitioner must adopt a "what if" stance toward anti-psychiatry in the beginning. This does not represent such a radical departure as it initially seems. Most psychotherapists are willing to suspend skepticism and refrain from value judgments about the objective accuracy or validity of a person's self-reports, at least in the beginning of treatment. It is difficult to fathom a process of psychotherapeutic change that does not begin with empathic acceptance of the other's operative world view. It is only logical, then, to extend this same consideration to a psychotic person. The fact that such a person's world view is alien from one's own in form as well as content makes such a task difficult. However, it does not warrant the practitioner's setting aside empathic skills and dismissing the other's world view as a manifestation of "first rank symptoms" or some such thing.

Consider the phrase "lack of insight" as it commonly appears in reports about persons diagnosed with schizophrenia. Lack of insight is typically associated with the phrase "into one's illness" and it implies that one's mental impairment has an objective reality that can be reliably agreed upon by most mental health practitioners familiar with that person, if not by family and friends of the individual as well.

When the affected person does not also acknowledge that consensual reality, he or she is said to show lack of insight.

From a practitioner's viewpoint, lack of insight typically portends a more guarded prognosis, lowered expectations of the person, and ultimately less effort expended to understand the person in light of this most basic of practitioner/recipient disagreements. The practitioner anticipates that such a person will refuse his or her ministrations; thus when noncompliance occurs it does so with elements of a self-fulfilling prophecy. In partial remedy of this difficult state of affairs, practitioner traditions have semantically elevated "lack of insight" to the status of psychological traithood as possessed by the impaired person. By attributing its existence to the impaired person alone, the practitioner is relieved of any burden of ongoing negotiations with the resistant person.

What is habitually overlooked is that such a "lack" has no verifiable existence beyond an impaired person's willingness to disagree with a practitioner. It is interactional and not psychological in nature, and it may have many meanings: conceivably the impaired person is aware that something is wrong but is reluctant to acknowledge this because of revulsion for the stigma of mental illness, or because of fear of hospital-based confinement and interventions, or because of symbolic associations between such an admission and one's important life themes, or because of personal pride, or because of some combination of the above. In light of this, it is not entirely facetious to question whose lack of insight it is, anyway.

In a *zeitgeist* of civil liberties and least restrictive treatment, it is difficult to separate lack of insight from rejection of the patient role, which Minkoff (1987) identified as the major legacy of deinstitutionalization. Statutory mechanisms such as the dangerousness standard for civil commitment have abetted the rejection of the patient role. Many psychotic individuals who have resisted the efforts of family, mental health practitioners, and police to have them take medications, attend socialization therapies, or be hospitalized discover that their right to "fly out of formation" (R.D. Laing's metaphor) is upheld by the courts as long as one is not a danger to self or others. For both better and worse, the mainstream has signaled these people that they need not subscribe to practitioner insights about their conditions so long as no one is endangered by their behavior. Many of them see little inherent benefit in acceding to such insights amidst a culture whose vernacular offers no quicker way to voice generic disrespect than to dismiss a person as "crazy" and his or her assertions as "insane." It is not surprising that so many psychotic individuals, their cognitive processes already impaired, interpret courts upholding their civil liberties as justification for not submitting to mental health treatment or accepting the patient role that such treatment would impose.

Something of a backlash against this has materialized in the literature of the 1990s (Lamb et al., 1992). Armat and Peele (1992) have argued for an "in need of treatment" standard for civil commitment. This in effect would expand the power of courts and mental health practitioners to impose the patient role on persons who are not covered by the dangerousness standard. Hospitalization has begun to lose its negative connotations with the quiet acknowledgment that institutionalization once provided asylum, respite, and low demand conditions to people who were too impaired to cope without them (Bachrach, 1993; Lamb, 1992). Lamb (1992) recently drew parallels between the plight of the mentally impaired and that of the developmentally disabled. Brain-as-diseased-organ (Armat & Peele, 1992; Torrey, 1992) has begun to nudge the biopsychosocial model further into the biological realm. Lamb and Weinberger (1993) have championed the linkage of conservatorship with case management. Appelbaum (1991) has proposed that a psychotic person sign an advance directive (akin to a living will) while he or she is asymptomatic. This would legally authorize the person's psychiatrist to restart anti-psychotic medications if the person relapses into an active psychotic state and refuses to take them voluntarily. Civil commitment to outpatient treatment is also receiving more attention now than it has received in the past (Miller, 1992).

Many of these developments remain in the dissemination or debate stage at present. Unless/until these become standard practice—and probably beyond that time—the street practitioner will need to remain open to suspending her or his expert knowledge in favor of antipsychiatry notions as an empathic premise of outreach work. This has some redeeming features, one being that it creates room for novel interventions (e.g., "submarine germ warfare" specialist). Another is that such a perspective forces the practitioner to attend to the adaptational strengths of the psychotic persons who operate within a street culture. He or she is likely to conclude that some of these people not only adapt adequately to a street person's role but also prefer it to a mental health patient's role.

SOCIAL SELECTION REVISITED

As previously noted, communities and regions vary in the degree of their neglect of severely impaired persons. The extent of that local neglect, as reflected in the availability of treatment and housing programs for the mentally impaired, shapes the size and nature of the psychotic component of a local street culture.

Still, some limited generalizations about this subgroup of people may be offered. The street practitioner will encounter few chronically violent and/or disorganized psychotic persons because these people tend to remain institutionalized in hospitals or jails. He or she will also encounter few of the high functioning individuals with schizophrenia. These are people who experience only time-limited psychotic episodes, and/or who respond well to medication, and/or who are blessed with supportive families and social networks. None of these types are prevalent on the streets. In low neglect regions, street practitioners will encounter only a few of the passive, submissive psychotic persons who readily defer to authority figures and external structure. Whether it is by virtue of impairment severity, personality factors, insight into their impairments, or some combination of the above, these people are readily integrated into community-based treatments and supportive residences that provide them with a valued buffer between themselves and the demands of the mainstream world.

Thus, the psychotic person who endures amidst a street culture is not so dangerous or disorganized as to require institutional controls. He or she tends to not have a good treatment record with medications, and to be alienated from family and support systems (and such estrangement may be a long-term consequence of an anti-hospitalization era's deferral to families that they tolerate and adjust to the psychotic behavior of an aberrant member beyond what was healthy for the family as a whole). The psychotic street person tends not to be submissive, compliant, or deferential to authority. To survive on urban streets and in urban jails with the adaptational handicap of psychotic symptoms requires that one not be docile or easily led. For such individuals, lack of insight into their deficits may belie keen insight that disclosing or acknowledging such deficits either threatens a loss of autonomy or increases the person's vulnerability. These people are not easily socialized into the patient role and reject the rules that many community-based treatments and supportive residences would impose upon them: mandatory medications taken at scheduled times, mandated individual and group treatment sessions, preassigned roommates not of their own choosing, forced abstention from cigarettes, alcohol, and sex except under highly restrictive conditions. Some resent supervision of their disability stipends and their lives in general by case managers. Others resent the stigmatization that comes with living in a congregate residence with other persons who are mentally impaired.

Beneath these protests bubble motives of personal pride, self-determination, and privacy. Such motives may receive mere lip service when a mentally impaired person is discussed. Consider Joyce Brown, a forty-year-old woman with untreated psychosis who staked squatter's rights to a particular street corner in Manhattan and subsequently became the most famous of mentally impaired street persons (Cohen and Marcos, 1992; Cournos, 1989). She lived there for more than a year despite symptoms and self-care deficits that were so extreme that Project Help moved to hospitalize her with the public support of New York City's mayor. This triggered a national debate about what to do with homeless, mentally impaired persons. This debate's varied themes touched upon the assessment of competency in psychotic persons, the right to retain civil liberties versus conforming to community standards of acceptable behavior, the right to refuse a treatment that would ameliorate symptoms and make one more acceptable to the public, and the difficulty of managing such persons in supportive housing programs (Cournos, 1989).

There is no shortage of academics, legal experts, and policy analysts willing to address these issues in the abstract. But the street practitioner must be able to see the trees through the forest. Consider the following excerpt concerning Joyce Brown's clinical presentation, ". . . she prided herself on her independence. Her stubborn refusal to accept medications could thus have been characterological and not based on her primary illness." The terminology "characterological" and "not primary illness" suggests that the woman's refusals and the motives which underlay them amounted to something of secondary importance. These are primary concerns to the practitioner-of-last-resort, who must view "stubborn refusal" as a sign of ego strength and elevate the preservation of that ego strength to an equal footing with all other intervention goals. The fact that Joyce Brown and many other psychotic street people derive personal pride from defiance-based behavior must neither be challenged nor lightly dismissed.

Along the same vein, it is important to recognize that many psychotic persons of the streets possess key adaptive skills that enable them to live independently (however marginally) on the fringes of society. These survival skills are overlooked by researchers who sample the population to tally demographics, diagnoses, and disabilities. They are also missed by passers-by who observe a psychotic street person pick up a discarded cigarette butt from the ground. People are moved to sympathy and perhaps revulsion by such behavior and can scarcely imagine what other miseries and humiliations street people must endure.

But not all psychotic street people will light up and smoke the butt right off of the ground, and those who do so often display good judgment in their choices of locations to eat, sleep, and elude predators.

Many collectors accumulate butts in their pockets and later squeeze their contents out onto inexpensive rolling papers, thus producing their own cigarettes at minimal out-of-pocket cost. As with collecting aluminum cans, such activity is goal-directed, consumes time, and provides something of a benefit to the community at large. It represents acquiescence to the scavenger role left open to them by the mainstream culture. Koegel et al. (1990) referred to it as a hunting-gathering subsistence strategy.

One can argue that less glibness and more indignation are in order here. But empathy by the street practitioner begins with the recognition that butt collecting bothers observers more than it does participants. Schizophrenia entails significant impairment in social interest and emotional rapport, thus rendering a person unable or unwilling to compete for the social rewards of love, friendship, sex, procreation, and family. Material wealth and intellectual achievements are precluded by cognitive aspects of the impairment. In the final analysis, tobacco is one of few autistic pleasures available to withdrawn and severely impaired people. Ironically, members of the mainstream culture who are galled that anyone would stoop to such depths in order to smoke tobacco have also underwritten such behavior by supporting the taxation of tobacco products beyond the ability of many psychotic (and other) street persons' abilities to purchase them.

Other street adaptations elicit anger rather than sympathy. When surplus clothing is plentiful and accessible in the Twin Cities, a number of psychotic (and nonpsychotic) street persons acquire their clothing at free stores, wear such clothing until it is thoroughly soiled, and then throw it away after having obtained replacements at a free store. This is often viewed as wanton waste, and yet the availability of surplus clothing balanced against the various costs of doing laundry predict such an outcome. For many psychotic people, the cognitive impairments associated with schizophrenia render a multiple-step task like laundry difficult to complete successfully. The various costs of laundering include the time involved, the three-to-four dollars to purchase soap and operate the machines, and the necessity that one carry the clothes around in a backpack and endure their bulk and weight throughout the day because of a lack of clean and safe storage space. Finally, there are the self-esteem costs of stares and other forms of disdain brought on by one's entry into the laundromat in street person's guise. From the street person's viewpoint, the three-to-four dollars seem better spent on cigarettes or other here-and-now pleasures.

Some adaptive skills of psychotic street persons appear only when they are least desired, that is, least desired from the standpoint of a street practitioner who has already determined an urgent need for treatment.

> Keefe was a white man in his early twenties who was first encountered in a drop-in center. He sat alone, smiling and talking jibberish toward pages of old sheet music and notepads spread out on the table before him. Part of the outreach approach with him had been to invite him to play an old piano kept in a back storeroom. He had eagerly accepted the invitation and played well, but also so loudly that he had to be stopped because of disturbing the rest of the center. He was angry and even physical while being led away from the piano.
>
> In time it was learned that Keefe was a dual diagnosis person (schizophrenia and marijuana abuse) whose SSI checks were administered by a case manager. This case manager had placed him in several day treatment centers and supportive residences. Keefe always withdrew from day treatment centers when they wouldn't allow him free rein on their pianos or leave him alone to write his music. In the various residences, he would light cigarettes, stand them up on their filters on top of mantles and such, allow them to burn down (which would leave long ashes perched atop the filters,) and talk to these "cigarette people" at night. Given the fire hazard this created, staff would confiscate Keefe's cigarettes and offer to dole them out one at a time to him. He would then demand all his cigarettes back and move out instead. The case manager professed to be out of options for Keefe, who also refused to take prescribed anti-psychotic medications: only marijuana helped him to write his music. It was his ambition to compose enough music that he could move to Los Angeles and become an apprentice to the composer Paul Williams, whom he had first seen on the television show, *Hollywood Squares.*
>
> It was in describing this plan to a psychologist that Keefe was at his most sociable and most coherent. His agenda in sharing this was to talk the psychologist and case manager into advancing him money from his SSI check for a bus ticket to Los Angeles. During the course of this bus ticket discussion, the psychologist tried to persuade Keefe as to the wisdom of restarting anti-psychotic medications so that he could get himself organized before embarking upon such an important mission. "I know, I know," Keefe would say, but then he missed two psychiatric appointments which the psychologist had arranged for him. She finally insisted upon taking him to such an appointment herself and was encouraged when Keefe readily complied with this. He muttered jibberish to himself during the car ride and continued to do so even as they went through the emergency room doors.
>
> But when Keefe sat down to talk with the psychiatrist he was calm, coherent, and goal-directed. He spoke none of his jibberish. He neither showed nor acknowledged any of the behaviors that the psychologist had observed of him previously. His responses were pointed,

> clipped, and unelaborated. He claimed that the only kind of help he needed was the sort that would get him to Hollywood and a meeting with Paul Williams. However, at the end of the interview he graciously volunteered that if he ever needed medications or hospitalization, he now knew to come. to this place.
>
> Back in the car he ignored the psychologist's questions about this dramatic reversal and resumed talking jibberish again. Less than a week later, Keefe was observed sitting alone with his music in the drop-in center again. When approached he proved to be working on a less-than-coherent petition that he be given a chance to play the piano there again.

Keefe possessed more self-control and internal personality organization than his previous behavior had suggested. Neither the case manager nor the psychologist had paid much attention to what Keefe had said during his more coherent periods. His prominent positive symptoms and the case management conundrums that he posed had diverted attention from the fact that he somehow survived on the streets despite being psychotic. If he had been viewed through lenses other than diagnosis and impairment history, perhaps they would have purchased him a bus ticket to Los Angeles—a round trip one with the return trip offered on a "just in case" basis. Perhaps giving him such a ticket before the visit to the psychiatrist would have yielded less suppression of psychotic behavior. The team might have even called ahead for directions to Paul Williams' office and considered whether or not to inform Williams' representatives as to who Keefe was and why he was coming. Given the absence of threats and a history of dangerousness, what was the compelling reason for not aiding Keefe with his quest? The outcome of that quest seemed a foregone conclusion, but although likely to go unrewarded, it would not go unanswered. With return ticket in hand, Keefe could always return home afterward to tell his sponsors about it. Thus a better therapeutic alliance and openness to interventions which would impact upon his psychosis were possible. Such a strategy is not without the risks of Keefe's victimization or hospitalization during his travels. However, those risks were present in his home city as well, and because he had already displayed an ability to suppress his psychotic signs according to the demands of one situation, it seemed reasonable to predict that he could do so for another.

The adaptational manipulation of psychotic signs is not confined to withholding them when mental health practitioners are around. At times it is in a psychotic person's best interests to flaunt them when a mental health practitioner is around.

> Daphne was a black female in her early thirties whose face showed both the ravages of life lived with schizophrenia and a striking beauty that predated the onset of mental impairment. She had ignored a number of outreach overtures by declining to respond in any way until the practitioner moved on to someone else. One morning she was encountered in the lobby of an emergency shelter that was renowned for violent incidents and poor security. Again she ignored an outreach attempt, this time by staring out the window until the male practitioner retreated. A huddle of four men had been watching this, and one of them called out to the practitioner, "What's-a-matter, did you strike out with Crazy Jane? Next time give this a try." With that he and the three others approached Daphne, cooing and leering and sounding catcalls mixed with laughter.
>
> Daphne suddenly whirled around from the window with her eyeballs two-thirds exposed. She hissed at the men like a cat, inadvertently spitting on two of them who were so startled by this that they jumped back. Her color seemed to have lightened and veins had popped to the surface around her cheekbones in a frightening transformation. Their withdrawal was immediate and swift, although all four men managed to slow down and avert eye contact as they passed the practitioner, this being a face-saving gesture after their collective defeat. When the practitioner looked back to Daphne, she was staring out the window as before. He stepped forward and complimented her on her self-defense. She did not acknowledge this either. She lingered for a few minutes and then walked past him and outside where she got onto a bus. Her face had returned to the bland expression that it had possessed prior to the incident.

It was widely thought that Jerry (p. 52) had also been able to survive unvictimized on the streets of the Twin Cities because of his forbidding appearance and mannerisms. Koegel (1992) described a sixty-six-year-old man who protected the contents of his shopping cart by loudly engaging in meaningless "spaceman talk" whenever a stranger neared it. He also observed that poor hygiene, a disheveled appearance, and multiple layers of clothing "may . . . reflect a storage problem, lack of access to bathroom facilities, or even an adaptive solution to the challenge of protecting oneself against predatory intentions" (Koegel, 1992, p. 8–9). Schizophrenic persons who value a minimum of social contact are also well served by poor hygiene. It is often thought to be evidence of poor judgment, but poor hygiene may in fact be an operant behavior that is reinforced on a continuous basis by the solitude it insures.

The converse of sensitivity to adaptive skills is sensitivity to maladjustment. Both assessment orientations represent something of a divergence from the traditional office culture focus upon symptoms, signs, unconscious material, and cognitive or intrafamilial dynamics. It is not so much the case that traditional assessment methods do not apply to street work as it is that street persons may not cooperate for them. In such instances, the street practitioner cannot revert to traditional office culture practices of suspending the treatment relationship until the psychotic person is ready to comply or cooperate. Instead, he or she continues an ongoing assessment of the psychotic person's ability to adjust to his or her surroundings, an assessment that may have to be based on casual contacts with and observations of such persons when the practitioner is out on the streets, plus whatever is passed on about the person from other members of the street culture. This latter, "grapevine" data are directed to the street practitioner as soon as he or she is accepted by the culture. Its reliability varies widely but it is not to be summarily dismissed.

Most street people and those who serve them show a high tolerance for deviant behavior that does not endanger others. Thus the persons who are referred to the street practitioner by these sources typically display prominent vulnerabilities; mental health symptoms alone are seldom a referral factor except to shape the decision that a person be sent to a mental health practitioner rather than some other kind of intervener. When confronted with severe vulnerabilities or adaptational failures, the street practitioner must take actions that either supplement residual adaptive skills or prevent adaptational deficits from further expansion. At times, this may mean intervening in the absence of a well-established treatment alliance or over the protests of a resistant psychotic client. Benign neglect, as occurred with Jerry, can have tragic consequences.

An example of limiting the expansion of adaptational deficits occurred when the psychiatric social worker obtained emergency weekend accommodations for "Crocodile Dundee" (p. 90). On the pragmatic level, she provided this person with food and shelter for the weekend and a Monday morning appointment with a case manager familiar with the Social Security bureaucracy. At a conceptual level, she recognized that a man dressed in garish attire who arrived on an ill-conceived odyssey with suitcase decorations loudly proclaiming his vulnerability—such a man was effectively advertising his "prey" status for all who would see. A voucher to a supervised shelter until Monday served to minimize this exposure to predators.

The adaptational dilemmas posed to and by Crocodile Dundee, Keefe, and others introduce a sensitive topic widely referred to as "Greyhound Therapy" (Bachrach, 1992; Breakey, 1992). The lore among many street workers and health care practitioners is that case managers from "other" localities place their vulnerable and expensive-to-treat persons in positions such that these people are only too eager to accept a one-way Greyhound bus ticket to any destination. When such a person disembarks at a destination, he or she is usually guided by Traveler's Aid or the police into the local public mental health system wherein the entire difficult-and-expensive-to-treat experience begins anew. This is presumably abetted by the fact that the psychotic person has been warned by the previous locality not to sign an informed consent release, or not to remember prior program or provider names and addresses. The brunt of the receiving locality's frustration and anger is then directed toward the psychotic person, and invariably there is at least a temptation to "solve" the problem by Greyhounding him or her back to the original location, again with a one-way ticket.

Such practices do occur, but certainly Greyhound therapy lends itself to much countertransference distortion as well. The fact is that psychotic persons who ride Greyhound buses are no easier to stereotype than are the psychotic persons who eat at drop-in centers. Some travel for the normative reasons of taking a vacation or making a fresh start. Perhaps they have been told that the receiving locality treats the mentally impaired better or offers more in the way of entitlement or welfare benefits, as had formerly been true in the Upper Midwest. "Crocodile Dundee" was engaging in what he thought to be effective problem-solving behavior. Other people hope to end supervision of their finances by unwanted payees or conservators. Such persons reasonably conclude that moving to a new city would mean a new payee or perhaps no payee at all. And there are persons like Keefe whose treatment might be better served if permitted to pursue their own American dreams via Greyhound therapy. A common denominator underlying each of these motives is this: Most psychotic persons who live independently are poor, and poor people travel by bus.

A white male of forty-two arrived in St. Paul on a bus. He said he was fleeing Utah's Jack-Mormons who were presumably taking over his mind in a "piecemeal" fashion. (Jack-Mormons are those Mormons who do not honor their sect's strict codes of behavior.) Without funds or friends, he was sent to a homeless shelter where his obsessive inquiries about local Mormons drew the attention of a social worker who referred him to a touring psychiatrist. Upon providing them with his name, the man quickly claimed that it was an alias. He was cold, remote, vigilant, and yet he could see that his beliefs might be delusional and a product of his younger years of marijuana abuse and not following strict Mormon teachings. He refused to provide further history or more personal access to himself because a hospital had once labeled him with "paranoid schizophrenia" and the Jack-Mormons were presumably using this label against him.

A strange negotiation evolved wherein the psychiatrist provided treatment for this man's schizophrenia even as the man insisted upon help in having that noxious label removed from his record. An agreement was struck that the man would engage in a trial of anti-psychotic medications over a period of several weeks. In return he provided his real name so that his hospital summary could be sent for. When it was received, it did verify that he had been diagnosed with schizophrenia. Then, at the man's direction, the psychiatrist wrote a letter to the hospital explaining the man's unhappiness with the label and requesting that the diagnosis be changed retroactively so that he could no longer be harassed with it (interestingly, by this time the man no longer spoke about the Jack-Mormons at all). The psychiatrist signed the letter, put his phone number on it, and placed it in a stamped envelope in the man's presence. He allowed the man to take the letter and mail it to the hospital himself. The man returned later to thank the psychiatrist, but also showed him another Greyhound bus ticket. He left town the next day.

No hospital would change a diagnosis on the basis of such a letter, but nothing is gained by increasing the person's insight in this regard. The risk of this intervention is that the man coded the experience into memory as a certification that he did not have a mental impairment. However, the man himself did not insist upon such language in the letter, and he had faithfully taken the medication for "bad nerves" that he blamed on the harassment by the Jack-Mormons. The psychiatrist hoped that his counterpart at the next Greyhound stop would not see fit to induce insight or challenge the man's world view by brandishing the term "schizophrenia" in his presence.

The contracting and deliberating with this person around medications involved brief, repeated contacts with the man over several weeks, during which time the man's ability to stay clothed, fed, sheltered, and nonvictimized were continuously assessed on an informal basis. The man functioned adequately in all of these realms, and when he chose to leave the cities there was no cause to restrict him from doing so. He had demonstrated that his freedom to continue his travels should be honored despite paranoid schizophrenia. Unfortunately, the street practitioner is often forced to draw conclusions about adaptational skills and vulnerabilities from a database of fewer contacts, more hearsay, and less cooperation from the psychotic person.

Another problem is that a treatment program or facility that might otherwise help to maintain a psychotic person's adaptive skills or shore up his or her vulnerabilites may be non-existent or have no openings. Some programs maintain de facto selection biases against homeless persons by requiring a series of intake appointments with different team members who then must schedule a full staff meeting to collectively discuss their impressions about the person. In the meantime, the adaptational deficits and failures of the psychotic person may persist or become worse. The final insult occurs when the person is ultimately rejected by the treatment program he or she has been waiting for (assuming that the person's condition has not deteriorated during the waiting period).

A VULNERABILITY STANDARD

Under such circumstances, hospitalization becomes an intervention option. Some psychotic people have learned how to anticipate impending acute episodes, or to accurately assess their own needs for asylum or refuge during the early stages of psychological storms. Other hospitalizations must be initiated by the street practitioner on an involuntary basis. Many mental health practitioners have distaste—if not disdain—for involuntary hospitalization (Kiesler, 1991). But the bleak ways in which many homeless psychotic persons live render it a more palatable intervention choice for them than it is for one's office culture recipients. In fact, the opposite danger can arise wherein a practitioner is tempted to treat his or her own tolerance conflicts with respect to psychotic symptomatology and human misery by hospitalizing them away.

Once a decision to hospitalize is reached, the street practitioner may expect pressures arising from within the local mental health system to block it. The dangerousness standard of civil commitment safeguards civil liberties, but it has also come to serve as a legal haven from which cost containment and other anti-hospital ideologies exert influences which are not necessarily in the best interests of a psychotic person. In such an adversarial context, the street practitioner who initiates a hospitalization must do so with strong convictions that it is appropriate, and also be armed with vividly explicit and logically compelling data to justify such a decision. It is to serve as an aid in such decision making that a vulnerability standard is proposed next. It may be applied in situations which involve vulnerable or skill-deficient psychotic persons who fall short of meeting a literal application of the dangerousness standard. Its elements are derived from a more connotative than denotative sense of dangerousness, and the street practitioner can not at all be assured that an admitting officer or a commitment court will respect such a definition. Still, its criteria reflect behavioral exigencies that are unique to street cultures and consistent with an ecological appreciation for homelessness. Admitting officers and courts may choose to overlook or downplay these exigencies, but the street practitioner may not.

Unlike the "in need of treatment" standard, the proffered vulnerability standard does not emphasize signs, symptoms, or disease entities. It addresses failures or losses of adaptive capacities in the unique context of a street culture which entails (1) close-quartered, communal living with unknown and unchosen others, and (2) ongoing dependence upon sources of life support that are not amenable to one's own control. Application of the standard assumes that the identified vulnerabilites are neither time-limited in nature nor are of a type that can be predicted to resolve spontaneously. It also presumes that the provision of refuge, asylum, or residential treatment in a site which is less restrictive than hospitalization has already been ruled out.

Failure to Scavenge

This refers to a failure to take advantage of necessary and available food, clothing, shelter, and medical care. It is a criterion that is already codified in many states' commitment statutes, although commonly it is subsumed or overshadowed by the application of the dangerousness standard. Failure to scavenge encompasses those psychotic street persons who are cognitively unable to retain and follow simple directions in order to convey themselves to provision sites. Profound deficits often signal the presence of an organically based psychotic condition, which in turn may be related to physiological deprivation or disease. Misuse of prescribed medication or street drugs can also give rise to such conditions. Thus some of these presentations may prove to be self-limiting or amenable to prompt medical attention. There are also runaways from psychiatric institutions and other custodial settings who function well enough to effect an escape but not well enough to sustain themselves in the street culture.

Regardless of etiology or duration, cognitive impairments that are severe enough to preclude effective scavenging behavior impose vulnerabilities which require intrusive attention. The more common failures to forage are those that do not so much reflect cognitive deficits as a psychotic person's tendency toward social avoidance and withdrawal. All entitlement programs have application requirements to qualify someone for provision of welfare, food, clothing, and shelter. Such requirements typically demand that an individual be able to wait with others in a public place, perhaps to tolerate a milling crowd, and ultimately to answer a series of questions posed by an official-looking stranger who may seem judgmental as he or she asks one to recall difficult dates and numbers under something of a time pressure. This may be sufficiently stressful for a psychotic person that he or she will withdraw or phobicly avoid a situation that strikes others to be a mere inconvenience or hassle. Such psychotic persons are prime candidates for outreach teams who can deliver requisite provisions to the person, or provide staff who can explain, assist, and take relevant applications in shelters, drop-in centers, and other low visibility places to which psychotic people retreat. Psychotic persons who cannot or will not cooperate with this degree of assistance may need to be hospitalized and treated until they can. Such a hospitalization is comparable to a "treatment to competency" mandate in forensic psychiatry.

Some street persons spurn available provisions in order to sleep in abandoned cars and so on (Susser et al., 1992). Often such choices represent goal-directed behavior motivated by pride or third-stage acculturation to homelessness. People who are adaptively skilled at this know how to avoid both the attention of mental health practitioners and escorted trips to detox centers, jails, and emergency rooms. Severely impaired psychotic persons are not skilled enough to elude such attention over an extended period of time. The street practitioner needs to become familiar with the common physical signs and symptoms associated with malnutrition and frostbite. Each is a severity indicator for immediate hospitalization and compelling evidence in the event that a civil commitment action becomes necessary later. Layers of clothing during hot weather, inadequate clothing in cold weather, foul body odor and poor hygiene—each of these must be carefully assessed on a person-by-person basis as to whether it represents an adaptational asset or deficit.

Prey Salience

This refers to the tendency of some psychotic persons (Crocodile Dundee) to advertise their deficits in ways that invite predation. When such persons are not beaten up for their money or sex, they are beaten up for not having any money or for providing poor sex. Some street predators are sadistic toward their "prey" because the latter detract from the macho swagger that predators like to associate with the streets. Other predators view these individuals as ready-made displacement objects, and still others view them as an opportunity to indulge thrill-seeking violence without fear of consequence. Whatever the case, such individuals must be provided with asylum at minimum. At times, this may need to be done over their own protests.

A man who suffered from bipolar disorder entered a drop-in center and proceeded to flash a large wad of bills around. He gleefully announced that these were a back payment he had just received from Social Security. When a street practitioner tried to intervene, the man forced a twenty dollar bill into her hand and said, "I've just bought your silence so shut-up already." He turned away and proceeded to hand out another twenty to a stranger who had just entered the building.

A psychotic woman came to a drop-in center dressed in a bizarrely provocative way that brought hoots and catcalls from the mostly male patrons. These brought a beamy smile to her face, and when the man closest to her slapped his knee and beckoned that she sit on it, the woman readily complied. The man was stunned by this, and by the raucous applause from the others. The woman smiled as if these cheers were for herself, and she resisted when a social worker (who already knew her) pulled her off of the man's lap and led her away. When the social worker addressed her by name, the woman indignantly pulled her arm away and said, "No, that's not my name!" She retreated in a huff toward the man on whose lap she had been sitting.

Peer Antagonization

While poor hygiene and dress may be reinforced for those psychotic persons who desire to be left alone, such a reward is lost if a person's hygiene becomes so bad that communal living arrangements are threatened.

Hector was a white male of twenty-five who suffered from schizophrenia but not (according to him) from life on the streets. He was delighted when he won a lottery that awarded him a thirty-day stay at a church shelter. This meant that he could store his possessions there for the duration and not have to worry about sleeping arrangements on a night-to-night basis. (The shelter staff privately acknowledged having rigged the lottery in Hector's favor in the hopes that mental health interventions would be facilitated for Hector with his whereabouts thus stabilized and a psychologist visiting the shelter on a regular basis. Hector had previously missed all mental health appointments they had made for him.)

After reading an article on AIDS, Hector refused to take a shower or change his clothes throughout a summer's heat wave. Seven days of pleading and cajoling (from shelter staff) and muttering and threatening (from fellow shelter guests) failed to budge Hector from his resolve not to use communal bathroom facilities. On the eighth day of this siege, when shelter staff were otherwise occupied, a group of guests forced Hector into the shower with his clothes on. They turned the water on and held the door shut until he agreed to throw out his old clothes and put on the new ones they had rummaged for him. Although unhurt, Hector protested the incident furiously and demanded

> to see a legal aid lawyer. The shelter administrator assigned three-day suspensions to the other guests involved in the incident, but levied a permanent suspension against Hector until such time as he agreed to come to the shelter in a clean and presentable fashion. This is virtually impossible for even a motivated street person to accomplish on a regular basis, and Hector adamantly refused to comply, insisting that all public facilities were breeding grounds for the AIDS virus. When confronted with the observation that his own hygiene was such that he seemed a more likely breeding ground for the virus, Hector smiled back and said that at least he knew where his odor came from.
>
> Word of the incident spread to other shelters which refused to admit Hector except under the conditions imposed by the first one. Although it was summer and there was little peril from the weather, Hector's adaptational skills were such that he was likely to fall prey to predators if made to live outside of the minimum protection of a shelter.

Many referrals to the street practitioner from shelter staff center on the disruptions that psychotic individuals bring to a closely quartered dormitory environment. Homeless shelters serve a varying mix of strangers each night, many of whom are not mentally impaired and have little sympathy or patience available for those who are. Sensory assaults like Hector's are just another insult to these people. Sleeping within several feet of such a person on a cold, musty gymnasium floor is a running commentary on one's self-efficacy, particularly if it seems likely to continue night after night after night. The guests, then, are in alliance with shelter staff in expecting the mental health practitioner to do something about this.

> When all else failed, the psychologist warned Hector that he would feel compelled to involuntarily commit Hector to a psychiatric hospital if he did not agree to clean himself up for another shelter. This worked, ostensibly because Hector had become convinced that hospitals were more virulent breeding grounds for the virus than were shelters. Over time Hector continued to refuse on-site mental health interventions and to rotate among various shelters for short-term stays. At times, his hygiene would deteriorate again. Whenever this threatened to proceed beyond some ill-defined tolerance point, the psychologist was summoned to threaten Hector with commitment again. This would result in another short-term behavior change and no more calls from shelter staff for a while.

It is interesting to speculate to what extent Hector's stronger association of the AIDS virus with hospital bathrooms than with shelter bathrooms represented another sign of schizophrenia versus an accommodation-by-delusion to the forces that were aligned against him.

If he had not capitulated, the psychologist had been prepared to follow through on his threats to commit Hector (this was the same psychologist who had failed to hospitalize Jerry during the previous winter). If poor self-care/hygiene jeopardizes one's suitability for and safety within a communal living environment, and the person in question is too mentally impaired to survive without that degree of protection, the behavior represents a significant adaptational failure due to increasing the person's prey salience.

Another kind of impaired judgment is making racial slurs in a shelter, especially when members of the targeted group are present. If the psychotic person's condition is obvious to all, an isolated slur may be overlooked by members of the targeted group if it is neither long, loud, clever, nor repeated. However, once any of these ill-defined thresholds is crossed, tolerance by members of the targeted group is tantamount to endorsing the message. Thus they must retaliate against the perpetrator regardless of his or her defenselessness or impairment.

Shelter staff move quickly to stop such behavior and may turn to the mental health practitioner for a solution. Some other shelter may have a racial mix that is not so salient or threatening to the psychotic person. One shelter provided an isolated sleeping area next to a furnace for a psychotic female guest. Staff knew from experience that she would not make racial slurs if she were segregated in this way. However, such accommodations are not always available, and most shelter providers are understandably loath to consider any accommodation short of expelling the offending person. Psychotic persons can sometimes be reasoned with or convinced to suppress this behavior, or to heed threats of hospitalization such as the one made to Hector. But such actions may not produce a cessation of the behavior, for example, a livid psychotic person responds to such confrontations with a tirade that this is America and he or she has a right to voice such opinions. If the person lacks the adaptive skills and support system to survive outside of the minimal structure of the shelter, and if no other place of asylum or refuge is available, the practitioner may have to hospitalize the person for his or her own protection. Deferring such actions to a police department such that the psychotic person is taken to jail (where presumably he or she will show the same poor judgment) simply sets the person up for greater retaliative peril there.

It bears repeating that hospitalizations in which the intervention goals are limited to the provision of asylum or refuge for vulnerable individuals will arouse opposition from mental health and court systems. Weeks after such an involuntary hospitalization first occurs, a libertarian advocate or the psychotic person's court-appointed public defender is likely to argue successfully that even a psychotic person in America retains the right to give money away to strangers, to dress provocatively and titillate indiscriminately, and to publicly voice one's opinion as to the inferiority of other racial groups. If such arguments lead to a psychotic person's discharge from the hospital, the street practitioner need not necessarily consider this a failed outcome. At the time of the critical incident(s) which had led to the hospitalization, the street practitioner had been able to afford to defer such considerations to the controlled confines of the courtroom more than he or she could have afforded to risk the psychotic person's endangerment or exploitation. Even a brief, incomplete hospitalization is likely to discharge the psychotic person in better physical and mental health than when the person went in, owing to the protective (when not nurturant) aspects of most institutional milieus. Treatment alliances and compliances are sometimes negotiated and forged among the psychotic person, the person's attorney, and hospital practitioners during such involuntary admissions; if, in the service of this, the street practitioner comes to be cast in the role of "bad cop" by all concerned, so be it. Moreover, less restrictive treatment alternatives that are acceptable to the psychotic person may suddenly become available, either because the hospitalization itself qualifies or prioritizes the person for such alternatives, or because courts and their satellite agencies retain the power to materialize such alternatives when the practitioner can not. Finally, consider that a follow-up study of persons involuntarily hospitalized by Project Help in New York City revealed that 43 percent of those contacted still resided in hospitals, 44 percent resided in community residences or residential programs, and only 12 percent were back to living on the streets (Cohen & Marcos, 1992).

Thus, the street practitioner should not be discouraged from applying a culture-specific vulnerability standard if it connotes a type of dangerousness to self or others which is unique to life in a street culture. Psychotic people have always had at least intermittent needs for asylum, and these used to be well (if excessively) met by the state institutions. Years of benign neglect toward treatment-resistant, nondangerous psychotic persons have led to their asylum needs becoming increasingly met by jails and prisons. Hospitals are more appropriate for this than are jail cells. Minkoff (1987) has gone so far as to suggest that an intermediate or long-term hospitalization may be necessary to effectively socialize some treatment-resistant persons into a role and frame of mind wherein these people accept the reality of their chronic and severe impairments. He suggests that until such socialization occurs, the probabilities of noncompliance and revolving door admissions will not be significantly reduced.

In conclusion, it has been estimated that 5 to 7 percent of homeless persons would benefit from psychiatric hospitalization (Dennis et al., 1991). Such an estimate is best interpreted both ways. On the one hand, it argues against a return to wholesale hospitalization and institutionalization of psychotic individuals as a solution to their short-term or long-term homelessness problems. On the other hand, it suggests that between 1 in 14 and 1 in 20 of the street persons whom the street practitioner encounters will be appropriate for hospital treatment.

TREATMENT AND HOUSING ISSUES

Homelessness is a variable that compounds the problems of treating psychotic persons even when treatment resistance is not present. Improved reality testing may come with costs: Some persons with bipolar disorder prefer elevated and expansive moods to the leveling effects of medication that would clarify the dreariness of the streets (Lamb, 1982). A person with schizophrenia may value the therapeutic properties of antipsychotic medication, but the effects of dulled senses and slowed reaction times can undermine confidence in the ability to defend oneself (Breakey, 1992). Clozapine, a recent advance in antipsychotic drugs, offers the prospect of symptom alleviation without prominent side effects (Kotcher & Smith, 1993; Reid, Pham, & Rago, 1993). But because clozapine also increases the risk of a serious blood condition, a weekly regimen of diagnostic blood tests is required with this treatment. Leaving aside the possibility that the nature of phlebotomy may intersect with a psychotic person's delusional beliefs, it remains a formidable undertaking for a street person to comply with weekly blood draws given his or her shifting whereabouts, lack of safe storage space, and frequent practice of packing and unpacking behaviors. As for dispensing pills and concentrates by prescription, predators will steal and sell these—and desperate psychotic persons have been known to do this also.

Still there have been anecdotal reports of medication compliance among street persons (Torrey, 1988). One large scale study involved an original sample of 193 shelter residents who were treated and followed in Philadelphia (Arce, Tadlock, Vergare, & Shapiro, 1983). All of these residents were evaluated by psychiatrists and 41 percent of them were prescribed psychotropic medication. An impressive 86 percent of this subsample complied with their medication regimens and displayed subsequent clinical improvement. Arce and his colleagues were surprised by this high compliance rate, which they also credited with the cancellation of a sizable number of involuntary commitment actions.

This particular shelter occupied abandoned floors of an operating general hospital. Arce et al. speculated that the residents may have been more compliant with medications in such a setting because of mistaken assumptions that they were in a hospital and thus it was part of the patient role to do so. Although this explanation was ultimately dismissed, a related one is more compelling: because of the physical proximity of the shelter floors to psychiatric services, this sample of psychotic people enjoyed ready access to those mental health practitioners with exclusive credentials to select and prescribe medications. The dearth of psychiatrists in settings that serve the indigent often means that other practitioners must perform evaluative functions and conduct the initial stages of assessing medication readiness. Many nonphysicians thus come to acquire a wealth of incidental knowledge about the indications/contraindications of various medications and their side effects. However, it is doubtful that medication readiness can be fostered equally well when relevant knowledge has been acquired incidentally and grafted onto one's practitioner identity versus acquired systematically and as an integral part of one's practitioner identity. It seems reasonable to infer that psychiatrists develop subtle confidences and competencies in these matters which have a significant effect on compliance rates and therapeutic effects above and beyond the "primary" chemical actions of the drugs (Meichenbaum & Turk, 1987). The shelter served by Arce et al. provided a temporal and geographic proximity of person to psychiatrist that removed the necessity for intermediaries and temporal delays in the treatment process. The findings suggest that medication compliance among homeless psychotic persons will be enhanced when psychiatrists take to the streets rather than defer early stages of compliance readiness to nonphysician colleagues.

Arce et al. (1983) offered yet another explanation for their high rate of medication compliance, "This compliance seems to be related to offering treatment in a setting with minimal structure, where few demands are made on the residents" (p. 816). This description is at odds with the spirit that has dominated the community mental health movement during its first 25 years. "Aftercare" programs have typically subjected psychotic persons to formalized treatment plans with specific goals and target dates for reaching those goals; however, due to shortcomings that were both fiscal and conceptual, such practitioner-driven regimens have not accomplished widespread alleviation or neutralization of psychotic impairments. In response, a more recipient-driven ideology has arisen. It promotes advocacy and self-empowerment, clubhouse socialization schemes, and deletion of the "patient" label for that of "consumer." Community mental health centers are now evolving into community support programs (CSPs) that are less tied to office culture locations, traditions, and practices. CSPs call for practitioner presence in clubhouses and other such sites, and they have been characterized as "asylums without walls" (Minkoff, 1987). Most CSP philosophies call for services and environments to be tailored to the mentally impaired individual's unique needs. They do not promote denial of adaptational deficits, but neither do they challenge nor focus on them. They promote positive self-esteem and acceptance of impaired status without expectation of or pressure to change or improve. Such developments have necessitated corresponding shifts in practitioner roles. Thus, case management is in ascendance while "primary therapist" is in something of a decline. Although job specifications for the case manager role are not yet universally agreed on, a first book devoted exclusively to the subject recently appeared (Harris & Bergman, 1993).

There have been corresponding changes in models of housing for the severely impaired as well. *Supportive* housing is the term now used to distinguish residential alternatives for the mentally impaired that are owned, operated, or otherwise controlled by mental health treatment programs and systems. These include board-and-care facilities, halfway houses, specialty-licensed adult foster care homes, and so on. The roots of supportive housing were in deinstitutionalization policies that anticipated thousands of discharged persons requiring a practitioner-controlled series of transitional residences until each was sufficiently prepared for independent living.

The new ideology argues that many mentally impaired persons would be better served by a *supported* housing approach (Carling, 1990). Supported housing entails that (1) mentally impaired persons reside in "normal" non-aggregate dwellings that are devoid of the stigmatization typically associated with congregated supportive housing, and (2) this normalized housing is not administered by or for a mental health treatment system, but (3) flexible support and treatment services are available to meet the individual needs of each mentally impaired individual. Carling (1993) and Tanzman (1993) recently reported that supported housing is now a clear preference of consumers and their families over supportive housing. It undoubtedly will have greater appeal to psychotic persons who reject the patient role or otherwise show lack of insight. In the vignettes that follow, the major sources of support for two psychotic persons were untrained nonpractitioners. These people assumed their protectionary roles because the psychotic persons in question shunned mental health practitioners and programs.

> Phael was a 38-year-old man who had been diagnosed with chronic undifferentiated schizophrenia for years. He resided in a proprietary boarding house which provided him with a small sleeping room, a communal bathroom at the end of the hall, and three meals a day. It was two blocks from a drop-in center and Phael spent his days and years going back and forth between the boarding house and the drop-in center. His SSI check went to a mental health case manager who served as his payee. This man paid Phael's room and board expenses and arranged for the rest of Phael's money to be doled out to him for cigarettes over the course of the month by the day-shift caretaker of the boarding house. Thus, Phael could count on receiving some predictable number of his own cigarettes each day without smoking his money away at the beginning of the month and not having any left over at the end. However, the daily allotment never satisfied him: Phael would smoke them up in the morning and spend the rest of his day begging cigarettes from others or scavenging butts out of ashtrays in the drop-in center. A positive side effect to his begging was that it forced him into contact with drop-in center staff and touring street practitioners who could thereby monitor his mental and physical condition. Otherwise, Phael would scarcely speak to them. He related to his case manager only as a dispenser of money. A psychiatrist visited Phael once a month at the boarding house to tend to his medication needs, but Phael had little use for him either. His main support person was the day-shift caretaker who had taken it upon himself to look after Phael and the elderly residents of the boarding house. This caretaker was a man with less than a high school diploma who saw to it that medications were supplied for and administered to Phael. It was he who would dole out the cigarettes and take Phael to the urgent care center when Phael was sick or had been robbed and beaten up by predators on the walk between the boarding house and the drop-in center. If more complicated problems arose, the caretaker would call the case manager, the psychiatrist, or the drop-in center for guidance.

Phael had previously been resistant or nonresponsive to traditional aftercare programming, and yet never deemed dangerous or vulnerable enough to require long-term hospitalization. His room was always in shambles but never an olfactory or hygienic threat to his neighbors thanks to the caretaker, who also made a point of redirecting Phael when he tried to leave the building in bizarre clothing or clothing that was inappropriate for the weather. Except for the times when he was out of cigarettes, Phael registered no complaints about this life and expressed no desire that it be changed. The caretaker, the case manager, the psychiatrist, and the staff and practitioners of the drop-in center collectively insured that Phael's life in a nonsupportive environment was possible.

Phael probably represents the exceptional case of a gravely impaired psychotic person surviving outside of supportive housing or an institution. A more typical "street" version of supported housing would involve a less impaired person.

> Jesse was a black male in his fifties who suffered from paranoid schizophrenia. He was delusional but remained well organized as long as he went unchallenged in his control of conversations and their premises. Under these conditions, he himself would outreach street practitioners rather than vice versa, usually to make flirtatious remarks to the females and sarcastic remarks to the males. He was so predictable in this as to be amusing and even endearing, until one female practitioner who felt quite safe with him gently inquired as to whether or not Jesse had ever received psychiatric treatment. Jesse exploded at her in a vicious verbal harangue, replete with death threats, until other street persons in the lobby forced Jesse out onto the streets to calm him down.
>
> The alarmed practitioner called the boarding house where Jesse resided. The proprietor was not surprised to hear of the outburst as every roommate he had ever paired with Jesse who had so much as muttered something about Jesse's being crazy had received the same treatment. The proprietor's solution had been to assign Jesse the smallest room in the building to himself and force three people to share the largest room. Thus, he neither lost money nor violated any building codes while ensuring that Jesse could stay there undisturbed. Over the years, the street people had learned to tolerate Jesse without "pushing his buttons." Thus, Jesse was never at a loss for partners in his spades games at the drop-in center and was alone only when he chose to be alone.
>
> The practitioner decided not to seek Jesse's involuntary hospitalization; she merely steered clear of him for a while. In time her faux pas was either forgiven or forgotten (she wisely decided not to press Jesse for clarification on this). Eventually he resumed his flirtatious remarks to her and even invited her to play as his partner in a game of spades.

Supported housing is more a philosophy than a treatment method. It may materialize serendipitously or planfully in transient hotels, SROs, apartments, and so on. It is what families provide when they allow a mentally impaired person to remain in the parental home. It is a potentially more flexible and economical approach than supportive housing because treatment dollars are attached to a person rather than to a facility. Resources are typically allocated through a case manager to the individual person's adaptational needs (some of which are episodic and time-limited) rather than to the ongoing maintenance of twenty-four-hour supervision and structure which may not always be necessary. In Phael's situation, there were occasional crises which required multiple interveners; in Jesse's situation, the mere removal of roommates was sufficient to minimize the frequency and severity of symptoms and with it the need for service utilization. Again, it is worth noting that although it was Jesse's wont to complain of many things, delusional and otherwise, he never complained about his life or demanded that it be improved. Being permitted to verbally harass mental health practitioners without reprisal, being given a single room, and being granted the license to be controlling and delusional as long as he harmed no one—each of these conferred some respect and dignity upon a man whose life lacked an anchor in reality. For their part, the various street practitioners grew content to do informal mental health check-ups of Jesse as he flirted with or berated them. It was ironic but true that as long as these inappropriate ritualistic behaviors were in evidence, the team did not have to worry about any adaptational slippage on Jesse's part.

This is not to suggest that supported housing, informal or otherwise, is a panacea or some final solution to the homelessness problems of the mentally impaired. Even as Jesse has continued to live this lifestyle for more than a decade as of the time of this writing, follow-up of Phael's status yielded an uncertain outcome. Phael's caretaker took ill and was forced to quit his work at the boarding house. The boarding house itself closed down months later with little advance notice being given. Not surprisingly, Phael's condition worsened at that time and he was recommitted to the state hospital. After being stabilized there, he was discharged to another boarding house that was run by a support figure like the previous caretaker. Phael disappeared soon afterward and had not been seen in more than six months at the time of this writing. In retrospect, his original supported housing arrangement had been so delicately tenous that he proved unable to later adjust to a reasonable facsimile of it.

One must wonder how adaptable Jesse will prove to be if forced to move to a location where a new landlord is unwilling to accommodate his need for a private room. It is out of concern that such a hard transition may ultimately occur that the practitioner team continues to be available for Jesse's outreach comments and spade games.

There will always be a contingent of psychotic individuals who need the over-arching structure and active treatment provided by supportive housing and/or traditional community mental health aftercare services. A state-of-the-art view of supportive housing models has been provided by Bebout and Harris (1992). These writers thoughtfully argue for an alignment of various housing models for the severely impaired along a continuum that is defined by peoples' varying needs for external structure and external loci of control. Bebout and Harris note that their continuum can accommodate supported housing models as well. Such an integration is desirable for more than practical reasons: As things currently stand, supported housing advocates are championing their approach as superior to the previous one. Such a tack is reminiscent of the "community treatment = good; hospital treatment = bad" mentality from the heady early days of the community mental health movement. It must be hoped that the consumerism/supported housing movement will not breed another such false dichotomy, thus creating a new brand of "cracks" for psychotic persons to fall through.

CHAPTER 6

Disability and Its Flashpoints

An important service that the mental health practitioner can provide on the streets is to facilitate access to relevant disability programs, most notably the federal one known as Supplementary Security Income (SSI). The process of qualifying for SSI and the bureaucratic hurdles that must be endured along its way are a forbidding prospect for a mentally impaired street person (Craig & Paterson, 1988; Koegel et al., 1990; Morse, 1992). So baffling and detailed are some of the procedures that many lower functioning street persons need assistance just to fill out the forms. Providing such assistance may be tedious for the practitioner but it may also be a productive outreach interaction. Psychologists and psychiatrists who have limited volunteer time to donate to the cause of homeless persons can make a valuable contribution by going to shelters and drop-in centers to perform SSI-formatted examinations. The government has traditionally paid private practitioners to perform these examinations on disability applicants who do not have a regular treating physician or psychologist. Unfortunately, such an examination usually needs to be scheduled weeks in advance to accommodate the office culture practitioner. The hardships discussed earlier that are imposed on homeless people by such advance appointments induce many of them to miss their examinations, and they are subsequently denied disability benefits. The "once-a-month" volunteer practitioner can circumvent this by taking the examination to the street person at the shelter or drop-in center.

SSI enables a qualifying disabled individual to receive a monthly disability benefit when there is no significant earnings history of Social Security deposits from which to draw. In conjunction with related state and local contributions, SSI benefits bring with them medical insurance under the auspices of state-administered medical assistance programs. Other benefits may be accessible through the policies and practices of local governments. These include qualification or prioritization for rent subsidy programs, low-income housing, food stamps, public transportation passes, and so forth. Monthly stipends from SSI are significantly higher than those of state and locally funded welfare and disability programs, and SSI is not as time-limited and subject to change and requalification as are most local programs. The SSI recipient can realistically entertain thoughts of a stable housing situation, even if it is only at a subsistence level or slightly above that (Craig & Paterson, 1988). Benefits also move geographically with the recipient whereas state and local sources of support do not. Beyond these obvious benefits lie more subtle, psychological ones that alter a person's perceptions of his or her life and impairment(s).

> Diane (p. 16) was alternately seduced and bullied through an extended SSI application and examination process. This was carried out by a team of practitioners over a series of contacts, all of which took place in her beloved lobby of the public library. She would only take part in these contacts when the weather was too bad to play shuffleboard in the park. She was resistant throughout; code words and outright deceptions were used to safeguard her pride and keep the process moving on. Once she began to receive benefits, she promptly changed residences, bought better clothes, and separated from her friend Linda and the library lobby. She began to respond more positively to the mental health team, consented to take an MMPI, and then accepted antipsychotic medications and enrollment in an industrial therapy program. These changes took place over a matter of years rather than months. However, four years after the original SSI interaction, she was sociable, relatively asymptomatic, and she was sustaining a part-time job as a telephone receptionist for a nonprofit organization.

This was a situation in which cognitive dissonance was forced upon a "lack of insight" person by making her apply for and receive disability payments. The dissonance was subsequently resolved by Diane's coming to behave in ways that suggested new insight into her impairment. Other street persons experience their assignment to disabled status with palpable relief, or as a vindication of past work failures and self-doubts. Some street people adamantly refuse SSI. Recall that Joseph (p. 68) declined to apply for SSI and constructed a "chumship" pretense to justify what entitlement funds he did receive. He chose the material hardship of poverty to the psychological hardship of acknowledging his impaired status in order to reduce his poverty.

Through many different channels, then, SSI can serve to minimize the frequency and severity of psychological distress and maladaptive behavior. Until broad-based societal interventions with the homelessness problem produce "forest" solutions for it, assisting mentally impaired individuals to qualify for SSI is something that a street practitioner can do to curtail homelessness on a "tree-by-tree" basis. For those street persons so affected, this is no mean feat.

Unfortunately, there is little consensus as to how disability should be defined among the mental health professions, and even less as to the circumstances under which such a social safety net should be strung. Many see disability programs as havens of disincentive and irresponsibility that benefit too many people whose impairments are either of dubious severity or are confined to deficits of conscience and integrity. From the other end of the spectrum, Kiesler (1991) and Schutt and Garrett (1992) have called attention to government initiatives of the 1980s that pared the disability rolls and increased the number of false negatives (i.e., truly disabled persons who were no longer supported by disability benefits). In the backlash of human and political misery which followed, the pendulum was pushed back in a way that dramatically increased the number of people found disabled for reasons of mental impairment (Kennedy & Manderscheid, 1993). In addition to shifting political winds, there are periodic "60 Minutes"-type investigations that trumpet atypical errors (fraud, checks lost forever in the mail, mindless follies perpetuated by government workers, etc.).

All of the above factors contribute to rampant cynicism and reflexive government-bashing among mental health practitioners as well as others. As a citizen and taxpayer, the street practitioner has as much right as anyone to develop and advocate his or her own stance about the philosophical underpinnings, political aspects, and bureaucratic requirements of such government programs. In the day-to-day conduct of street work, however, one's legitimate sociopolitical attitudes represent potential countertransference influences in the assessment of disability. Federal disability regulations do stipulate guidelines and procedures that serve to anchor the practitioner's thinking and reduce the impact of subjectivity. However, the influence of subjectivity can never be completely eliminated and, in the realm of mental impairments, one must rely heavily upon the self-report of the street person even as other medical fields lend themselves more readily to objective findings and laboratory evidence. Once the word is out in the street culture that a certain practitioner performs SSI examinations, that practitioner can expect to be approached by persons with questionable stories and presentations that are not easily verified by independent data sources. Such dilemmas leave the street practitioner in a different quandary than his or her office culture counterpart whose experience with disability applicants is confined to persons who are already known from a treatment context. The street practitioner with a "first contact" person is more susceptible to the influence of countertransference issues upon the disability evaluation process.

Other problems posed by disability evaluations for government programs include those of bureaucracy and documentation. It is easy to lose sight of the fact that both of these policy instruments were well-intentioned at the outset, having been intended to uphold accountability to the taxpayer and equality of treatment for all applicants. Unfortunately, such respectable aims now work their ways down through the bureaucracy to the practitioner and applicant as a deluge of paperwork, multiple appointments, telephone calls, voice mail responses (the latter being a particular hardship for street persons who must borrow telephones). Temporal delays are perpetrated by unseen workers with disaffecting words like "case" and "examiner" in their job titles. Fortunately many social workers and nonpractitioners are sufficiently versed in the ins-and-outs of SSI to help the intimidated street person negotiate the labyrinth. Some take applications on site in the shelters and drop-in centers.

Such adaptations do not alleviate the greater problem of generating sufficient quantity and quality of evidence to permit a reliable conclusion as to a street person's being disabled or not. Records of past mental health treatments offer the best documentation of the presence, duration, and severity of a disabling condition. Unfortunately, many mentally impaired street people have been too poor, too burdened, too ashamed, or too "lacking in insight" to have presented themselves for mental health treatment in the past. Others with ongoing paranoia about hospital commitment, being "snowed with drugs," and so on, may choose not to acknowledge a mental health treatment history even when it is in their best interest to do so. Given these and other circumstances (e.g., treatment records too distant in time or place to be remembered or acquired), the burden of providing sufficient evidence to establish the presence of a disabling mental impairment falls to street practitioners who have observed the client in either traditional interview contexts and/or during daily, incidental contacts while touring street culture sites.

Some mental health practitioners believe that a one sentence conclusionary statement to the effect that an applicant is disabled or not disabled should suffice as documentation of disability. Others dislike the roles of information gatherer, report writer, and form signer when these are performed on behalf of a government program that does not pay free market rates for such services. Still others argue that they have been trained to assess and intervene with mental health problems, not evaluate disability, and when they are forced into a disability assessment role they perform it reluctantly.

Street work is different. The author is aware of numerous occasions in which a referral source convinced a resistant street person to "try out" a psychologist by first requesting that psychologist's assistance with a disability claim. One psychologist who spent an hour helping an intoxicated, illiterate, psychotic man to fill out an application form saw this develop into a good treatment alliance (p. 184).

Such a first contact is analogous to a blind date, with SSI as the common starting point of interaction between street practitioner and street person. The subsequent practitioner-street person interactions in the pursuit of disability status may define therapeutic issues to be developed in later contacts after the disability question, per se, has been addressed. The process is seldom a predictable one.

> Flory was a chronically angry woman in her mid-thirties whose place of refuge was an attic in a dilapidated carriage house behind a cloistered convent. She wandered the streets with an aggrieved demeanor and a small dog on a leash who looked better fed and taken care of than she did. Flory's chronic anger was about the termination of her parental rights to children who (presumably) lived in another state with their father. As she told it, someone had labeled her a paranoid "schizotonic" as a pretext for taking her children away from her. She told this story wherever she went to whomever would listen, including mental health practitioners who were always offered it with more volume and affect.
>
> Flory was thus a person for whom the appropriate outreach attitude entailed the street practitioner listening to her bitterness about mental health matters without taking umbrage or becoming defensive. She would also rail about street sites that would not permit her to bring her dog inside with her, and about the Social Security Administration (SSA), which she accused of being determined to find her not disabled, even though her nerves had obviously been ruined by the termination of parental rights action. She refused to attend two consultative examinations which SSA scheduled for her, and she refused to give them informed consent to pursue records of prior mental health treatments. When both of her claims were denied because of lack of sufficient evidence, she began to feature SSA in her daily harangues of persecution.
>
> Most street people were too fed up and irritated with Flory to listen to her more than once, but she was such a pathetic sight with her laments and her dog that she never entirely lost their sympathy. The willingness of touring street practitioners to endure her plaintive refrains on a daily basis minimized her nuisance value to others (and thus also achieved some public relations benefit for the mental health team). Eventually Flory consented for one of the psychologists to submit a report on her "ruined nerves" to the SSA in lieu of attending another one of their scheduled consultative exams.
>
> So predictable and regular was Flory that when she stopped coming to street sites months later it was noticed immediately. When her dog was found wandering the streets without her, a check-up of the carriage house attic revealed her wrapped up mummy-fashion in a blanket on her cot. She was almost catatonic in her lack of responsiveness. An ambulance was summoned to hospitalize her, and, as she was removed to a

stretcher, it could be seen that she was clutching a crumpled check from Social Security that was in the amount of thousands of dollars (probably a "windfall" back payment check covering all prior months for which she had been adjudged disabled).

It seems reasonable to speculate that the awarding of disability benefits contributed to the onset of the psychotic episode, insofar as this represented a profound upheaval of the persecutory premises by which this woman organized her world. (Flory was subsequently committed to a state hospital and not encountered on the streets again.) Whatever the case, this woman's deterioration makes clear that the psychodynamics of disability are not a foregone conclusion. Changes as dramatic as hers are unusual, but some moderate degree of destabilization is common when a person is first found disabled.

DISABILITY STANDARDS

Before turning to psychodynamic issues in greater depth, the technical aspects as to what constitutes a finding of disability according to the SSI and SSDI (Social Security Disability Insurance) programs must be examined. Although SSI and SSDI are distinct entitlement programs, they invoke almost identical evidentiary, regulatory, and procedural requirements, and they are administered by the same state-sponsored agency, a Disability Determination Service (DDS). The following orientation to the disability determination process highlights the kinds of information that are most useful to the DDS so that the mental health practitioner may better assist both street persons and the DDS.

First, the submission of a two-line statement to the effect that a particular client is disabled or not disabled by schizophrenia will not satisfy the programmatic regulations governing the DDS. Federal regulations call for a finding of disability which is documented by medical evidence and objective findings rather than practitioner judgment. Thus, it is in an applicant's best interest for the street practitioner to articulate and submit evidence which supports the disability conclusion rather than submit the conclusion, per se.

Once the relevant evidence has been gathered by the DDS, a team made up of a claims examiner and a psychiatrist or psychologist assesses the evidence according to a three-stage process. The first stage is the establishment of relevant signs, symptoms, and laboratory evidence (including psychological testing, if available) that document the presence of a mental impairment. The diagnostic criteria that govern the DDS in this first stage were adapted from DSM III-R. The only special stipulation governing this first-stage evidence is that the person who establishes the diagnosis in the field be a psychiatrist or psychologist. Mental health practitioners of *all* training backgrounds and credentials are qualified to submit evidence bearing on the second and third stages of the adjudication process.

As a rule, fine diagnostic distinctions (e.g., paranoid vs. chronic undifferentiated schizophrenia; borderline vs. narcissistic personality disorder) are not critical to the DDS once the presence of a generic diagnostic category (e.g., schizophrenia or personality disorder) has been established. Co-existing impairments need to be identified and substantiated, but it is not imperative that the street practitioner determine which one is primary, which one gave rise to the other(s), or what relative contributions of biological predispositions, psychodynamics, and/or social forces gave rise to each one. At this first stage of the evaluation process, the DDS merely needs to accumulate sufficient evidence to convince a putative independent reviewer that the mental impairment(s) alleged by or attributed to the applicant do exist. To satisfy DDS requirements for this first stage of evaluation, it is sufficient for the psychiatrist or psychologist to substantiate an applicant's depression with a report of signs and symptoms (e.g., sleep and appetite disturbance, suicidal thoughts, antidepressant medication being taken, MMPI scale 2 *T*-scores) and a reasonably detailed history of the condition.

Research has shown that psychiatric diagnosis per se is not significantly correlated with inability to work (see Anthony & Jansen, 1984). Instead, it is one's past work history, one's ability to get along with others, and one's ability to concentrate and sustain involvement in goal-directed behavior that are most indicative of the capacity to work. The second and third stages of the evaluation process thus address the impact of the diagnosed condition on the applicant's psychosocial functioning and work-related psychological capacities. These impacts are often more difficult for the DDS to establish than is the psychiatric diagnosis. Street practitioners from all disciplines are in an excellent position to provide evidence in these areas by virtue of their contacts with and observations of street persons adapting to the ongoing demands of street culture.

This second stage of the evaluation process (i.e., the impact of a mental impairment upon psychosocial functioning) is programatically divided into four realms: activities of daily living, social functioning, concentration-persistence-pace, and decompensation episodes. Evidence pertaining to these realms is routinely sought from applicants and their significant others, but a practitioner's observations of these areas will contribute to the coalescence of a functional picture of the applicant to the DDS team. The DDS team that makes disability decisions does not have face-to-face contact with the applicant. As such, vivid descriptions of functioning with concrete, evocative examples (e.g., "X can't seem to remember the rules of the shelter. Staff are frequently exasperated by having to explain these over and over to her.") contribute more to the process than comparable factual statements (e.g., "X's concentration is moderately to severely impaired on an ongoing basis").

Activities of Daily Living

This refers to such things as dress and hygiene, daily routines and behavior patterns, leisure pursuits, and so on. The appropriateness of dress and hygiene must be gauged with an eye toward the standards of the street culture and its limited availability of bathing and laundry facilities. Capacity for goal-directed control of one's day-to-day affairs is a critical assessment category. The alcoholic person who thinks to bury part of his alcohol at night for consumption in the morning in order to combat *delirium tremens* until the liquor stores open is showing more goal-directed behavior than the one who repeatedly shows up drunk at shelters or drop-ins that explicitly prohibit anyone with alcohol on his or her breath. From this perspective, the alcoholic man who works the temporary agencies every day to keep himself in liquor by night is different from the alcoholic man who is begging on the streets or is found alone by police and taken to a detoxification center every evening. Performing volunteer work and performing as middleman in drug deals are roughly equivalent in that each attests to a capacity for self-structured, goal-directed behavior.

Social Functioning

This encompasses casual observations of a how a street person interacts with significant others, peers, staffs of the culture sites, and so on. Whether the person gravitates toward, against, or away from others, and the person's history of same are often more relevant to assessing this realm than how the person relates to the practitioner during a one-on-one interview context. Some persons have high social interest but poor social skills, while others have good social skills but low social interest. The schizophrenic person who spends a day at a social center sitting alone in a corner smoking cigarettes is different from the schizophrenic person who accepts invitations to join card games there.

Such differentiations are of greater value in disability determination than are distinctions among schizophrenia versus schizoaffective disorder versus bipolar disorder.

Concentration, Persistence, and Pace

This is a realm in which interview observations that address a person's ability to track conversation or perform adequately at mental status exam tasks (e.g., digit span, serial sevens, recalling three objects after five minutes) are relevant. Incidental observations that address time periods of two hours or more are especially valuable: can the person concentrate for one plus hours at a game of chess or watching a feature length movie with peers?

Deterioration Episodes

Time-limited episodes of poor functioning that occur during work or work-like situations is the final category. A history of the person's psychiatric condition is important here in terms of what stressful circumstances triggered hospitalizations, precipitous job losses, school failures or withdrawals, and the like. In this realm, frequency counts and dates have great evidentiary value. Psychotic decompensations, panic attacks, and other kinds of acute episodes that take place during volunteer work, temporary labor, waiting in line at the welfare office, or in any other worklike situation are pertinent data in the evaluation of this realm.

If available evidence suggests to the DDS that a street person is "markedly impaired" (as defined by SSA) in two to three of these four realms, a finding of disability will be rendered. Again, a street practitioner who is convinced that such marked impairments exist will serve the process better by submitting appropriate documentation rather than simply forwarding his or her professional opinion as to the presence of "marked" deficits.

A street person may also be adjudged disabled when the mental impairment does not cause marked impairments in psychosocial functioning. This occurs when "moderate impairments" reduce a person's work-related functional capacity to a degree that the person is unable to sustain the performance of a routine, repetitive, one- to two-step task over an extended period of time. This analysis of residual functional capacity is the third and final step in SSA's disability evaluation process. According to federal guidelines, there are four basic work-related functions that must be present in order to conclude that a person is able to sustain a routine, repetitive job.

The first requirement in this third stage is that a person be able to *understand, remember, and carry out one- to two-step instructions.* Few persons are so impaired as to preclude this (those who are tend to be maintained in inpatient or other highly controlled settings). However, the person who cannot follow a simple medication regimen without becoming confused, and the person who becomes lost during a two- to three-block walk to a well-marked destination are providing evidence that bears on this realm. The testing of a person's ability to remember and perform two- to three-step commands, in sequence, can also be incorporated into a mental status exam.

The second work-related capacity to be assessed is the *ability to sustain mental effort at a simple task over an extended period without frequent breaks or disruptions due to symptoms.* People who cannot sit through a feature length movie without losing its train of thought, those who become paranoid at a work site as the social situation begins to feel familiar, those who fatigue early and quickly due to depression, and those who are unable to complete an MMPI at one sitting despite adequate reading abilities—all of these people are displaying significant deficits in this realm. In contrast, the alcoholic man who drinks all night but is able to get up in the morning and get himself to the labor pool so as to be able to afford his alcohol the next night is displaying residual functional capacity in this area. This is an assessment realm in which historical information and casual observations of a person's functioning amidst the culture are more germane than behavior during a particular interview.

The third realm of residual capacity for work pertains to a person's *ability to maintain the superficial social relationships required by a non-public-contact job, and the ability to adapt to ordinary levels of supervision.* Persons who become embroiled in repeated conflicts with authority figures across different settings, and those who are either insensitive or nonresponsive to the effects that poor hygiene has on others are displaying behavior that is relevant to this category. Over reaction to constructive criticism is another relevant observation here—again, concrete examples are preferred to abstract statements.

The final category is the *ability to adapt to expectable changes and stressors which frequently occur in the workplace.* This category addresses people who are so fragile as to be unable to tolerate deviations from routine, or whose frustration tolerance is so limited that they explode or withdraw in response to the slightest provocation.

It is critical for the street practitioner who offers observations and evidence in these areas to be able to link the deficits in question to the DSM IV condition that has been diagnosed. Does the "Axis II" person who quits a dishwashing job because it is boring or not worth the money do so because of motivational factors which are independent of the personality disorder per se? Definitive answers to such questions are difficult, and it is not the job of the street practitioner to tease out the various determinants of disability-related behavior. However, it is imperative that he or she be able to articulate some linkage between the mental impairment(s) and functional deficits which are reported to the DDS.

Finally, the DDS informs all applicants that responsibility for disability decisions rests with the DDS and not with the practitioners who submit relevant evidence. This effectively shields the practitioner from reprisals by applicants who are angered upon being denied disability benefits.

COUNTERTRANSFERENCE REVISITED

Sean was a white, alcoholic man in his late thirties when first found disabled by DDS on the basis of multiple failures in various chemical dependency treatment programs. The documentation included records of numerous appearances at various jails and detoxification centers where police would take him after he had passed out on the streets at night.

Sean's case came up for review five years after the initial award. During that interim, his admissions to chemical dependency treatment programs, jails, and detox centers had dropped to zero. DDS staff inferred that such changes suggested significant medical improvement. After Sean failed to appear for a scheduled examination, the DDS terminated his SSI benefits. One hour after having received this notification, a panicked (and intoxicated) Sean burst into a drop-in center where he had heard that "those shrink types" hung out. He was desperate not to lose his SSI benefits and be out on the streets again. He pleaded shamelessly in public that his daily drinking pattern had not changed a whit during the five years.

Ultimately the psychologist determined this to be true. Sean's drinking had not changed, but his support system had. He was no longer a solitary drinker with only police to clean up after him. His SSI payments had enabled him to take an apartment where he joined a domiciled bottle gang whose members occupied a majority of the rooms in the run-down building. He and his buddies confined their drinking to each other's flats, pooling money at the end of the month and sending out the most sober one for liquor when necessary. They generally tolerated each other's passing out in the wrong apartment although there had been occasional fights and feuds. Sean came to feel less distress about his alcoholism over these years and had lost all interest in "taking the cure."

Even though Sean's chemical dependency was as disabling as ever, the shift from solitary to bottle gang alcoholism had provided him with a support system that removed the necessity for police and treatment center interventions. It had also removed all incentive to pursue sobriety as well. For this latter reason, the psychologist who submitted a report to the DDS as to the illusory nature of Sean's medical improvement did so with both professional and personal reluctance. Sean's SSI benefits were restored.

A mental health practitioner may be forgiven his or her misgivings about contributing to Sean's reinstatement. Most would recoil from Sean's request, but this would merely pass the problem on to someone else. The reality is that Sean's argument is one with merit, given the way in which current federal regulations recognize alcoholism as a disabling impairment. It is not the province of the practitioner to selectively address such situations on the basis of privately-held beliefs about their merits. It is better to find a silver lining, and there is one here: the cessation of SSI benefits would have returned Sean to the streets and thus also reinstated the financial and "burnout" costs to police, detox personnel, and other service providers whom Sean's behavior had burdened in the past. Many street practitoners come to view such silver linings as more than rationalizations.

Thus, this sort of cognitive dissonance may be easier to resolve from a countertransference perspective than that caused by unavailable or unconvincing clinical evidence. During single contact disability assessments, the practitioner must wonder to what extent his or her sympathies are being courted. Questionable signs and symptoms should be attributed exclusively to the street person or couched entirely in the street person's own words (e.g., "X reports visions of the Four Horsemen of the Apocalypse, three times a day and twice on weekends"). Most people with intent to malinger know what signs and symptoms to report or acquiesce to, but they are usually less attuned to matters of psychosocial functioning and residual functioning capacity for work. Thus, a practitioner sometimes receives or elicits reports about manifold symptoms which are embedded in a lifestyle context of structured daily routines, an absence of problems relating to others, and few difficulties in concentrating on things that interest the person. Finally, the street practitioner need not feel compelled to resolve inconsistencies in the data or impose a definitive conclusion upon them. The task of resolving inconsistencies can be left to the DDS which usually has access to multiple evidence sources about the applicant.

In some circumstances, the street practitioner may choose to be forthright with a person as to how skeptical he or she is about the person's alleged disability. Informing some people that minimal evidence of disability is apparent may be received with surprising relief. It may also lead into a productive discussion of why the person had stopped seeking work.

> James was a black male in his mid-fifties who lobbied extensively for a psychiatric resident's statement in support of his SSI claim. His was an Axis II condition at worst, and he was jocular and cagey about his alcohol use. Yet he sought to be the resident's intermediary with black street people, referring them to her and singing her praises at informal meetings and card games where the subject would come up. The resident ultimately composed a statement in which James' allegations of serious symptoms were couched entirely in his own words. Her observations upon his lifestyle, his ability to relate to others, and his ability to concentrate during their conversations and upon projects of his own which he set his mind to were of equal prominence in the report.
>
> She also allowed him to read the report in her presence. After he had approved it in full, she put the report into a postage paid envelope, sealed it, and handed it back across the table for him to mail. After he had accepted it, she offered to tell him what she *really* thought, which was that she did not personally see him as mentally impaired to any significant degree in spite of all of the symptoms he had reported to her. His response was a broad smile and a loud rejoinder, "To be honest with you, doc, I'm glad to hear you say so." After a pause he asked if she had ever tried to find a job being black and 52 and no diploma. After her "no," he cleared his throat and they settled back into their chairs for a 45-minute session. He offered her his hand to shake at the end of the hour, and then had to return ten minutes later because he had left behind the envelope that had originally been his only reason for meeting with her on that day.

The street practitioner must remain open to the prospect of a therapeutic alliance beginning in an unpredictable way. Still, it would be misleading to suggest that occurrences such as the one above are typical or even frequent. In fact, it is more than likely that a practitioner's candor about such matters will trigger anger or hostility. One's sense of empathic contact with the person is the best guide as to whether or not such an interview has potential to move beyond its initial purposes.

For each person like James, there will be perhaps two like Sean—dislikable characters who view a mental health practitioner like they would a "one-night stand." That is, they eagerly appeal to the practitioner for disability purposes and later decline to acknowledge him or her once the disability enterprise has been completed. Such behavior (and the practitioner's reactions to it) are seldom relevant to the question of whether the person is disabled or not. Such behavior is also irrelevant to the practitioner's charge of eliciting evidence which bears on the disability question. There are some hard realities to accept: the most dislikable of antisocial characters may be so severely socially impaired as to be intolerable in any workplace, while a victimized and traumatically stressed woman somehow retains the capacity to perform in the workplace despite her ordeals and travails. It is critical for the practitioner to keep in mind that SSI disability is a criterion-referenced decision rather than a competitive one. Staying aloof of the emotional pulls associated with the assessment task is desirable. Some cognitive adjustments are helpful:

1. Adopt an attitude during the assessment that one will never know its outcome or have further contact with any of the parties involved in it. The detachment and task-centered focus of a consultant is optimal.

2. If one accepts the "single session" disability assessment role—and it will be at both the applicant's and DDS' delay and expense if one defers it to others solely because it is difficult to perform well—one must expect that mistakes will be made. However, spontaneous symptom remissions in response to disability awards do not necessarily represent mistakes. The street practitioner will undoubtedly encounter such before-and-after changes while on tour amidst the culture, but he or she should never assume that these spontaneous recoveries necessarily expose exaggerators and malingerers who are now "dropping their cover." Many such remissions reflect new-found relief, renewed optimism, and other therapeutic impacts of SSI benefits as discussed at the beginning of the chapter.

3. The fact that a person may deign to lie or exaggerate does not mean that the person is not disabled. If the street practitioner comes to process all clinical data through a cognitive construct such as "malingerer," he or she is likely to filter out and not report evidence which is inconsistent with that construct. It is not hard for a markedly impaired street person to rationalize the exaggeration or manipulation of data to the remote and faceless (sic) government bureaucrats who had denied his or her claim once before. Such temptations are not unlike those which appeal to middle class persons as they fill out their tax returns.

4. When the practitioner's conflicts over whether or not to report something of dubious validity cannot be entirely resolved, it is best to give the applicant the benefit of the doubt. This suggestion is not made in endorsement of any fiscal, political, or philosophical position. Rather, it reflects sound clinical judgment as to the profound stressor which homelessness is. Because a disability award offers promise for

ending or avoiding homelessness, probabilistic judgments which maximize false positives (i.e., those truly nondisabled persons who are found disabled) are preferable to those which maximize false negatives (i.e., those truly disabled persons who are found nondisabled). Again, because the DDS renders its judgments on the basis of evidence obtained from a number of sources, the final word on doubt resolution rests with that agency.

5. Last, it is better to live with doubt than to resolve it by editing clinical reports through the sieves of political or moral beliefs (e.g., housing is a natural right). While the "natural right" position may be valid for the street practitioner *qua* citizen, its seepage into disability evaluations forwarded to the DDS will undermine the practitioner's credibility with that agency and detract from the import attached to the practitioner's future submissions.

The challenge of maintaining credibility with entitlement agencies while addressing the survival needs of street people is particularly important in situations which involve low income housing. Here the practitioner's signed statement may enable a mentally impaired individual to bypass waiting lists or move immediately into such housing. In this circumstance, the housing authority may require an assessment from the practitioner as to both the extent of mental impairment(s) and the person's ability to adapt to the communal living demands of an apartment complex. A cavalier attitude on the part of the practitioner toward communal living issues may lead to problems in the housing complex.

A psychologist was asked for a statement about a schizotypal woman's ability to live unsupported in an apartment. The woman in question had not been hostile nor had she shown positive signs of schizophrenia. She was able to see to her own needs on the streets by getting herself to shelters at the appointed times and eating at drop-in centers. She politely refused to submit to a formal psychological evaluation. Even so, the psychologist predicted that she would not pose any serious problems, and he sent a statement to the housing authority to that effect.

The psychologist proved to be wrong in his prediction. The woman hoarded leftover food under her bed. She also hoarded newspapers, plastic wrappers, and other such debris. The smell mounted until it offended others who pressed the housing authority to investigate. The mass of newspapers violated fire codes. When the woman refused to remove them she was evicted.

Even before the eviction was final, the housing statements of *all* psychologists began to be returned by the housing authority with a stamp "insufficient documentation." When pressed for an explanation, the housing authority indicated that the guidelines which governed it had been "reinterpreted" such that the signature of an M.D. was now required on all such statements.

THE PARADOX OF PRIDE

A more vexing situation is one in which a psychotic or otherwise severely impaired person is too proud to countenance the fact that his or her condition is disabling. He or she may attribute poor functioning to victimization by family, friends, other mental health practitioners, The System, etc. Such persons drain sympathetic support figures of funds and overuse emergency resources even as they refuse to relinquish their illusions of personal adequacy. Eventually their sources of support become exhausted and wash their hands of the person, perhaps with a send-off to the effect of "you have to at least apply for SSI before I'll help you out again." The psychotic person may well withdraw from the relationship at this point and construe it as yet another example of benefactor-turned-persecutor. Eventually his or her only reliable benefactors are police officers and emergency room personnel. Ultimately he or she may be psychiatrically hospitalized or treated (perhaps self-treated) with Greyhound therapy.

Ideally such persons could be found disabled without their knowledge or consent (their financial support could be "laundered" to them through channels which are more acceptable than disability). However, the administrative, legal, and philosophical questions raised by such a practice are daunting, and many avenues of potential abuse would be opened. At times, there are quick and painless accommodations to such persons. Recall the rapid compliance which was obtained from a range of agencies (including the DDS) to help with the "submarine germ warfare" situation (p. 65). Practitioners and agencies were willing to accept this as a qualifying diagnosis when the woman refused to authorize the release of any clinical reports which did not assign that diagnosis. The psychiatrist called the DDS in the woman's presence and enlisted their collusion by suggesting that the unusual diagnosis be used in place of "#295.30" (the DSM IV number for paranoid schizophrenia). This is a matter of constructive sociopathy being applied in the opposite direction.

Lyle was a black male of thirty-five who approached a psychiatrist seeking a psychological fitness statement in "multiple, high resolution, Xerox copies" so that he could append these to all of the job applications he planned to be submitting over the next six months.

Pressured speech and ego inflation were apparent within fifteen minutes, and Lyle himself ventured that he had "50% insight" into his problems. By this he meant that his"other half" believed he was a superman and it was this other half that had gotten him into trouble whenever he would be hired. He was usually able to get hired and to favorably impress employers during his initial weeks on a job. In fact, he was able to focus his energy sufficiently to exceed the production standards set for him. Invariably, however, he would become arrogant and condescending toward fellow employees who could not keep up with him. He would also expand into meddling, usurping, or superseding stances with supervisors until he was fired. His first such experiences had occurred with his parents and siblings in the family business. His "other half" had nearly ruined the business by conducting speculative after-hours deals when no one was around to supervise him. When this came to light, Lyle was expelled not only from the business but from family membership as well.

A string of such job failures, hospitalizations, etc., were attributed by him to this "other half." Medications taken while in the hospital would subdue the other half so well that Lyle would see fit to stop medications when he was discharged or, in an experiment of his own design, he would take half of the dose or the full dose half as often. When he engaged the psychiatrist, however, he was desperate for work and not treatment. He was living out of an abandoned car and winter was fast approaching. Lyle shunned the available supports of the local street culture because "they're losers" and he, most assuredly, was not.

At a second visit, the psychiatrist was able to convince Lyle that appending such a fitness statement to job applications would only serve to draw unwanted attention to his other half because most people who apply for jobs do not make such statements. This logic appealed more to Lyle than did the psychiatrist's countersuggestion that Lyle apply for 50 percent disability even as he continued to look for work. At first Lyle declined this, but he came back for a third visit three weeks later and announced that it was only fair to hold his other half accountable for a fair share of his support. He also noted that the nights had gotten colder in the car and he was still unhired. ("It's my clothes, I think. I must look like a street person to them!") He filled out the SSI application form alleging "50% disability only, please. Thank you!" The past medical records acquired by the DDS were compelling enough that Lyle was found disabled without needing a statement from the psychiatrist. Because the regulations governing SSI do not include allowances for partial disability, Lyle received full benefits even as he continued to assume that he was receiving only 50 percent. The psychiatrist decided that this lack of insight would go unaddressed. Lyle soon had his own apartment, food stamps, a medical card—and a new resistance against treatment ("Mr. Superman is pulling his weight now. There's no sense in adding insult to injury by taking lithium, too.") On the other hand, he was delighted by the laundry facilities of his apartment complex as these helped him to be more presentable for job interviews.

Multiple contacts with Lyle suggested that this "other half" was an ego-stabilizing attribution rather than an identity delusion or a dissociative state. From the standpoint of treating a resistant individual with bipolar disorder, the psychiatrist's approach yielded little beyond a good alliance. However, from the standpoint of increasing quality of life and reducing vulnerability to predators, the seduction of Lyle into applying for SSI was an unqualified success. The key juncture occurred when Lyle refused appropriate treatment and the psychiatrist did not "terminate" him for this. Instead, the goal of providing necessary financial supports was pursued and achieved because of the psychiatrist's willingness to support Lyle's rationalizations for his impairment. When the objectives of treating a mental impairment conflict with those of providing basic life supports, the former must be sacrificed in the interest of the latter.

For individuals like Lyle, pride matters that stir an opposition to disability are not magically resolved by the SSI award. Lyle's psychiatrist remains concerned that Lyle will refuse SSI checks if he ever comes to know that he is receiving full benefits rather than half. The psychiatrist's plan in that event is to advise Lyle to cash the check first and send half of it back rather than reject the check outright. It is the psychiatrist's hope that the inconveniences that this will pose for Lyle, coupled with Lyle's own appreciation for his improved standard of living on full benefits, will induce him to develop another rationalization for why he should keep the whole check.

Upon receiving her first SSI check, Diane (p. 124) began a compulsive search for odd jobs. She also began to call for appointments with the social worker who had walked her through the SSI application process (during all previous contacts the social worker had needed to outreach her). At these appointments, Diane would query the social worker as to how much she could earn on the side without forfeiting her SSI. On one visit, she asked him if he didn't think she could afford to go over that limit. The social worker told her that he did not think she could afford to jeopardize her SSI.

At their next visit, Diane arrived in an irritable mood rather than the frantic one she had displayed at prior appointments. She reported that she had stopped doing odd jobs. She also reported a dream of the previous night in which the social worker had appeared in a military uniform and had been barking orders to a lot of people.

A finding of disability can create a new set of problems even as it solves old ones. Focal psychotherapy which addresses a person's adjustment to disabled status may be indicated, and this may need to be provided on an outreach basis through informal channels. It is always a mistake to overlook a person's need to "work through" such a change of identity and status.

PAYEESHIP PROBLEMS

There is no arena in which the issue of personal pride is more salient than that of representative payeeship, wherein the checks of a disability recipient are sent to a family member, friend, or social service designee for management on behalf of the disabled person. The determination that an SSI recipient is unable to manage benefits in her or his own best interest is made by the DDS, although it is typically based on the opinion of a treating/examining physician or psychologist. Many SSI recipients who are disabled by drug addiction or alcoholism are automatically designated for payeeship status. If a recipient wishes to be removed from payeeship status (so as to receive his or her checks directly), a treating physician/psychologist must submit a statement to SSA to the effect that the person is now capable of managing the benefits in his or her own best interests.

Unless one knows a person well over an extended period of time, the street practitioner is in a poor position to make an informed decision in this realm of assessment. There will be many such requests, however, particularly when it becomes known that the practitioner performs SSI exams or is otherwise a resource person in the area of disability. In most respects, the "first contact" assessment of ability to manage benefits poses the same difficulties as a first contact assessment of disability. However, the backdrops of the two are different in one key respect. In the disability assessment situation, the person is not receiving benefits and is thus already experiencing the ravages of homelessness or is at risk for doing so. In the payeeship situation, however, benefits are already being received and (hopefully) administered in a way that prevents homelessness, regardless of whether the disabled person likes the way in which this is being done or not. Thus, except when there is reason to believe that the disabled person is being exploited by the payee, there is no cause to assume that the disabled person's quality of life will necessarily be improved by undoing a payeeship assignment.

To the contrary, there may be many reasons to project that the possibility of homelessness may be *increased* by undoing a payeeship. A person's pride and self-esteem should not be reinforced when homelessness seems a likely by-product. For example, most representative payees know to pay for a chemically dependent person's room-and-board as soon as the SSI check arrives. Left to their own devices, addicted persons are inclined to spend the check on chemicals and binges at the beginning of the month, thus rendering themselves resourceless for its duration. Some psychotic persons—particularly manic ones—are prone to engage in comparably foolish bouts of impulsive spending, perhaps splurging on cigarettes and caffeinated beverages that render the sedating effects of medication easier to cope with. Both of the above groups are also vulnerable to predation. The disbursement of government checks at the beginning of each month is a high profile date in a street culture's cycle. Predators gravitate toward liquor stores and check cashing establishments at such times. While a benefit of the doubt may be extended to a homeless person in the disability assessment process, there is little justification for extending this when it comes to rescinding a person's assignment to payeeship status.

However, this is not to say that such requests by street persons should be responded to with a flat, "no." Rather, the practitioner should acknowledge that there is no way in the course of a single interview to determine how well someone is able to manage money in his or her own best interests. The practitioner can suggest that the person make once-a-month return visits for a time to provide the practitioner with an accounting of income and disbursements for those months as a way of showing that he or she is up to the task of managing benefits. The practitioner can also request references to attest to the person's abilities in these realms, and these references should include the current payee whenever possible. Such demands will not deter the driven, determined individual who is indeed up to the task of managing benefits. These demands will dissuade the impulsive individual who can not sustain such a task. Most persons who are alcohol or drug addicted fall into this latter category.

The course of a payeeship transaction is less predictable with a psychotic person. Whether motivated by pride, impulse, autistic schema, or resentment of the payees who control them, some of these people take payeeship matters into their own hands and attempt to solve the problem by self-prescribed Greyhound therapy. Upon arriving in a new city, the person will either seek out a mental health practitioner or display symptoms in a way that brings him or her to a practitioner's attention. He or she may then tell the practitioner of exploitation by the current payee, or pronounce that payee too distant, given the psychotic person's intention to relocate to the new location. The practitioner is assured at some point that the psychotic person can manage his or her money if only given the chance to do so.

Such presentations and stories must be viewed with skepticism. The person's permission to allow contact with the current payee should be sought; demurrals attributed to forgetting the name or phone number of the payee are to be viewed with cynicism (if a person is not so psychotic as to warrant hospitalization, he or she is typically not so psychotic as to forget critical information about the payee who formerly administered his or her financial resources).

Debra was a woman in her forties who bussed into the Twin Cities from Providence, RI, to retire closer to "my Scandinavian roots." She claimed to have recently been awarded social security *retirement* although this was not consistent with her age or her negative symptoms of schizophrenia. Even after a computer check indicated that she was not on SSDI, she continued to maintain that this was not so. She did accept her social worker's offer to put her up in a shelter at the county's expense until her checks started to arrive at her new post office box. A psychologist was also called to interview Debra. She offered a diagnosis of residual schizophrenia. Debra declined to consider treatment.

Three months later, Debra was still at the shelter at the county's expense. She had made no complaints and had bothered no one. When the social worker followed up with the SSA office of the eastern region, it was learned that Debra's benefits were originally to have been assigned to her mother in Providence as payee. However, when Debra had learned of this plan, she had moved west and the payeeship paperwork had been stopped. According to records, all checks had been written in Debra's name and had been forwarded to her Twin Cities address.

Debra did not respond when confronted with this information. The social worker made Debra take her to the post office box where they discovered a three-month accumulation of mail including three monthly disability checks made out to Debra. Debra maintained that she had forgotten to check her mail, but in saying this she was as flat and indifferent as she had been to everything else. She protested mildly when the psychologist signed her into payeeship status with the county, but soon acquiesced to that arrangement, just as she had acquiesced to all other things done on her behalf since she had arrived.

Debra had displayed some savvy in her manner of evading the original payeeship assignment, but she also showed poor judgment in her contentment with living a vouchered existence. Her mother was eventually contacted, and she provided a social history good enough that when Debra later experienced an acute psychotic episode, it proved possible to stabilize her and move her into a board-and-care residence without a hospitalization.

From the standpoint of clinical management, then, this outcome must be considered a good one. However, such a conclusion must be tempered by a consideration of various administrative and economic facts. The bed occupied by Debra represented one less board-and-care bed available for psychotic persons who were indigenous to the Twin Cities. The three months of vouchered expenses were not recovered. Whatever benefits which Debra derived by virtue of eluding mother-as-payee may well have been achieved in Providence with a better choice of payee in the first place.

Such issues are often raised by financial workers, program managers, and elected officials. They are also raised by indigenous street persons who take a dim view of actions that encourage the immigration of transient street people to their locality. Because street practitioners sometimes lose sight of such attitudes and issues, the following is offered as a first approximation of procedural guidelines to follow with impaired persons who would immigrate to a community. If a transient psychotic person is assessed to be highly vulnerable, or to have prominent positive symptoms, or to be genuinely distressed in conjunction with a compelling story of payee exploitation—under any of these circumstances, a compelling case can be made for a practitioner of the host city to facilitate at least a temporary relocation of the person at the host city's expense. On the other hand, for those psychotic persons with residual or remitted conditions who display little distress or vulnerability and intend to depend immediately and indefinitely upon the host community for their financial support (sometimes referred to as "Easy Rider's syndrome")—for such persons, a bus ticket back to their point of departure is always defensible and sometimes the intervention of choice. The key question in prescribing Greyhound therapy is whether or not such a decision is based upon a careful assessment of the person or a reflexive exercise of local policy.

CHAPTER 7

Single Session Interventions

At the end of the interview with the psychologist, James (p. 135) left behind the envelope containing the very report that had been his reason for seeking the psychologist's services in the first place. James' SSI application was eventually denied and he subsequently declined a caseworker's offer to assist him with an appeal of that decision. Shortly thereafter he dropped from sight and was not encountered again; despite this, it seems reasonable to conclude that something changed within James during the course of that interview, given his original presenting problem and the nature of his memory lapse. His leaving the interview empty-handed suggests that he was in psychological possession of something which, for the moment at least, was of greater importance than the statement addressing his allegation of disability.

Psychotherapeutic change may be set in motion without an ongoing alliance and repeated contacts. Thus the once-a-month volunteer who does not do disability evaluations can still have an impact if persuaded to try. In fact, single sessions are more the rule than the exception in street work. No street practitioner can ever assume that a second session will occur with a homeless person simply because that person asks for one and seems likely to attend it. The rumor mills of street culture spread "good-jobs-quick" schemes on a frequent basis, and the dulled miseries and seeming endlessness of street life endow these rumors with magnetic appeal to those who would hear them. Short notice (and no notice) geographical moves across city, county, and country are not unusual. A telephone call to the practitioner canceling the second session may not come.

Practitioners are advised to adjust their expectations of multiple sessions work accordingly. Some may also need to revise their doubts about the value of single sessions. Distinctions have always been drawn between short-term and long-term psychotherapy, but few practitioners have asserted that a single session can serve any purpose beyond intake or diagnosis. Even when a first session (or perhaps some later single session) is pivotal compared to all others of a particular series, it is rarely highlighted as such. Time-honored traditions of psychotherapy value the whole over the sum of its individual parts. Another traditional belief is that as the number of sessions increases, so does the depth of therapy and the probability of a meaningful positive outcome.

But traditions are one thing and research findings another. To date, the presumed positive correlation between the length of psychotherapy and quality of outcome has not been empirically demonstrated with any consistency (see Garfield & Bergin, 1986). To the contrary, a scattering of case reports and follow-up studies have quietly accumulated to challenge at least one corollary of the "more is better" tradition. That corollary is the belief that the failure of a person to return for a second interview typically reflects either a poor treatment alliance or inadequate motivation on the part of the person. Such single session persons are traditionally referred to as "dropouts," even though the literature now suggests that they not be burdened with the negative connotations of that term (Bloom, 1984). For example, Breuer and Freud (1895/1957) reported a single session treatment success with a woman who suffered from anxiety attacks. Other one-session case studies have depicted successful insight-oriented interventions with a variety of somatization disorders (Groddeck, 1951; Reider, 1955; Rosenbaum, 1964; Tannenbaum, 1919). Cognitive-behavioral approaches have proved successful with simple phobias (Fassler, 1985; Ost, 1989) and post-traumatic stress disorder symptoms (Kellner, Singh, & Irigoyen-Rascon, 1991; Shapiro, 1989). Albert Ellis (1989) reported a successful single-session treatment of suicidal depression by rational-emotive therapy. There are also reports of successful marital therapy (Seagull, 1966) and family therapy (Kaffman, 1963) by way of single sessions.

The findings of follow-up studies have also been encouraging. Bloom (1981, 1984) reviewed six independent investigations in which a variety of recipients were contacted between six months and eight years after a single mental health interview. Each of these studies demonstrated that significant therapeutic benefit was common after a single contact. Two of them found single contact recipients to have had better outcomes than those who had participated in extended courses of treatment (Edwards et al., 1977; Rosen & Wiens, 1979). The Rosen and Wiens research included two untreated control groups who did not improve on the criterion variable (reduced utilization of medical services) as well as the single session group had done. The classic outcome research by Cummings and Follette (1976) can also be cited. Their subjects included a subsample of eighty emotionally distressed persons who, as a result of a single psychotherapy interview, demonstrated a 60 percent reduction in medical services utilization over a subsequent five year period.

Bloom concluded from his review of this literature that (1) single contacts have been demonstrated to be therapeutic, and (2) they have this effect independently of whether or not the practitioner had initially intended them to be therapeutic. That is, therapeutic effects accrue even when the practitioner intends or perceives a first (single) session to be only evaluative in nature. It must be observed here that the post hoc nature of these follow-up studies cannot conclusively establish the nature of single session effects, nor the conditions under which these are most likely to occur. In most of these studies, it is not clear to what extent subjects were pre-assigned to single session groups versus permitted to define themselves as dropouts by failing to attend otherwise planned second sessions. However, two follow-up studies do address dropout subjects exclusively: Littlepage, Kosloski, Schnelle, McNees, and Gendrich (1976) found that their mental health center dropout subjects rated services as highly as did those who formed extended alliances with practitioners and terminated treatment in ways which met practitioners' expectations. Silverman and Beech (1979) reported follow-up data in which 70 percent of a community mental health center's dropout subjects claimed to have been satisfied with the services provided to them.

The work of Moshe Talmon (1990) represents the first systematically planned implementation and follow-up of single session psychotherapy as a treatment modality of choice. Among a sample of 60 single-session persons treated by Talmon and his colleagues, 58 percent agreed that they did not require any sessions beyond the initial one. In follow-up contacts which occurred from three to twelve months after a single session, 88 percent of this subsample described themselves as either "improved" or "much improved" since that session. Seventy-nine percent of this subsample reported that the single session had been sufficient to meet their needs.

Both Bloom and Talmon cite a number of reports which document that single session encounters are quite common. In some settings, one session is the modal number of contacts between recipient and practitioner. It may be that practitioners' expectations are violated more frequently by single session encounters than are their recipients' treatment needs. As Jerome Frank wrote in his preface to Talmon's book: "A closer look at dropouts from all forms of psychotherapy, however, reveals that most patients who quit after a single interview do so because they have accomplished what they intended and that, on the average, such patients report as much improvement as those who stay the prescribed course" (Talmon, 1990, p. xi).

However, one must still consider that the philosophy that has given rise to single session therapy is managed mental health care. Most persons served by managed care are middle class people who possess jobs and health insurance benefits. One must question whether such gainful employment and related achievements attest to a level of adaptive skill or ego strength which is not often encountered in the street culture. Indeed, Talmon (1990) frequently alluded to the fact that the natural recuperative powers of the person must be counted upon to continue the practitioner's single session work.

How limited are the natural recuperative powers of street people? They are certainly limited among the psychotic people of the street culture, as well as others whose homelessness mainly reflects social selection mechanisms. Limited recuperative powers also characterize those who have reached the third stage of acculturation to street life, that is, people who have accepted homelessness as a verdict and final resting place for themselves. But there are many others on the streets who have not lost self-consciousness along with self-esteem. Socioeconomic decline and psychological decline do not go hand in hand—at least, not in the beginning. To the contrary (and consistent with crisis theory), acute homelessness creates a readiness for change which is subject to influence from outside sources. The prognosis is good when someone is encountered in the first or second stages of homelessness, that is, while he or she still struggles to resist self-definition as a street person. Lorion and Felner (1986) have endorsed the single session approach as a viable option for practitioners who work with persons of low socioeconomic status.

Robert was a burly Native American in his late twenties who was met in a shelter while scowling and cursing in the direction of a white female staff as she walked away from him. He did not stop his muttering as a white female psychiatric social worker approached. She had originally intended to walk past him, but stopped 15 feet short of him and moved to one side as he continued his tirade. Eventually he stopped and asked her what she thought she was staring at. She replied that she was just being careful not to walk into someone who was already in the middle of an emotional storm. Robert changed his tone to that of aggrieved victim as he explained how he had just been upbraided for having given away two cigarettes to a fellow shelter guest whom he had just met. (This violated a shelter rule which had been designed to discourage a common form of predatory extortion.)

Robert was not an extortion victim. He was new to the shelter from "the res" (reservation) and claimed that no rules had been explained to him. "What do they think I am? Like I'm one more drunken Indian or some shit like that!"

The social worker listened for a while. She did not seek any history nor try to offer the shelter's point of view. Once Robert's emotional storm began to subside, she thought to admire the intricate bead work in the necklace which he wore. Robert lightened up immediately and emptied his pockets which were filled with other beadworks which he had intended to sell at a Native American festival in the east. He'd had a falling out with his associates during the drive to that festival and they had dumped him at the roadside when he had fallen asleep.

He invited her to his room to see more of his work. She declined by alluding to shelter rules "against that too," but invited him to bring the rest of his work down to show her in the lobby. This he was delighted to do. She had him lay it out before her within view of the front desk where the staff member who had angered him earlier was now working. Because his work was good, it caught that staff member's eye, and she walked over to admire it. The social worker left Robert with that woman soon afterward, making a point to remind her that Robert still needed orientation to the unusual rules of shelter life.

This intervention was therapeutic on several levels. First, Robert's preemptive and incorrect conclusion (incorrect in this instance, at least) of racial bias was short-circuited. The social worker's admiration for Robert's craft bolstered his morale, and her drawing the staff member in to be part of Robert's self-esteem boost reduced the tension between those two. This other woman later became instrumental in Robert's finding a job and moving out of the shelter (in fact, she ultimately became a romantic partner to him).

Thus, in "treatment plan" language, this social worker's opportunistic and understated intervention consumed forty-five minutes and (1) interrupted an instance of maladaptive thinking, (2) provided a stroke of emotional support for Robert, and (3) reduced tension and thereby achieved some measure of milieu therapy for the shelter.

An alcoholic man asked to see a psychologist during the latter's visit to a chemical dependency treatment shelter which served homeless men. He complained of vivid, frightening dreams which woke him up almost nightly. He was unable to remember these dreams afterward.

The man took two minutes to present this information and then sat back expectantly in his chair. When the psychologist deduced that nothing more was forthcoming she casually remarked that dreams often reflect thoughts and feelings which a person shuts off during the waking hours.

This ten-second statement stirred the man to verbal action: "I've been shutting off my feelings for years with alcohol," he exclaimed. He then talked for ten minutes in a monologue about how bound and determined he was to proceed through more than one step (of treatment) this time. He seemed to draw an emotional lift from being allowed to soliloquize in this fashion. The psychologist confined herself to nodding and said nothing until the man stood up and thanked her profusely for "all you have done for me."

This man presented a troublesome symptom and he was offered a perspective on it which fit well within the subjective context of his ongoing world view and sense of self. It struck the psychologist that *any* such new perspective would have worked equally well, and that she could have achieved the same outcome by saying that alcohol cessation disrupts sleep cycles which had previously been governed by alcohol consumption. In any event, the symptom lost its troublesome quality immediately; the man's subsequent monologue contained many of the earmarks of a stress inoculation procedure. All in all, it was a display of spontaneous recuperative powers that required very little from the psychologist to be activated.

This last vignette is typical of ways in which addicted persons make use of street practitioners. Talking with a mental health practitioner strengthens resolve not to use. It represents a new response to environmental cues (the physical and social aspects of the street culture) that had previously elicited and reinforced chemical use. The addicted person who uses a practitioner in this way tends to be in the proselyte stage of indoctrination to a chemically-free life. He or she may be out and about on the streets shortly after discharge from primary care to aftercare status. The practitioner need only serve as an attentive listener to be helpful. It is not stimulating work for the practitioner: Addicted persons often call forth the precepts of the Alcoholics Anonymous ideology as if these were the Scriptures. In fact, some do so with a fervor that is tiresome to those with scientific backgrounds, and the practitioner may feel as if he or she is the sole audience member of a pep-rally-for-one. Nevertheless, if one's purpose is to assist street people, then lending tacit support to such an ideology through one's attentive presence is an appropriate stance for the practitioner to take. By doing so he or she extends the same respect for freedom of religion that is usually afforded to office culture persons.

The nature of single session contacts is such that one seldom receives feedback as to the value of a session to the person. The above instance was an exception: two weeks later at the same site, another man from the treatment program asked to see the psychologist upon referral from the first man.

He, too, had trouble with dreams—flashback dreams to his days as a soldier in Viet Nam. These had started on a night after the man had returned to the treatment shelter from an A.A. meeting off the grounds. He had walked into the climax of one of the *Rambo* movies being shown on VCR in the commons area of the shelter.

After five minutes of inquiry, the psychologist concluded that the man suffered from post-traumatic stress disorder (PTSD). The man had experienced a full-blown PTSD syndrome shortly after having returned home from the war, but the symptoms had tapered off with time and he had not experienced any such symptoms for ten years.

In this instance, the psychologist chose to explain how long-term memory is like a library that includes many lost and forgotten books. The movie had functioned like an entry number from the card catalogue of the man's library and this had brought back memories from the war. The man found this explanation convincing and added that it brought to mind another "lost" memory about how nervous he had felt years ago when *The Deer Hunter* and *Apocalypse Now* had been released simultaneously. He had avoided those movies then and now reckoned that he needed to be more careful to stay away from war movies in the future.

Most practitioners who have worked with PTSD victims or Viet Nam veterans would not find the above problem unusual. If anything is unusual here, it is the fact that this man had not been offered such an explanation for bad dreams and flashbacks in the 20 years since the war had ended. This highlights an important fact that cannot be overlooked: practitioners encounter many persons in the street culture who are undereducated, alienated from the mainstream culture, and/or preoccupied with ongoing economic survival problems for periods of years. These and other factors foster a limited psychological-mindedness among street people as a whole, but it is wrong to conclude from this that they cannot acquire psychological-mindedness. This veteran displayed a capacity to integrate the psychologist's explanation into his world view by his spontaneous recall of his anxiety response to Viet Nam War movies he had seen earlier. Such behavior would meet most technical definitions of the "working through" process of insight learning.

Talmon (1990) has suggested that mental health practitioners grow to underestimate the novelty and value of knowledge and insights that they themselves have discussed and worked through extensively with supervisors, colleagues, and previous recipients. Such complacency tends to be reinforced as one is repeatedly exposed to the saturation coverage which such topics now receive on television interview shows, talk radio, magazines, and so on. It is also reinforced if one works with better educated persons who have the leisure time to be exposed to this media saturation. The net effect is that the practitioner comes to view certain knowledge to be self-evident among society as a whole. Perhaps this explains why practitioners have so consistently underestimated the value of single sessions to "dropouts." It may well be that the questions and formulations that a practitioner makes in a first interview are sufficiently novel and provocative to trigger a viable change process which many people can carry forward on their own.

Talmon (1990) emphasized peoples' recuperative powers in accordance with humanistic traditions of thought. He paid little heed to the fact that in the act of dropping out after a single session, the person is also asserting control over the treatment. Such recipient control may not be a bad thing (unless the person comes to feel that he or she cannot contact the practitioner again because of this behavior). Nevertheless, most mental health practitioners who have been trained outside of the humanistic tradition (along with many who have been trained within it) believe that it is necessary for the practitioner to maintain control over the timing and dosage of sessions. After all, it is the practitioner who is the expert, formulates the treatment plan, and so on. This works fine as a basic postulate governing treatment alliances in most circumstances. However, such expectations must be modified when the premise of interpersonal engagement is either outreach or the more ambiguous context of making oneself available to recipients on the latter's own territory. Territory always cedes elements of control to its holder; these effects are subtle but powerful, and some recipients regard them as more basic than those ceded to the practitioner by virtue of his or her training and expertise. Street practitioners must always be attuned to these matters and willing to yield to them. Conceiving oneself as a "personal problems consultant" rather than as a psychotherapist may help in many instances; dismissing difficult people as resistant or noncompliant does not.

It is doubtful whether many street people ever reflect on such matters. Some seek merely the generic, cathartic relief that comes with being able to tell one's story to a sympathetic ear. This sort of agenda is not so prevalent among office culture persons, most of whom have family, friends, and significant others who are willing to listen sympathetically to them. Indeed, such office culture people usually seek psychotherapy *because* mere sympathetic listening has not proved sufficient to reduce psychological pain. At the first interview, then, the practitioner can often assume that something more than sympathetic listening will be required to reduce the other person's psychological distress.

This is not an accurate assumption on the streets. By definition, street persons have become sufficiently alienated from family, friends, and other sources of support to lack ready access to sympathetic ears. Patient listeners are in short supply on the streets. Everyone has his or her own tale of woe which he or she believes to be worse than the next person's. Newly homeless persons are often jolted by the disdainful reception that telling one's story receives from others who have been on the streets longer. A common response theme is righteous one-upmanship, for example, "If you think your story is tragic, wait until you hear *my* story!" Thus the street culture has its own complacency problem, and this fuels the collective demoralization and social alienation that already prevails there.

The sympathy taboo does not apply to interactions with those from outside of the culture. The street practitioner comes to learn that the indulgence of sympathy deserves more therapeutic respect than it typically receives. It may function as a first avenue of emotional connectedness, out of which springs other emotional transactions and bonds. Thus, the street practitioner must be willing to meet this need when chosen to be a listener. It is a readiness that becomes difficult to muster after one has heard a litany of tragic stories and begins to habituate to them.

A psychiatric nurse was regularly stationed in the cafeteria of a shelter during off-meal hours due to an absence of office space elsewhere. While interviewing people there, he would often observe a quiet, slow-moving man in his early sixties wiping off tables in the background. The man wore a paper food service hat and a white apron. He would ignore the nurse and others and keep a proper distance from conversations. No one ever seemed to mind this man's presence during their contacts with the nurse. Twice the nurse asked someone about him and both times he received the same response: the person would turn around to look and then exclaim, "Oh, that's just Cookie." The nurse came to regard Cookie as a fixture of the place, which he was: Cookie had been cleaning up the shelter's cafeteria after meals for as long as any resident could remember. He did this for all three meals, seven days a week, and received his room and board in return for his labor. Nothing else was known about the man because he kept to himself.

On one slow morning, the nurse arrived and exchanged the usual mundane smiles with Cookie. He sat down at his regular table and began to work on paperwork to pass the time. Cookie walked up to the table and asked, "Busy?" The nurse shook his head and pushed the paperwork to one side. Cookie sat down and leaned forward on his mop handle as he said, "I think it's time to be moving on." The nurse asked if he could help in some way. Cookie looked at the floor and shook his head. "It was twenty years ago tomorrow when my Mayday come in."

"Mayday" referred to a police dispatcher summoning him from a truck stop on a stretch of I-80 in rural Nebraska where he was working as a diesel mechanic at the time. He was also an auxiliary police officer,

> and on that day he was dispatched to the scene of an accident to direct traffic while sworn officers attended to the accident itself. He recalled having slapped his suction cup siren to the roof of his car before heading down the interstate. He arrived to find a smoking pile of demolished cars. Some were still on fire, and it was some time before he looked back over his shoulder while directing traffic and saw that his wife's car had been among them. She and their two children had been killed in the accident. There had been five deaths in all and, within a week, the police department released a report that said that the accident had been caused by his wife having failed to brake. Cookie had been working on her car's brakes that morning, and he recalled having rushed through the reassembly because he had feared being late for work at the truck stop.
>
> Hearing this story rendered the nurse speechless, even close to tears. Cookie thanked him for listening and hoisted himself back up with the mop handle. He then pointed to the door to indicate a person waiting to see the nurse. Cookie moved out of the shelter on the next day and was not seen again.

Cookie obviously wanted an audience for a private agenda, which was never made clear. One may speculate that it was to help him endure an anniversary reaction and a decision to change his life at that time. For present purposes, however, a follow-up of the psychiatric nurse is more relevant. After this session with Cookie, he could not listen to the stories of other homeless persons with his normal degree of patience. Cookie's story represented the epitome of tragic life events, and the nurse found himself increasingly curt and detached to "all other comers." He began to tell Cookie's story to others in the course of clinical contacts, and it was not until one person got up and walked out in response to this that the problem of habituation became apparent to him. He last spoke of Cookie's story to a group of coworkers at an after-hours social gathering. Their understanding and support were sufficient to alleviate his habituation problem (for the time being, anyway).

There are also opportunities to make clever and sophisticated single-session interventions in street work.

> Larry was a proud, strapping white male in his late fifties who asked to speak with a psychologist at a shelter after the latter had been introduced by staff at one of the nightly community meetings. Larry had been divorced for two weeks and a shelter resident for one. He had come to see the psychologist because "everyone" thought that he wasn't making progress in getting over this divorce and he was beginning to think so, too. He hadn't been eating or sleeping and his energy always flagged when he went out to the temporary agencies to work in the mornings.

It soon became clear that Larry was not one who would normally open up or "unload" about such things. He labeled himself "one close-to-the-vester-with a stiff upper lip," and he smiled in adding that he was just like his father before him. The divorce had occurred after 28 years of marriage and was presumably amicable. He had decided to leave his home (a tourist town near the Badlands of South Dakota) because he could not stand the small town gossip and questions that people kept asking him about the divorce. He had taken five hundred dollars and his pick-up truck and driven to Madison because he had heard that there was work there. He reported no prior problems with mental health or chemical dependency, although he recalled having been "sorely grieved" when his first wife had died in a car accident when he had been twenty-three. He had raised their three children "on my own and successfully" (the incongruence of this statement juxtaposed against a second marriage of 28 years was not resolved). He was proud to say that all three were doing well on their own, and it had been a matter of pride to him not to tell any of them, not even his favorite daughter, about having left home. It was his plan to call them after he got himself back on his feet, but the shelter staff and others had "hollered" at him that he was in bad shape and had better call his daughter now.

He smiled a brittle, quivery smile while saying this part. Given Larry's world view, the psychologist surmised that such a smile was the last thing which Larry had going for him. The psychologist declined to join the chorus urging Larry to reach out to his daughter for help. Instead, he agreed with Larry that it was only a matter of time before he got back on his feet, and that he could probably put up with the bad sleep and the low energy until then. On the other hand, based on the little that Larry had told him about the daughter, the psychologist worried how she would hold up under not knowing his whereabouts for who-knows-how-long? Was she used to not hearing from him for weeks or months? Would she be mad or disappointed if he didn't let her know, or wouldn't let her take care of him? "You know women," the psychologist said, "they need to be taking care of things and people even what don't need it. She might get to feeling deprived."

"Yeah, womenfolk are like that," Larry said, his eyelids and lips quivering again. He lapsed into silence for a while, and then abruptly got up and left the room. The psychologist phoned the shelter the next day to check on him. Staff reported that he had finally called his daughter that morning and then had left the shelter for her place with all of his belongings.

Many single session interventions proceed beyond the generic provision of support. Problems are solved or (re)framed in ways that let persons like Larry solve them on their own. The traditional practice of completing indepth evaluations and detailed histories before intervening is probably not needed in many instances. Reflexive adherence to such a practice runs the risk of alienating a street person who comes into a first session under the private premise that he or she will be giving the mental health practitioner just one visit's chance before moving on. For many such people, engaging in an extensive historical review of the presenting problem represents an unwanted confrontation with a failed past, regardless of the practitioner's good intentions.

Still, one cannot conduct such sessions according to the spontaneous spirit of an encounter group. And given the current state of knowledge about single session impacts, traditional first-session practices will likely yield beneficial effects without a preplanned therapeutic purpose. There is also a middle ground position for practitioners who wish to experiment with single session work but prefer more license for doing so than the literature currently provides. It is this: the street person may be asked early in the interview how many sessions he or she can devote to solving the problem, and whether or not he or she would prefer to join the practitioner in trying to solve the problem in that session alone. Yielding an element of control to the street person is a therapeutic gesture in and of itself.

CHAPTER 8

Intermittent Psychotherapy

Many street persons do not expect single sessions to meet their needs. Some are willing to schedule return visits or attend office culture clinics, but the majority prefer to know when and where the practitioner will be available for additional sessions as the person deems these to be necessary. Circulation of a regular tour schedule or designated night(s) of the week/month at a particular site provides sufficient continuity of care for them. Giving the homeless person voice and control over sessions is also a gesture of empowerment and a bow to the exigencies of life in the streets. To some, this small empowerment is more than symbolic, given that the experience of power is so rare in street culture. This sense of powerlessness inclines many street people to rationalize their irresponsible behaviors and blame them on The System.

Ceding control over treatment also means that the temporal spacing of visits is determined by the street person rather than the practitioner. It means that some session lengths may be measured in minutes, others in hours (Susser et al., 1992). The sites of sessions may also rotate if one is a touring practitioner whom street people know how to locate on any given day. Treatment plans are seldom written because the goals shift too frequently.

The best label for such a semi-structured treatment format is intermittent psychotherapy. Some practitioners would argue that this format does not meet enough definitional standards to be considered "true" psychotherapy because of its fluctuating parameters and the large extent of recipient control. Perhaps it is better characterized as an adaptation of traditional psychotherapy to the lifestyle demands of street culture. The street practitioner strives to achieve the same goals as in traditional psychotherapy, but does so by tailoring formats, venues, and methods to be more culture-specific.

A FALL GUY

The following 20-session treatment spanned a period of two years. Meetings occurred at four different sites as determined by the street person (pseudonym "F.G."). The range of session lengths was 15 seconds to 27 minutes. These durations and the temporal gaps between visits are highlighted for illustration purposes. At the outset of treatment, F.G. was a 32-year-old man of mixed racial descent and borderline to dull normal intelligence. He was poorly socialized and his interaction style seemed driven by a need to cover up his obvious limitations and project the machismo that he aspired to. He was not good at this, and his public blusters of competence were either ignored by his peers or elicited taunts and mockery from them. F.G. said that he began living on the streets after having served two years in prison for an unspecified offense. When asked about this offense, he became so agitated in his assertions of innocence and of having been framed that the topic was dropped and not raised again. In retrospect, the likelihood that he had been framed seemed quite high in light of his lame, even pitiable displays of machismo, his field dependence and suggestibility, and his general lack of forethought and wherewithal to anticipate (much less outwit) those who would taunt him in the shelters and drop-in centers. In short, he was a prototypical "fall guy" who claimed to have emerged from prison to find that his family had left town with no forwarding address. "Who needs 'em?" was his editorial retort about this.

Session 1—15 seconds. F.G. calls out, "Hey, shrink!" after a community meeting at a shelter where a psychologist had just been introduced to the group. The psychologist makes eye contact and nods to him. F.G. smiles back but waves him off.

Session 2 (2 weeks later)—20 minutes. F.G. appears happy when he comes to see the psychologist in a back room after another community meeting at the same site. He provides the background information that was presented earlier. After talking for a while in a virtual monologue, he announces that his number is about to be called for the shower line and he gets up and leaves.

F.G.'s agenda is not clear. Asking for it is met with a befuddled shrug and, "I don't know, just to see if it would help." One suspects that his low social standing among his peer group renders his isolation greater than that of most others. His demeanor is lackadaisical, flippant, even chirpy. For the psychologist, this is rather tiresome to encounter in the evening after a long work day. However, forebearance is a form of clinical acumen on the streets where one works with persons who seldom last long in office culture settings.

Session 3 (4 weeks later)—15 minutes. F.G. invites the psychologist to sit down with him at a drop-in center. He is mildly agitated and complains about all of the drunks who sleep next to him on the floors of the shelters and how he's moving out to the country where he will sleep outdoors and bus into the city to work his job at a downtown fast-food restaurant. The psychologist allows him to ventilate and then offers some basic cognitive awareness and redirection training about anger problems.

Session 4 (8 weeks later)—25 minutes. F.G. is seen in a different shelter upon referral from staff after his verbal altercation with another resident had almost come to blows on the previous night. This other man had not been made to see the psychologist and this angers F.G. all the more. In the first five minutes, he protests his innocence and stresses how dangerous he can be when pushed. He asserts that the other man had provoked him first. After he calms down, the psychologist suggests that they identify and rehearse better coping responses for the next time that someone provokes him. F.G. engages productively in this effort, but at the session's end he invokes the "code of the streets" and says that he must answer violence with violence. The psychologist neither challenges nor endorses this.

It appears that the psychologist's effort to teach anger control and stress inoculation methods were appreciated by F.G. It is important to observe that the psychologist accepted F.G.'s blaming of the other man, and also F.G.'s labeling himself as dangerous. Doctrinaire cognitive therapists might find fault with such a permissive stance here, particularly on the self-labeling issue. However, illusory and/or maladaptive self-statements are best left alone when these support a fragile semblance of self-esteem and self-respect.

Note that no extensive history of this man's presenting problem has yet been attempted. In fact, F.G. has not articulated a presenting problem beyond the here-and-now crises that have arisen around his getting along with his peers. Since another altercation may mean that F.G. will be put out onto the streets, the psychologist must invoke here-and-now methods to prevent this. It is also worth noting that F.G. had a limited attention span and always terminated sessions before 30 minutes had elapsed. To this point, there have been four contacts which have totaled 60 minutes.

F.G.'s fantasy of living in the country and bussing into the city to work at a fast-food restaurant is unrealistic. For the brief tenure during which he held this dishwashing job, F.G. was forced to stay in the shelter because the job did not pay him enough to live anywhere else. He eventually quit the job because he was going to "lose it" and "waste" his boss who had complained about the condition and smell of the clothes that F.G. wore to work.

The scenario of the shelter staff setting up the psychologist to be a judge, jury, and sergeant-at-arms without his foreknowledge is not an uncommon one. At first practitioners abhor such practices, only later to see how these can be turned to one's advantage in working with difficult persons (see Chapter 9).

Session 5 (7 weeks later)—5 minutes. F.G. asks for a visit at a drop-in center. He is visibly upset and shows a form letter from the DDS that he can barely read. It says that a part of his disability application had been due two weeks ago. The psychologist calls the DDS immediately and obtains an extension for F.G. and a clarification of what F.G. needs to do to remove the deficiency. F.G. is reassured by this.

Session 6 (4 weeks later)—27 minutes. F.G. is agitated by shelter events again but comes self-referred this time. He says the other men had played a trick on him to frame him for the disappearance of some property belonging to the shelter director. He voices paranoid and murderous rages toward his unidentified tormentors. The psychologist talks F.G. down and then walks him through a series of concrete, problem-solving steps that will serve to distract and subvert F.G.'s paranoid thinking and restore a more appropriate cognitive set for the situation at hand. This intervention succeeds in changing F.G.'s agitated anger into a muted, muttering one. The psychologist ends the session by suggesting that F.G. meet with him again tomorrow. F.G. does not appear the next day as prescribed.

Session 7 (3 months later)—2 minutes. The psychologist unexpectedly encounters F.G. at a drop-in center and asks about the resolution of the last crisis. F.G. seems to not want to talk; the psychologist persists and draws out a sheepish admission from F.G. that the missing property had turned up and F.G.'s paranoid conclusions had been unwarranted. The psychologist tries to seize the moment as a working through opportunity, but F.G. tunes this out, perhaps reading an "I told you so" message to this which had not been intended. The psychologist backs off and says "see you around."

Pride that is seldom validated by one's social environment is easily piqued. The invitation by the psychologist to work through the incident was probably experienced by F.G. along the lines of parental condescension. It also occurs several months after the original incident, a time lapse that certainly extends beyond the normal "relevance span" of F.G. (and many others as well). The psychologist's "see you around" at the end is meant as more than a colloquial ritual. It conveys an implicit assurance to F.G. that he had not been judged or rejected and would be welcomed back to talk again.

The psychologist does not comment on F.G.'s "no-show." In other contexts, a no-show would be viewed as an issue that needs to be addressed for the sake of the therapeutic alliance. In a street context, it is more likely that raising the no-show issue will be taken as a criticism which itself can lead to a unilateral termination by the street person. Hence, it is not addressed; this is a matter of adjusting one's expectations to a new culture rather than imposing preconceptions that are more valid in one's host culture.

Should not the psychologist have clearly defined treatment goals for this person after seven visits? Thus far, all contacts have been crisis interventions, and F.G. has not asked for help with housing, or for a supportive statement for disability, or for anything else. The psychologist does learn from casual questioning (conducted while on hold during the telephone call to the DDS) that F.G.'s disabling impairment is "schizophrenia—and I'm a psychopath!" The application for disability had been initiated by a social worker prior to F.G.'s release from prison.

Session 8 (4 weeks later)—2 minutes. F.G. drops by the table of a drop-in center where the psychologist is sitting. He complains about the smell of Jerry (p. 52). The psychologist tells him that everything that can be done is being done for Jerry. F.G. scoffs about such persons needing to be arrested. The psychologist argues instead for compassion and tolerance. F.G. laughs and walks away.

Session 9 (1 week later)—1 minute. F.G. stops by to announce that he has been awarded both SSI and SSDI. He is elated by this and the psychologist congratulates him.

The brevity and informality of these contacts belie their importance to the therapeutic alliance. F.G.'s expressed contempt for Jerry parallels the street culture's contempt for F.G. Thus Jerry can be viewed as a metaphor for F.G. himself, and F.G.'s approaching the psychologist is indirectly about their relationship, that is, whether or not the psychologist views F.G. with the same contempt that F.G. has experienced from his family, his fast-food supervisor, his peers, and so on. The psychologist passes this test. Six days later, F.G. shares a happy moment with the psychologist. The source of that happiness is predicated upon something that F.G. has in common with Jerry, his scapegoat and stand-in.

Session 10 (5 weeks later)—1 minute. At the shelter, F.G. seems needy when he takes the psychologist aside. However, he stays only long enough to let the psychologist know that he's still waiting on his disability payments to begin and that he will not be needing to have a payee.

Session 11 (6 days later)—5 minutes. F.G. begins with a complaint of headaches but steers quickly to "subconscious stress" which in turn steers to the fact that his disability checks haven't started to arrive yet. The psychologist writes down the name and number of a social worker who knows how to check on such things, but F.G. scoffs that he has already talked to her and she didn't know anything either.

Session 12 (5 days later)—14 minutes. F.G. approaches and the early talk is about his anxiety and concern over when and whether his disability benefits will arrive. He pulls out his award letter from the DDS which he looks at and slaps for emphasis—its ragged condition suggests that he has done this many times before. Nevertheless, he rejects the psychologist's offer to call the DDS for him, reminding him that he already has a social worker to do that. He then announces that he has a date next week, his first one since prison. He is nervous and talks about his nervousness a while, but before the psychologist can say anything, he pronounces himself to be fine and volunteers that there is no reason for the psychologist to start doing "that stress inoculation crap again." He leaves.

As previously discussed, adjustment reactions to disability awards are not uncommon. "Talking down" a person or calling the Social Security office on his behalf will often reduce some of this anxiety. F.G.'s declining the psychologist's offer to call Social Security and his shifting the conversation into the dating realm suggested a need to keep the psychologist in a role of counselor or therapist rather than something else. It also injected a theme of normalcy to replace one of disability.

Next he disparages the psychologist's prior interventions. The psychologist later speculated that here F.G. had been striking back at some perceived disrespect in the psychologist's offer to make the call for him, perhaps the implication that F.G. could not do so for himself. For a person who aspires to machismo, the immediate aftermath of having been adjudged "disabled" is cognitive dissonance. Note that a major theme of the brief Session 10 is to establish that F.G. does not need a payee, a point of honor and self-respect on the streets.

Session 13 (3.5 weeks later)—1 minute. F.G. comes to see the psychologist at a drop-in center. He hands him a subsidized housing form to be filled out by the psychologist to establish F.G.'s eligibility for same on the basis of his disability. The psychologist agrees to fill it out.

Session 14 (1.5 weeks later)—1 minute. F.G. drops off a second subsidized housing form and explains that the first one had not been received.

Session 15 (2 days later)—20 minutes. F.G. comes to the drop-in steaming that his first disability check had been sent to the wrong address. The psychologist offers empathic support but cognitive interventions do not seem necessary. He concludes at the end that F.G. is managing this stressor rather well under the circumstances.

Session 16 (5 days later)—2 minutes. F.G. comes to the same drop-in and announces with delight that he has been assigned to a unit of a desirable subsidized housing complex. The psychologist congratulates him on that success, and for having "kept your cool" the other day. F.G. responds to this compliment by muttering a slur about hispanic persons and then leaves.

Session 17 (1.5 weeks later)—1 minute. The psychologist sees F.G. in the drop-in and asks for an update on his housing plans. F.G. responds that he will soon go into a transitional housing program, a statement that perplexes the psychologist in light of the previous developments. But F.G. doesn't want to talk about it further. His mood is level and he seems to be baseline. The psychologist drops the matter and F.G. moves on.

Bureaucratic requirements, processing delays, and lost forms are other "adjustment reaction" stressors of street life. Based on his past experience with F.G., the psychologist decides not to call Social Security or do anything else of a "social work" nature unless F.G. specifically asks for this (which he does do in the matter of the subsidized housing form). Instead, the psychologist confines himself to a therapist's role of listening and providing an empathic outlet. This is by no means a hard and fast rule, and there are many situations in which stepping out of one's practitioner role to make a telephone call is exactly what is needed (as it apparently was in Session 5). However, what F.G. wants from the psychologist seems to have changed since that session.

F.G.'s rejection of the supportive compliment that the psychologist makes in Session 16 is also vexing. Upon being reinforced for his self-control, F.G. ignores the compliment and behaves in a way that suggests tenuous self-control. Perhaps he felt patronized. Perhaps he viewed self-control as inimical to machismo and "the code of the streets." Perhaps a hispanic man had been the latest to mock or taunt him. Whatever the case, he and the psychologist are not on the same track here, and this would not appear to be due to a lapse in skill by the psychologist. Again, street people are difficult to work with. If they communicated well and behaved in predictable ways, they would not be so alienated and hard to help.

Session 18 (5 weeks later)—1 minute. Psychologist outreaches F.G. in the drop-in after the latter had dropped from sight for a relatively long time. F.G. is in a new apartment now and professes to be doing fine. He mentions that he is due to get a disability check that day. He seems neutral about talking to the psychologist and drifts away.

Session 19 (3 weeks later)—1 minute. This time F.G. approaches the psychologist at the drop-in. He says that he is doing well (and looks it). Unfortunately, his checks are still being held up and are going to the wrong address. He casually mentions that he has a social worker who is looking after this for him.

Session 20 (9.5 months later)—3 minutes. F.G. approaches after almost a year's absence. He looks to be doing well and mentions having had a leg injury in a hot air balloon accident during the previous summer. He speaks of the boredom of just sitting around in his apartment but otherwise professes to be OK. The psychologist mentions a local clubhouse for the mentally impaired, but F.G. waves the suggestion off contemptuously, saying "that place is for crazies." The psychologist neglects to ask why F.G. is at the drop-in on that particular day. F.G. is not encountered again on the streets.

SUPPORT ORIENTATIONS

F.G.'s outcome was regarded by his psychologist and others as a successful intervention. A series of anger crises had been defused without leading to injury or to F.G.'s expulsion from a shelter (it is less clear whether he learned and internalized the cognitive interventions which had been taught to him). His acquisition of disability benefits and stable housing are best credited to unseen social workers, but the psychologist provided relevant assistance at various points and probably helped to render the delays more tolerable. Certainly the unconditional respect and empathy offered to F.G. were valued by him, given that 80 percent of the contacts were initiated by F.G. and none brought him any tangible gains. He behaved in ungrateful ways but was not rejected. What pride and positive self-esteem he possessed were affirmed. These achievements by the psychologist are noteworthy even if their contributions to F.G.'s ongoing adjustment are difficult to weight.

None of these achievements alters the fact that F.G. remained an individual at risk for an additional episode(s) of homelessness. Social safety net programs like SSI and general assistance are strung so tightly as to be easily snapped, and F.G.'s boorishness and poor judgment do not inspire confidence in his ability to develop his own informal safety net. And yet to have an episode of homelessness for such a man end with F.G. stabilized for an ongoing 12 months, and to have him contemplating his boredom rather than his admission to a jail, prison, or psychiatric hospital—this represents a positive outcome that is not to be minimized.

A support-oriented approach is appropriate for many of the low functioning, "social selection" members of the street culture. The approach is to support them in their efforts to survive in niches that they have carved out for themselves. Such support can take many forms and avenues. The practitioner "makes rounds" during his or her tours of the various sites, pausing briefly to address a greeting or question to each of the "regulars" he or she is tracking. If one of these regulars suddenly stops appearing, inquiries are initiated, as occurred with Flory (p. 127). When there are no competing demands for one's time, the practitioner sits down, plays chess, or joins a card game, perhaps agrees to "watch my back" for a PTSD-afflicted veteran who has been made to sit with his back to the door but is too proud or embarrassed to ask one of his peers to switch seats with him. Most supportive and collaborative activities are acceptable, provided that street persons do not perceive these as a means of "hustling" them to change or to begin formalized treatment. At times, a street person may perceive such a "hustle" into treatment where none had been intended. Reciprocity is the sole vehicle of trust among alienated people; some anticipate that treatment willingness is the catch or payback that the practitioner expects for any favors which he or she might perform for them. With some people, the street practitioner can capitalize upon this sense of "obligation;" with others he or she must work to dispel it. Knowing when and how and with whom to take one stance or the other represents another realm of clinical acumen for a practitioner-of-last-resort.

One working hypothesis of a support orientation is that a street person's lack of medical or psychological distress signifies that his or her particular niche may be a livable one, regardless of how squalid and unbearable it may appear to mental health practitioners, researchers, and other passers-by. This touches on the issue of whether or not people are homeless because they choose to be homeless, and whether or not one should cease efforts to help those who do so "choose." Such thinking may be bypassed with the recognition that the survival demands of street culture niches are onerous for anyone with psychotic symptoms, cognitive deficits, and other vulnerabilities to predators and privations. Monitoring such individuals with momentary but frequent check-ups costs little, but the practitioner must also be prepared to address instances of adaptive failure with an array of interventions. Hospitalizations can be averted if one has ready access to contact persons in agencies that can provide emergency supports without the delays necessitated by bureaucracies and appointments.

Thus, a support orientation on the streets entails:

1. Accepting people's acceptances of their particular niches and lifestyles on the streets, however intolerable these may appear to others;
2. Coming to understand what these niches are and what demands they make of their occupants;
3. Making casual, intermittent check-ups of these persons and assessing how well they are able to meet the ongoing demands of their niches; and
4. Supporting an adaptation until such time as the street person moves to a position where he or she will consider change-oriented treatments (medications, day treatment programs, etc.).

A psychiatric resident forged an alliance of sorts with a woman in her late fifties. This woman, who claimed to have never been psychiatrically treated, was a nurse veteran of the Korean War. Her prevailing delight was a delusional conviction that the CIA planned to assassinate Soviet premiere Gorbachev when he visited the Twin Cities in 1990. The resident never challenged the woman's delusion but wondered whether Gorbachev's surviving the visit would destabilize the veteran's paranoid rigidity and render her more available to change-oriented treatments. The two had roughly 25 contacts before Gorbachev's visit. During most of these contacts, the resident would listen respectfully to the woman's detailing the various permutations of the CIA plot.

On the day after Gorbachev's visit had ended without incident, the resident checked up on the veteran at the drop-in where they typically met. The woman was eating and initially paid the resident little mind. After small talk had been exhausted, the resident wondered aloud what the veteran made of the fact that the CIA had not assassinated Gorbachev "as planned."

The woman responded bitterly that, "they couldn't take him out because you blew their cover! You're the one who couldn't keep your mouth shut. You fouled clandestine ops (sic)—it was too risky for them to try with you talking about it to so many people."

The resident had in fact said nothing of it to anyone but her supervisor. Over the next several weeks, the woman goaded her publicly at various sites to admit to having blown the CIA operation. The woman's perseverance in this was unnerving as she thought nothing of interrupting the resident's contacts with other people. After consulting her supervisor, the resident decided to admit to the veteran that she had spoken to him about the plot and to no one else.

"I thought so," the woman had cried. "Now, the next time I give you some information about clandestine ops, you'll know to be more careful!"

Their contacts continued until the resident's rotation ended. In frequency and length, these contacts reverted back to the form of those that had taken place before Gorbachev's visit. However, now the veteran strived to "brief" the resident as to all she knew about clandestine operations and the need for secrecy. The resident assumed her former role of listening to these brief, often repetitious teachings. She also found the woman newly willing to answer personal questions about her living status and other such matters after each "lesson" was over. The woman came to rely upon the resident as a medical authority and as one who would extend her eligibility for general assistance checks (disability was "out of the question!" for someone who was still engaged in field work). When the resident finally left the rotation, the woman presented her with a going-away gift.

An interesting dimension of this therapy is the flexibility of the woman's delusional system in the face of disconfirmation by the outside world. In contrast, Flory (p. 127) experienced psychotic disorganization after her persecutory premises were violated by a disability award. Because there is no reliable way to predict the response of a given person to such a disconfirmation, one could argue that the resident should have waited for the veteran to bring the "nonassassination" up rather than introduce it herself. Even so, subsequent developments render it doubtful whether such a reactive stance would have made much difference. This veteran appears likely to have thwarted any confrontation in which her delusional system was framed as a problem. On the other hand, to the extent that it was used as a vehicle of communication, the supportive benefits of this therapy were made possible. There were more than 60 contacts between the resident and veteran over a six-month period. The majority of these lasted less than five minutes. At this rate, it was not difficult for the resident to make time available to the veteran two to three times a week in the drop-in center. The veteran never displayed psychological distress nor complained of it, and she appeared to be maintaining herself adequately on the streets despite her gender and psychosis. She never revealed much about the niche that she occupied. She declined to say where she lived because she was "operating under deep cover" and claimed to move among a series of "nondisclosable locations," never staying in the same one on consecutive nights. It is possible that she was not homeless at all: she showed several presentable changes of clothing and never acquired the telltale odor which the mobile lifestyle which she professed to lead would have dictated.

It is also important to consider the goodbye gift that she gave the resident at the end of the rotation. That this proved to be a book on espionage (purchased for less than a dollar at a public library clearance sale) may bring a knowing smile. But beyond this "signature," the gift reflects the importance of these intermittent contacts to the veteran despite an absence of therapeutic change. It appears that these interludes of controlled social contact represented an optimal dose of social involvement for a woman who needed her delusional premises to be accepted without challenge.

A psychiatric social worker was asked to intervene with Phael (p. 119) when he raised the collective ire of the drop-in center by gaining access to the free telephone and then refusing to relinquish it after his allotted 10 minutes. When other street persons confronted him in anger, he yanked the phone from the wall and barricaded himself in the men's restroom with it. The social worker coaxed him out with the promise of a cigarette and the use of her office phone in back. Phael eagerly consumed the cigarette first, and while dialing her phone, he pushed his plastic bag of butts across the desk to her and indicated that she was to do his cigarette rolling for him while he was occupied. At first he wouldn't say whom he was trying to reach, but after 10 wrong numbers, his frustration showed in sweat on his brow. Pointed questions from the social worker (who sat across from him, squeezing out his butts) yielded the following: on the previous holiday weekend, a local church youth group had volunteered to pick up homeless people and take them to a holiday dinner. Phael had been picked up by four girls who had apparently treated him like a king for the whole day and then dropped him off at his boarding house that night. Phael claimed to have fallen in love with the one named Sherrie, and he had professed that love to her and asked her to marry him at the end of the night. He said that she'd laughed sweetly but hadn't given him an answer. He needed the phone to get his answer, but he had also neglected to get her last name or the exact name of the Lutheran church from which she had come. He was now proceeding to call all Lutheran churches, which numbered close to one hundred in the Twin Cities. He dialed them alphabetically, and when someone would answer, Phael would bark for Sherrie into the phone without a greeting or preamble.

Even as she continued to squeeze out the butts, the social worker decided to lie to Phael. She told him that she knew that particular Sherrie and that Sherrie was already married and hadn't Phael seen the wedding ring on her finger? At first Phael was stunned by this news: he put down the phone and stopped dialing. The social worker volunteered that Sherrie had meant to be nice, and that she was nice, and Phael wouldn't want to get her into trouble with her husband by calling her like that, would he? Phael started to sob and then cry, and then he spread his arms apart to indicate that he wanted to be hugged. The social worker obliged him this, after which Phael abruptly asked for the return of his butt bag and left the room.

Over the course of the next two weeks, Phael was forlorn and miserable during rounds—but decreasingly so. The social worker shared the story with other service providers who knew Phael, and several of them sympathetically alluded to it in their "check-up" rounds with him. Eventually Phael reverted to his "normal" flat affect while scavenging tobacco.

Most practitioners find it difficult to justify lying and violating confidentiality practices as occurred here. The psychiatric social worker herself viewed these as distasteful, but still clinically indicated (the same attitudes she held toward hugging Phael and squeezing tobacco out of his butts for him). She knew both Phael and the local volunteer culture well enough to consider this love-at-first-sight story a likely event rather than a psychotic production. She also knew that the subtleties and complexities of interpersonal relationships and the signalings of same to be beyond Phael's comprehension. The lying was done in the spirit with which it is sometimes recommended for Alzheimer's victims, that is, to spare all concerned a stressful, time-consuming, and ultimately futile exercise in reality testing (Nash, 1991).

Spreading the word about Phael's experience among the drop-in staff and other practitioners enabled them to contribute to his "working it through." Brief visits with multiple practitioners are indicated for persons as disorganized as Phael. The context that justifies such nonstandard practices includes his blatant disregard of the rules governing the use of a scarce resource (free telephone), his damaging that resource when confronted, and his barricading himself in the bathroom. If not resolved immediately and decisively, such behavior was likely to eventuate in Phael's victimization or hospitalization.

CHANGE ORIENTATIONS

Most systems of change-oriented psychotherapy can be adapted to street work and intermittent contacts. Many a street person who was psychologically intact before an episode of homelessness retains the cognitive abilities to benefit from these approaches. Often episodes of homelessness are precipitated by social pressures (e.g., divorce, unemployment) rather than by social selection forces (e.g., pre-existing Axis I conditions). This can create start-up problems for practitioners of all systems: When a recipient's attributions to explain his or her homelessness emphasize external loci of control, it becomes difficult to shift away from these to address internal loci of control. This problem is compounded by the fact that the publicness of homelessness renders it a constant source of emotional distress. Awkward and disdainful glances, both real and imagined, are drawn by one's bedraggled appearance and backpack. The street person has no refuge to withdraw to for "licking the wounds." Given constant scrutiny and minimal privacy, many street persons develop heightened tendencies toward projection, rationalization, and other externalizing defenses.

Thus, regardless of one's theoretical orientation, the street practitioner must anticipate sessions in which a street person fixates upon his or her victimhood. The practitioner must be prepared both to accept this and to permit the street person time to elaborate upon it under respectful conditions. The practitioner need not agree with the recipient's stance nor reinforce it, but respect is a sine qua non. It may not be possible for a street person to consider internal loci of control until after external ones have been aired.

Unlike the support-oriented approach described above, change-oriented therapy relies minimally on outreach and maximally on the street person's approaching the practitioner on site to request session time. Most persons who approach the practitioner only to rant and rave about government policies, the lack of affordable housing, and so on, do so knowing that the practitioner is not in a position to do much about these forces. Repeated diatribes of this type from the same person serve latent purposes, perhaps being a "warm-up" of sorts or a testing of the practitioner for underlying prejudice. Instead of yielding to boredom or frustration over such behavior, the practitioner is advised to scan it for possible transitions from the manifest material to the private matters that would better explain why the street person has sought the practitioner out. The ability to facilitate such a transition in ways that are neither too abrupt nor interpreted as "finger-pointing" represents another facet of clinical acumen in street work.

> A clean, relatively well-attired black man in his late forties was a frequent drop-in center patron who would sit quietly at a table for hours and read the newspaper without talking to anyone else. He was referred to a psychiatrist by staff after he complained about needing to see a V.A. psychiatrist again for a recertification of his service-connected disability. He was a Viet Nam War veteran who was cynically furious at

the V.A. and the military. With articulate but bitter understatement, he described having been a medic who "cracked up" from a daily routine that included hauling away buckets filled with amputated limbs and helping to treat officers whose tents had been "fragged" with grenades by their own men. He had been returned to the states and discharged as psychiatrically disabled. In the two decades since the war, he had bristled at each request that he return to the hospital for recertification, and at various times his benefits had been threatened because of his delays in doing so. He had steadfastly refused all treatment opportunities in the V.A. system, including their informal street outreach program. At his last exam, the psychiatrist had commented on this and the veteran had interpreted it as a threat that he get into treatment or lose his benefits. This was a major reason why the street team's psychiatrist was recruited to see him.

The veteran spent three visits reviewing these matters with the psychiatrist who said little and listened much. At the fourth visit, there was a pause in his V.A. diatribe, at which point the veteran made a startling statement that he wanted to get back into the mainstream. At session six, the psychiatrist moved to shift the conversation away from the horrors of the war and the V.A. system to what the veteran had been doing since the war. The veteran began another cynical tirade, this time about past employers, women, and "male associates." At his next opening, the psychiatrist said, "those lyrics are new but it's the same melody that I heard before." He then affirmed an interest in helping the veteran get back into the mainstream, and suggested that the veteran's major obstacle to that seemed to be his adoption of cynicism as a way of life. This tongue-tied the veteran for a moment, but he responded that he had never thought of himself as cynical, only realistic.

At session seven, the veteran approached with a novel he was reading and said that there was a character in this book with whom he saw many personal parallels. Unfortunately, a crisis in the drop-in center at the time commanded the psychiatrist's attention, and the veteran was gone when he looked for him later. Next occurred a series of sessions initiated by the veteran over form letters from the V.A. about his delays in scheduling his recertification exam. The psychiatrist talked the veteran through his range of feelings and suspicions until ultimately the veteran scheduled and then went to his exam. While there, he signed up for a rehabilitation program, something which he had resisted doing for 20 years. But then he grumbled that he would refuse to take part in it unless they approved his request to become a graphic artist and rehabilitate him at the local art academy. As this grumbling grew into another diatribe against the V.A. system, the psychiatrist said, "there's that old melody again." The veteran stopped talking and nodded remotely.

At session 11, he reported that he had been turned down for the art academy but had been granted retraining dollars to go to college. He

> said that he had decided to go to junior college because his outlook had improved. Otherwise, he was as morose as ever and complained about all of the V.A. paperwork he was sure he would have to fill out just to get started. The psychiatrist refrained from another "melody" interpretation at this time.
>
> The veteran was seen briefly for two more times before disappearing from the drop-in center. Presumably he had started as a full-time student at a local community college.

This 13-session therapy spanned 10 months with sessions ranging in length from 1 to 65 minutes and a median length of 15 minutes. The initial session was staff-referred, seven of the next nine were initiated by the veteran, and the last two were one-minute outreach efforts with the veteran being busy with his newspaper and not interested in extensive contact. Only one session of 65 minutes exceeded the traditional "50-minute hour," and it was allowed to continue because it generated sufficient energy of its own—and because there were no other demands on the psychiatrist's time at that moment. All sessions took place at a table in the middle of the drop-in center.

Despite these irregularities and missed opportunities (the "novel character" contact), some significant change was accomplished. The willingness of the veteran to talk freely to a psychiatrist for the first time ever signaled that he was primed for change to begin with. But the psychiatrist's ability to have an impact was also predicated upon his patience in listening to the veteran's drawn out story over several sessions without imposing a focus or a treatment plan upon him. The veteran's droll, evocative articulation of his story was entertaining per se and made the psychiatrist's task easier.

Other people are not as primed for this kind of significant change. In fact, some may use a practitioner only to work through their doubts one final time, after which they embrace a third-stage street identity which is grounded in helplessness and victimhood. This is a regrettable outcome and is not always easily detected. The practitioner's empathic, nonjudgmental listening is sometimes solicited and then interpreted as tacit approval for "giving up."

Tacit discouragement of this process can be achieved by the practitioner's limiting session length and depth when its content suggests such motives. This is a rare practice in the 50-minute-hour office culture. It is a variant of the extinction principle and might well be termed "selective extinction." It is preferable to confrontation that would provoke transference distortions (e.g., "easy for you to say that I'm giving up when you've already got your house in the suburbs!"). Selective extinction keeps communication channels open, and the street person who is sensitive to these altered session qualities can always question them. The practitioner's exerting control over session length is a rare practice in the 50-minute-hour office culture. It is also a flexible tactic: The street practitioner may limit session length and depth with a markedly impaired person who has "lack of insight" and seeks out the practitioner for support in unrealistic ventures or aspirations. Session lengths and depths can be expanded if/when that same person is ready to work through the acceptance of lowered self-expectations which are more realistic. In fact, Minkoff (1987) has recommended such change-oriented psychotherapy be practiced with psychotic persons. Ideally such therapy would address these persons' rejections of (1) the patient role, (2) the reality of psychotic impairments, and (3) the appropriateness of lowering their self-expectations.

Some proud people who view the street practitioner as a potential catalyst for change may be loathe to admit this to themselves and to the practitioner. Instead, it is acted out in sessions.

> A particularly memorable man would take startling chances with self-disclosure at the start of a session. First, he would engage in the kind of soul-searching that energized his practitioner's efforts on his behalf. Then, when seemingly on the verge of a breakthrough, he would short-circuit the process by suddenly announcing another appointment that he had to leave for, or by claiming that the material about to emerge was "too private," or by asking the practitioner if "anything like that ever happen to you?" No matter how the practitioner responded to such feints, that particular session was effectively over.

The frustrated practitioner was left to reflect alone upon what had gone wrong. But after this pattern had been repeated several times, it became apparent that this was the man's modus operandi. The practitioner's regrets about the man's "two steps backward" at the end of each session needed to be considered in the context of the "three steps forward" that had occurred at the beginning. The practitioner also noted that although this man made frequent and regular appearances, he never once requested an appointment. He came to be seen as a man who needed to exert control over sessions in order to feel safe enough to make use of them. Such persons are not well-served within the confines of office culture parameters.

> Daniel was a large, white male in his fifties who spoke seldom and softly with a New England accent. He sought help for depression from a psychologist who toured the shelters. Daniel complained that life felt meaningless except when he indulged a compulsion to loiter outside of gay bars. He was quick to assert that he had never had a homosexual experience except for several years earlier when a gay man

whom he picked up hitchhiking had stroked his arm and then his genital area in a light, playful fashion. Daniel "blacked out" at that point, and when he returned to consciousness he found himself beating the man "to a pulp" on the side of the highway with two state troopers on his back trying to pull him off. His victim had been severely injured, and on the basis of the troopers' testimony, Daniel had been sent to the state security hospital for a year. His gay bar compulsion had begun upon his discharge from the hospital. He "drank my way" to the midwest, and because this had been a parole violation, he felt that he could not return home. As his gay bar compulsion grew stronger, he began to cut back on his drinking so that "I can keep my guard up." On most days, he would get up early to work the labor pools and then spend his late afternoons and early evenings "posted" against the wall outside one of these bars where he felt a curious sense of calmness, "sort of like someone's guardian angel." When he was run off of the premises, he would walk to another bar and post himself there until the curfew hour of his shelter for that night.

He met with the psychologist 15 times. The alliance was good but Daniel's psychological-mindedness was not and he was hypersensitive to questions about his sexuality. Twice during the course of these sessions, the psychologist was called by managers of gay bars who had tried to run Daniel off. Daniel had told them that he was there by "the blessing" of the psychologist and had given them the psychologist's phone number for verification. The psychologist demanded that Daniel stop doing this; while he agreed to do so, Daniel was obviously aggrieved and testy about having been rebuked for this. A third call came two weeks later from a police officer who had almost arrested Daniel after hearing him threaten to "rough up" a bar patron.

At the session after this third call, the psychologist told Daniel that he thought a recurrence of Daniel's violence was probable if Daniel continued to loiter outside of these bars. Daniel swelled with indignation and angrily protested that he was under control and that this was the only activity that gave him any relief "until you figure out what's wrong with me—if you ever do!" When the psychologist restated his concerns about another violent episode, Daniel became incensed and requested immediate assignment to a new practitioner. The psychologist agreed to this, but over the next several weeks he was unable to find someone willing to work with Daniel. Daniel still came by to check on the progress of this with the psychologist, and he would defiantly report that he had been to the bars every night of the previous week without any trouble having occurred. Eventually he dropped his inquiries about a new practitioner, but he would still come by to report his ongoing progress, which was "no thanks to you!" He had begun to enter the bars now and was "getting acquainted with those types." Such updates continued for several months, during which time Daniel reported that his depression was beginning to lift. There were no more calls from bar owners or police. After a while Daniel, stopped coming around, and the psychologist later heard that Daniel had left the shelter circuit after being invited to share an apartment with an openly gay man.

Daniel apparently underwent an unusual transformation in his sexuality. A catalyst in this change was the fact that his psychologist had proscribed certain behaviors. This prompted Daniel first to protest, and then to defy the proscription. Ultimately, he rendered the psychologist's predictions to be wrong. It is important to observe that, on the basis of the data available to him, the psychologist's conclusion about potential dangerousness and his recommendations that the loitering cease represented a reasonable course of action. In truth, his prediction may have been an accurate one, if not for the fact that the act of making that prediction to Daniel had elicited defiance-based change from Daniel.

Such change processes are rarely reported in the academic and professional literature. Many paradoxical methods hinge upon defiance-based change, but most of the time the practitioner serves as a proactive architect of this defiance. Such was not the case here; Daniel's change is better conceived as an unexpected instance of psychological reactance. According to this model, when Daniel's unfettered freedom to loiter was unilaterally curtailed by the psychologist, it motivated Daniel to display behavioral controls that negated the need for the restrictions imposed upon him. It seems clear from his many return visits to update the psychologist and his cessation of requests for a new practitioner that Daniel's "previous" therapy had not in fact ended. It had simply proceeded in an unusual direction.

But how unusual? Such change processes, unflattering as they are to practitioners, probably occur more frequently than their absence from the professional literature would suggest. Look instead to *Reader's Digest* and other such pop literature and one finds many so-called "miracle cure" testimonials in which the second or third sentence begins with the phrase "just when the doctors told me that there was no hope . . ." Norman Cousins'(1979) recovery from an incurable collagen disease was attributed to vitamin C, a positive attitude fueled by humor, and the release of endorphins. However, his autobiographical account suggests that reactance motivation was a first premise of his recovery: he refused to accept the "terminal" verdicts of the medical specialists who had examined him.

It is likely that psychological reactance represents a naturally occurring process, a "negative" placebo effect. Paradoxical therapists may have harnessed and systematized it, but nothing more. Of relevance to street work is the fact that reactance is more likely to exert influence among a culture with high levels of alienation, oppositionalism, and resistance vis-à-vis mainstream attitudes and modes of thought. If so, the evocation of protest behaviors from aggrieved street persons should not concern the street practitioner when the protest behaviors that appear have adaptive aspects. Positive outcomes may create cognitive dissonance for practitioners, but it will be unfortunate if efforts at such dissonance reduction preclude a better grasp of nonstandard processes through which resistant, alienated people come to change their behavior.

CHAPTER 9

Complications

Chemical dependency is a specialty field with its own treatment facilities, training tracks, credentialing mechanisms, and professional terminology. Most public health models reflect this in their bifurcation of mental health and chemical dependency service systems. This bifurcation is apparent even at the level of the practitioner: when addiction emerges as a problem in a mental health setting, it is not uncommon for the person to be referred to a chemical health agency for a separate treatment. In some settings, there may also be a cessation of mental health services until such time as the addiction has been successfully managed. This state of affairs extends to health care teams that serve homeless persons. Teams are typically funded by grant monies from sources grounded in this bifurcated model, such that chemical dependency specialists are budgeted and administered separately from a team's mental health component. Street persons with alcoholism and drug addiction are then seen to be the exclusive responsibility of chemical dependency specialists.

Even so, the mental health practitioner will have contact with a wider range and larger number of addicted persons than he or she would see in an office culture setting. Part of this may be attributed to the large numbers of addicted people in the street culture: Fisher (1989) concluded that alcoholism is nine times more prevalent among homeless people than among the general population. Another reason is the nature of outreach work itself. There are no screening or triage components that would direct addicted persons away from mental health practitioners. The more numerous contacts with addicted persons also reflect the fact that there is resistance to and alienation from traditional chemical health services in the street culture, a resistance that parallels the one that exists toward mental health services. Many addicted persons who are "in denial" or who claim to "have been burned before" or to be "fed up" or otherwise poorly served by chemical dependency treatment programs will logically turn to a mental health practitioner when they want help.

Thus, mental health practitioners must sometimes be prepared to treat addicted persons themselves (Ridgely & Dixon, 1993). However, many of them feel alienated from and resistant to the prospect of serving such people. The forces of specialization and bifurcation have unwittingly produced mental health practitioners who see themselves as lacking the requisite qualifications and experience for working with addicted persons. And there is another, more powerful source of practitioner resistance: the prevalent view that persons addicted to alcohol/drugs are less respectable than those who have other impairments, due to the greater elements of choice, motivation, and responsibility associated with addictions. Disease models of addiction continue to elicit skepticism despite research evidence that has established the genetic transmission of susceptibility to alcoholism (Cloninger, Bohman, & Sigvardsson, 1981; Goodwin, 1986; Shuckit, 1987). The various controversies surrounding disease models of addiction are complex and beyond the scope of the present work, but they do impact upon street work through the preconceptions and countertransference reactions that they foster among street practitioners. Both alcoholism and drug addiction have been found to attach "disreputable" connotations to homelessness, while non-addicted street persons are generally seen as deserving of assistance (Wiseman, 1987). Lubran (1990) surveyed chemical dependency specialists and found considerable resistance to treating addicted persons who were also homeless.

To what extent is the addicted person to be viewed as afflicted, and to what extent as responsible? From an armchair or lecture podium, most practitioners would choose to equivocate to this question. However, he or she will not be given time or cause to equivocate when solicited for help by an addicted person on the streets. Often the most convenient remedy is to refer the person on immediately to a chemical dependency specialist. However, such an approach is inconsistent with the role of practitioner-of-last-resort; also, many (if not most) addicted persons living on the streets know how to find their way to chemical dependency treatment if that is what they seek. When a mental health practitioner is consulted first, it suggests that there are resistances or other complexities that stand between the addicted person and traditional avenues to recovery. The street practitioner is thus advised to accept the role that is assigned to him or her rather than reflexively refer these people on to a chemical dependency specialist.

CHEMICAL DEPENDENCY: STREET TYPES

McCarty, Argeriou, Huebner, and Lubran (1991) have provided a historical overview of both legislative and treatment-based efforts to curb the co-morbidity of homelessness and chemical dependency. The fact that one-third to one-half of all homeless persons have a chemical dependency problem indicates that none of these initiatives has yet to achieve any significant success.

There are a number of street niches that can accommodate addicted people. Reference has already been made to "bottle gangs," small groups of addicted men and women who coalesce around the acquisition, consumption, and ritualistic celebration of alcohol and/or drugs. These groups foster a third-stage acceptance of street identity among their members. Their within-group norms and codes of conduct may extend to welfare fraud, petty crime, and serving as go-between or "mule" in the sale and distribution of illicit substances. They may prey upon other street people. The singular nature of crack cocaine addiction warrants attention in this context. Unlike the extended periods of intoxication, incapacitation, and recovery imposed by the abuse of alcohol or opioids, one dose of crack cocaine produces a cycle of intense high followed by intense withdrawal pain which together can span less than an hour. Crack is not as incapacitating as other drugs and it is readily available on the streets at a low price. Taken together, these considerations dictate a lifestyle of multiple predatory excursions during a single day, and these excursions need not be confined to well-to-do victims.

It is more common for the street practitioner to learn about these matters from a victim rather than from a predator, perhaps during a debriefing session conducted while the victim is receiving first aid for injuries. Direct contact with predators is infrequent because the recent use of alcohol or drugs is an exclusion criterion of many street sites. Moreover, many members of these dissocial groups disdain street culture sites. The presence of elderly and handicapped persons, as well as those with mental impairments, plus the providers and practitioners who serve these groups—all of these confer a decidedly negative status to these sites. The direct contacts that do occur between practitioner and predator will likely be incidental or confined to harassment humor aimed the practitioner's way in a crowded place. Rare calls for an assessment occur when an episode of crack cocaine intoxication is mistaken for a full-blown, manic episode. It is difficult to distinguish between these syndromes by reference to signs and symptoms. Both conditions impose cognitive diffusion, grandiosity, and a disinclination to cooperate with any interview process geared toward differential diagnosis. Crack cocaine intoxications tend to be briefer, but better diagnostic accuracy is achieved when the practitioner can find someone who is knowledgable about the impaired person's recent history and is willing to share that knowledge.

The street practitioner will have more contacts with another segment of addicted persons who overlap with the dissocial component. These persons operate from a third-stage acceptance of street life and chemical dependency, and they lack motivation to give up their chemical(s) of choice. They are often loners who seek out the street practitioner in pursuit of secondary gain, such as SSI or removal from workfare roles. This may engender practitioner resentment that must be set aside if chemical dependency is a recognized impairment of the entitlement program in question. If such is the case, the street practitioner may need to rationalize his or her enabling behavior of signing the form or writing the qualification statement. Perhaps he or she can realistically view it as reducing the probability of the addicted person's preying upon others. Mandatory assignment of the addicted person's benefits to a payee and reduced health service costs to the community as a whole have already been discussed in this regard.

The largest contingent of chemically dependent persons on the streets are those in the second stage of acculturation. They show varying degrees of motivation for recovery. Most communities have a variety of street sites and institutions that serve these people. These include residential programs, halfway and quarterway houses, gospel missions, AA clubhouses, and the like. While members of this component are easier to empathize with than are the previous two, they also tend to be more unstable and challenging. At one extreme are those persons who are enamored of their treatment programs, fervid "twelve-steppers" who take on life through an ideological lens and engage others mainly to ward off relapses between group meetings (p. 149). At the other extreme are "contrarians" who would defy the ideology and norms of treatment programs. The street practitioner can function as a safety valve or outside outlet for such people, sometimes by choice of the addicted person himself and sometimes by referral from a program that recognizes the need for such an outsider. Some of these contrarians prove to be "secondary gainers" who enroll in treatment for reasons that have little to do with sobriety. That they soon chafe beneath the ideology or program requirements is a reflection of their lack of optimal motivation. Others chafe for more legitimate reasons. Some find group treatment and the forces of group cohesion to be alien or threatening. Others develop "cabin fever" in response to requirements that they remain confined within the facility for an initial period of days or weeks. Still others do not feel at ease amidst the prevailing racial, gender, or educational backgrounds of the rest of their treatment group. Some complain of the "brainwashing" tactics that many of these programs seem to invoke, and others are angered by the infantilization that comes with living under house rules and

24-hour supervision with a staff who may not be much further along in the recovery process than they themselves are.

Many such reactions and complaints are legitimate, and a safe outlet for their expression contributes to the person's recovery. Unfortunately, most treatment programs that serve addicted street persons are too poorly funded to hire mental health consultants. Staffs tend to be composed of paraprofessionals, other recovering persons, and counselors whose training is exclusive to the precepts of a particular self-help model or circumscribed philosophy of recovery. Many of these people are not trained to deal with the carping complaints of addicted people who are mourning their lost chemical agents. Visits by practitioners who are outsiders serve to drain off the tensions of the milieu, regardless of whether the practitioner spends time with the staff or the residents.

Finally, there are many addicted persons who present with psychological concerns that have little to do with their particular forms of chemical dependency. Postponing such concerns until after chemical health is restored, or viewing these problems exclusively through the prisms of addiction and abstinence are mistakes that may undermine the person's recovery process. The street practitioner must strive to remain free of such myopia because few chemical dependency treatment programs are willing or able to do so.

DUALLY DIAGNOSED PERSONS

Dual diagnosis is the regrettable term applied to persons with problems of chemical dependency and severe mental impairment. It has been estimated that 10 to 20 percent of street persons qualify for dual diagnoses (Ridgely & Dixon, 1993; Tessler & Dennis, 1989). There is little consensus as to what constitutes a severe mental impairment in this classification. One prevalent view is that the mental impairment must be an Axis I disorder that manifests itself prior to or independently of chemical dependency. Some authorities have suggested that the coexisting mental impairment needs to be a major thought disorder like schizophrenia or a major affective disorder like bipolar disorder (Drake et al., 1991).

Definitional subtleties are moot to the street practitioner. By the time such persons are encountered on the streets, their impairments are intertwined beyond easy separation. Chicken-or-egg-first questions are perplexing: did the person's history of hallucinogenic drug use precipitate pre-existing vulnerability to schizophrenia? Does alcoholism represent an attempt to self-medicate depression or psychosis?

Do symptoms of psychosis and depression represent withdrawal signs or sequelae of long-term substance abuse? There are also interaction effects wherein a person's overall presentation is qualitatively different from what would be predicted from the sum of its parts. Finally, Minkoff (1987) observed that some of these people prefer the social role of addicted person to mentally impaired person. They may trumpet their signs of the former condition to divert attention away from the latter one.

An unfortunate contribution to this daunting mix of clinical issues comes from a public health system's difficulty in addressing the needs of people who do not fall neatly within the boundaries of its discrete categories. The forces of treatment specialization and bifurcation of resources serve to maroon dually diagnosed persons in a "no treatment" buffer zone between mental health and chemical dependency treatment systems. Given an overall climate in which the service needs of homeless people exceed the existing supply of health care practitioners to provide them, the bureaucratic correction factor of exclusionary criteria is used to create a balance between supply and demand. Responsibility for dually diagnosed persons is often jettisoned to the system other than one's own, even as one's counterparts in that other system are doing the same thing.

But this is not merely bureaucratic insensitivity. Many psychiatrists are understandably reluctant to prescribe antipsychotic and antidepressant medications to people who are prone to abuse alcohol or drugs. For their part, many chemical dependency specialists view antidepressant drugs as inconsistent with the abstinence principles that they proffer during treatment. Both sides find their work with homeless persons who are "simply" depressed or "simply" alcoholic to be difficult enough without additional complications. The consequent neglect of dually diagnosed persons extends to housing entities as well. Residential directors and landlords may feel capable of managing the manifestations of one condition, but not of the other nor of both.

Dually diagnosed persons are thus positioned to receive more rejections than treatments. Often rejections come couched in the form of a referral to the opposite health care system. Referrals are always easy for the practitioner to make and difficult for the street person to grasp and pursue, particularly those who lack transportation and telephone. These difficulties point up a more fundamental problems with referrals: just as placebo effects occur as a component of any treatment, frustration effects are an expectable component of any intervention that ends in referral. Referral to a specialist in an office culture practice may yield optimal care, but only for one who trusts mainstream medicine, grasps the referrer's rationale, and can tolerate the temporal delay and ongoing symptoms that must be endured along the way. Few street people possess all of these traits, and therefore referrals—even well-intentioned ones—are likely to reinforce a sense of alienation, discouragement, and the belief that one is being brushed off.

For all of the above reasons, the miseries and adaptational problems of dually diagnosed persons are perhaps the greatest among all segments of the street culture (Koegel et al., 1990). Koegel and Burnam (1987) reported that dually diagnosed persons were more likely than other street persons to prostitute for basic provisions and to be incarcerated by the police. Two independent studies of persons discharged from state psychiatric hospitals found alcohol and drug abuse to be strong predictors of homelessness (Belcher, 1989; Drake, Wallach, & Hoffman, 1989). Perhaps the only encouraging development on behalf of these people is the emergence of dual diagnoses as a clinical subspecialty unto itself (e.g., Minkoff & Drake, 1991). *Hospital and Community Psychiatry* (Volume 40, 1989) devoted an entire issue to the topic, and treatment programs that specifically address dual diagnoses among homeless people have been reviewed by Drake et al. (1991) and by Policy Research Associates (1993).

Present knowledge does not provide the individual street practitioner with any distinctive interventions for members of this group. He or she should anticipate "not my turf" battles over these people when trying to link them with treatment and housing programs. The plight of dually diagnosed persons also gives one cause to extend outreach activities beyond customary limits of convention and advisability. For example, there is a prevalent view across office cultures and mental health disciplines that interacting with a person who is in an intoxicated state is useless from a clinical standpoint. This is also an implicit premise of many street culture sites that have rules against persons entering their premises under the influence of alcohol or drugs. In actual practice, many sites tolerate people who have been drinking, provided that they are not disruptive to the milieu. Staff look the other way until there is trouble, at which time the alcohol/chemical use serves as an immediate justification for the person's extrusion from the site.

The street practitioner is urged to adopt a similar attitude toward a dually diagnosed person who has been drinking but is less than intoxicated or is well enough controlled not to draw any unusual attention. Such a person has probably learned to anticipate rejection and ejection when the first hint of his or her alcohol use has been discovered. The practitioner who does not reject an under-the-influence person in a reflexive manner is often rewarded with better reception when that person is sober. Moreover, some people who value machismo can only open up about the pain beneath their swagger after the disinhibiting catalyst of alcohol has been introduced. In such instances, the premise of mild intoxication (and sometimes it may be a faked intoxication) represents a face-saving way of allowing oneself to lose face.

A tolerant stance toward chemical use is always in order when there are clear signs of a co-existing mental impairment. But even in this context, discretion is the better part of outreach. Female practitioners need to be more conservative than males, given that chemical usage may well disinhibit sexuality before it disinhibits anything else. Another potential source of negative outcome occurs when the street person either forgets or otherwise decommits from what transpired while under-the-influence.

Nevertheless, a practitioner-of-last-resort operates according to the "nothing ventured, nothing gained" adage.

> A female outreach worker from the welfare department requested that a male psychologist stand by for deterrence purposes while she tried to help a somewhat intoxicated man in the back room of a drop-in center. The man was white and in his late twenties, and he claimed to need help in being reinstated to his SSI benefits. He preened and leered at the woman and paraded around the room, seemingly too agitated to sit while she made a telephone call on his behalf.
>
> The psychologist introduced himself only after the man mentioned having once been on prolixin shots (prolixin is a long-acting, antipsychotic drug that is often prescribed when noncompliance with oral medications occurs). At first the man waved the psychologist off with an intense look, as if they were rivals for the woman's affections. The psychologist did not ask probing questions, but neither did he leave. When the woman turned her attention to a second telephone call, the man walked over to the psychologist, "got into his face," and said that he needed more help than the woman was able to deliver. The psychologist then arranged for a time to meet later that day. Ostensibly this was to give the psychologist time to bone up on SSI matters, but in reality it was to allow time for the man to sober up.
>
> The man appeared for this appointment. He was not entirely sober but neither was he as much under the influence as he had been earlier. The psychologist did not comment on this. They were able to work for an hour and a half on a new SSI application, which compelled them to review the man's life and treatment history. At the end of the interview, the man ventured that he was supposed to be reinstated on prolixin "for the voices" (a reference to likely auditory hallucinations).
>
> This first intervention ultimately led to the man's linkage with a community support program for the mentally impaired and his "reinstatement" on prolixin. After being awarded SSI benefits, he acquired an SRO housing unit and lived there for the next several years. During that period, he was encountered drunk as often as sober, but he did not

lose his housing nor miss any of his prolixin shots (at least, such were his repeated assertions).

COLLATERAL INTERVENTIONS

In the above instance, the psychologist was first called to play the role of bodyguard. Good street work is opportunistic. It often materializes out of just such a role, or that of chess opponent, form signer, or "rescue" consultant for a shelter staff in crisis.

Some street persons will still choose others to bring their mental health problems to. Discussing mental health matters with a public health nurse or a generalist social worker may be more easily rationalized or legitimized in a street person's mind. Such "alternates" are also chosen because street people have had occasion to try them out in the past when seeking aspirin, vouchers, and so on, or because earlier life experiences had established such alternates as a class of helpful and responsive people. Many of the nurses, social workers, and others who choose to work with homeless people have excellent engagement skills, that is, they are empathic, nonjudgmental, and offer unconditional positive regard.

There is no cause for the mental health practitioner to be concerned about competition. The fact that an alienated, resistant street person finds *anyone* to confide in is cause for optimism. Problems do arise when alternates are reluctant to accept therapist roles assigned to them by street people. Some claim that this takes too much time away from their assigned duties, but many are simply frightened or perplexed by suicidal or psychotic talk and think that they are ill-prepared to deal with such matters. Still others—particularly nurses who have been trained in hospital cultures—refer mentally impaired people on reflexively, even over the person's protests and threats not to follow through. They seem not to appreciate the inherent rejection, alienation, and logistical hurdles that referrals impose upon street persons. It is unfortunate when referrals are dispensed like pills, or when they are made to serve a practitioner's need to be rid of a difficult person in a superficially legitimate fashion.

Some of these referrers should not be pressed into "alternate" service. However, others may be reassured to learn that untrained paraprofessionals have been shown to function as well as experienced professionals in psychotherapeutic roles (Berman & Norton, 1985; Hattie, Sharpley, & Rogers, 1984). The mental health practitioner should not promote out-of-role interventions except when it is clear that the street person in question will respond to no one but the person he or she has chosen. Even in these latter situations, the practitioner must remain available as a consultant to provide expert knowledge and guidance that will supplement the alternate's therapeutic skills.

At times, the mental health practitioner may be asked to function as an alternate in a medical intervention. His or her skills in human relations may be required to negotiate a street person's resistance to a medical procedure.

A Native American woman in her eighties had been ensconced for a decade in a single room of a boarding house which, over the course of her tenure there, had gradually evolved into the most dangerous of the community's shelters. She resisted being moved out to a nursing home, in part because the local media had publicized her story and rendered her something of a celebrity. Although never preyed upon by other shelter residents, she had developed severe cataracts such that she made daily errors when taking her many medications (something that she insisted upon doing for herself). She refused to consent to an operation for cataract removal, and after the medical team despaired of persuading her to do so, she was referred to a psychiatric nurse with the hope that she might be deemed incompetent enough to qualify for a guardian who would consent to the operation for her.

The nurse met with this woman three times a week for about six weeks. During these visits, he never mentioned the operation but did ask the woman about other aspects of her life and listened to the stories that the woman would tell. In later sessions, the woman began to repeat her stories, and when the nurse called her attention to this it clearly peeved her. Eventually, she raised the topic of the cataract operation herself. During the course of that discussion, the nurse wove in educational material about cataracts and operations for their removal (he had previously been coached by a medical nurse as to how to do so). At his 23rd visit, the woman consented to the operation, and she maintained this cooperative attitude over the two-week waiting period until the operation itself could be performed.

The street practitioner must know alternate therapists well enough to be able to endorse their performance of mental health work on a proxy basis. Repeated observations that an alternate undercontrols or overcontrols the various stress and countertransference reactions that are endemic to street work is evidence that he or she is not suitable for the proxy role. However, most medical and social service practitioners are trained to be attuned to the dangers that their judgments may be clouded by stress or burnout reactions from time to time.

The same cannot be said for site staff—the people who work exclusively and full-time with homeless people in shelters, drop-in centers, and the like. These people are not only vulnerable to burnout, but they are also ill-equipped and poorly supported in their efforts to resist its effects. They tend to be a diverse group, ranging from inexperienced, idealistic college students to jaded, cynical, ex-street persons whose jobs at the shelter maintain them one-paycheck-away from homelessness themselves. This motley mix of personalities and backgrounds is stationed forty plus hours per week on the front lines of the homelessness problem, and the military connotation of the phrase "front lines" is not mere metaphor. Street people often cast site staff in the roles of scapegoat and tar baby. Site staff are charged with absorbing the individual and collective outrage, alienation, and negativism of the street culture on an hour-to-hour basis. They serve as ready transference objects and represent The System to homeless people. Along the way, they must also maintain vigilance for weapons, drugs, and predator-prey confrontations. Their pay is low, their benefits are few, and their promotional opportunities are limited. Lofty social ideals and altruism that may have motivated them in the beginning are often transformed over time into cynicism and detachment. Turnover is high.

The mental health practitioner must strive to support this part of the culture because it contributes significantly to the overall humaneness of the street milieu. He or she must minister to the individual and collective burnout of these persons; one such avenue is to provide training in mental health matters on both a formal and informal (ongoing) basis. Many site staff begin their front-line work with archaic notions or ignorance concerning mental impairments. These states may be expressed through phobic avoidance of mentally impaired persons or through ridiculing and lampooning of them. Many site workers have also picked up culture-wide biases caused by mass media portrayals of the mentally impaired as excessively prone to violence (Gerbner, Gross, Morgan, & Signorielli, 1981). Many of them do not understand the mental-illness-and-dangerousness standards governing civil commitment statutes. They expect that any person who displays psychotic behavior qualifies for immediate hospitalization, and they look askance at a mental health practitioner who preaches tolerance for psychotic behavior and then departs the shelter without relieving them of such a burden. Moreover, because of rapid turnover, the practitioner can never assume that site staff need to be trained only once. The National Resource Center on Homelessness and Mental Illness can supply training materials and resources addressed to the varying sophistication levels of site staffs.

Street people who are referred to the mental health practitioner by site staff should generally be given priority over those referred by other street workers. Any intervention that addresses a site staff's needs can be expected to produce a ripple effect that will reach the street people whom they serve. Unfortunately, site staff often use mental health practitioners like bouncers or sergeants-at-arms. Thus, a practitioner arrives at a site to find a negativistic, perhaps hostile street person waiting to be seen, and this person indicates that shelter staff have informed him or her that he or she cannot remain there unless first cleared by the mental health practitioner.

In office culture settings, such unannounced, "strong-armed" referrals connote professional disrespect and are resentfully referred to as "dumping." Nor are mental health practitioners typically trained to pass judgment upon someone's fitness to reside in a shelter, a decision that is rendered all the more difficult by the context of a negativistic person being seen for the first time under conditions that induce resentment. Performing such an assessment well also require an excellent grasp of the shelter as a social unit.

However, upon further reflection and experience, the street practitioner learns that such strong-arm referrals from site staff represent an excellent outreach opportunity to intervene with difficult persons who would not otherwise find their way to a mental health intervention. First, one must infer that the person in question is at least marginally acceptable for continued stay in the shelter. If he or she had behaved in a way that was completely unacceptable, the site staff would not have waited for a mental health practitioner before expelling the person or calling the police. Milieu safety is a much higher priority for site staff than mental health interventions. The fact that a strong-armed person can be taken back with a mental health clearance signals staff's implicit judgment that he or she is not an imminent or serious risk to the shelter milieu at the time.

Once the above line of reasoning is applied, the mental health practitioner is relieved of the burden of a difficult decision. That is, barring unforeseen developments, the final decision in all such assessments will be to give such a person the benefit of the doubt and clearance to return to the shelter. Once this stance has been adopted, the mental health practitioner is free to conduct the clearance interview—with which the street person is already compelled to cooperate—in ways that serve outreach or treatment purposes. Resistances can be surfaced and addressed, a social history taken, or empathic exploration of a stressful life experience pursued. The mental health practitioner signals the positive clearance decision early in the interview to reduce the street person's anxiety; once the positive decision has been signaled and the person has been reassured of continued shelter, the practitioner is free to present the shelter's point of view on the person's behavior. He or she may also attempt to mediate the street person's conflicts with shelter staff, perhaps providing some informal training in the process.

The long-term effect of such interventions is the enhancement of the practitioner's reputation, thereby facilitating referrals and outreach efforts in the future. Thus, as was true for many other situations discussed earlier, strong-arm referrals have different implications in street work than they do in office culture settings. Such a statement can be taken as a guiding principle for the practitioner-of-last-resort.

CHAPTER 10

Summary and Disclaimer

As a method of summary and synthesis, the 58 vignettes which have been used to illustrate this book will be reconsidered as a set. The outcome designation for each vignette (positive, negative, or neutral) reflects the summary judgments of the practitioner(s) involved in each situation. Admittedly this is a selective sample of outcomes, but what it lacks in nomothetic representation is balanced by its didactic value for those who would meet homeless persons as individuals rather than as data points of a study sample. What is not well-conveyed by these vignettes are the periods of boredom and ennui that occur when one's outreach efforts are rebuffed and ignored, and the fact that, over time, intervention dilemmas will tend to repeat themselves. The present anecdotal approach has relied upon vivid, memorable examples of a phenomenon to drive home its essential nature. This may give rise to the overprediction of that which is colorful and the underprediction of that which is routine, a cognitive bias known as the availability heuristic (Hamill, Wilson, & Nisbett, 1980). The street practitioner is therefore advised to expect "down times" to street work when one will feel caught up in the quiet, milling desperation of the culture. Infrequent and short-lived doses of tedium and malaise will provide the occasional volunteer with a good empathic reference to the emotional climate of street life. But a burnout syndrome is likely for the "regular" who must endure more frequent and extensive periods of understimulation. Diversification in one's professional life and regular input from colleagues and students are the best antidotes for this.

Of the 58 vignettes, 32 were judged to have had positive outcomes, although many of these do not correspond to traditional indices of treatment success. Traditional indices include the removal, amelioration, and/or stabilization of a person's signs, symptoms, and distress; changes from pre- to post-treatment on scales and tests; self-reports of improvement or gratitude from recipients of treatment; and cessation or reduction in the utilization of treatment services and the costs associated with these. These success standards do not translate well into street work because the stressors of homelessness underwrite mental

TABLE OF VIGNETTES

No.	Outcome . . .	Retrieval Cue	Page
47.	+	Robert: beadwork display in the shelter	148
48.	+	A pep rally for two	149
49.	+	PTSD dreams and war movies	150
50.	−	Cookie: a mayday catastrophe	153
51.	+	Larry: womenfolk are like that	154
52.	+	F.G.: a fall guy	157
53.	+	Gorbachev's assassination	166
38b.	+	Phael: jilted by a church volunteer	168
54.	+	New lyrics, same melody	170
55.	+	Three steps forward, two backward	173
56.	+	Daniel: posted at the gay bar	173
57.	+	An intoxicated SSI applicant	184
58.	+	Cataract surgery	186

Legend: + = positive, N = neutral, − = negative.

impairments and are not subject to control by either the street person or the practitioner. When not removed or substantially reduced, these stressors continue to undermine coping skills and catalyze a person's vulnerabilities and predispositions to maladaptive symptoms and behaviors. Reliable support persons and systems with whom the practitioner might ally on behalf of the impaired street person are seldom available. And many street persons have not only failed to respond to known treatments, but have also developed self-expectations that project these negative treatment experiences of the past into the future.

Thus, the street practitioner adjusts his or her standards of positive outcome to fit a difficult context of care. Against such a backdrop, a subset of eight vignettes (5, 13, 22, 27, 38, 39, 53, and "Linda" of #4) were judged to have had positive outcomes, even though the achievements in question were limited to the formation of an ongoing alliance with a previously resistant person. No significant improvement in signs, symptoms, distress levels, or adaptational niches was achieved with any of these people. They changed little, if at all; what did improve was their estrangement from mental health providers. Forming such linkages ("alliances" is perhaps too strong a word) serves three purposes. First, the impaired person's ongoing adaptational abilities become available to ongoing review. Changes for the worse are more readily discernible and timely interventions can be made, as occurred successfully with Phael (38b) and unsuccessfully with Flory (41). Second, as new treatment options become available, a working relationship is already established within which such treatments can be initiated. Finally, when functioning well, these people provide practitioners with first-hand knowledge about how an impaired person adapts to a dangerous, nonsupportive culture (e.g., 33). This advances the ecological understanding of homelessness in a way that is less dehumanizing than affixing radio transmitters to people and tracking their movements electronically. This latter approach has been floated for consideration more than once by researchers. Ironically, its technology was first devised to study endangered species, and yet homeless people appear to be anything but endangered.

Most of the outcomes that were judged to have involved successful crisis interventions (6, 30, 31, 37, 38b, 48, 51, 52) averted a person's loss of or estrangement from an important aspect of his or her support system (i.e., shelter, drop-in center). These are not crises in the psychological sense of the term, and the methods used to remedy them as often resemble mediation as crisis intervention techniques. However, when working with people who lack adequate support figures and systems, the preservation of those supports that do exist is of highest priority.

Another group of positive outcomes involved practitioners contributing to the acquisition or preservation of entitlement program benefits (23, 25, 40, 42, 45, 46, 52), supported housing (40, 52, 57), or supportive housing (20, 46). Such interventions require that the practitioner identify and facilitate a fit between a particular street person and a particular niche. Entitlement programs generate resources that enable a street person to gain access to a better class of niches. This may be the only thing that some street persons will permit a mental health practitioner to help them with.

Only a minority of positive outcomes (17, 20, 23, 34, 43, 49, 54, 55, 56, 58) correspond with traditional standards of treatment effectiveness. Even then, some of these invoked treatment dynamics and tactics that are rarely seen in office culture work. Thus, the street practitioner may have to show patience and forebearance through an extended course of hazing (17). He or she may need to be content with changes based on psychological reactance (23, 56), with writing an out-of-state hospital to request a change in one of its discharge summaries (34), or with threatening to hospitalize someone if he or she refuses to maintain marginal cleanliness (37). Practitioners do not learn of such things in medical or graduate schools where positive treatment alliance is an implicit beginning to most treatment encounters. On the streets, a positive treatment alliance must be earned as often as it can be assumed. A first step in such earning is for the practitioner to respect the street person's resistance. Practitioner-of-last-resort is sometimes a submissive role that dictates that one follow rather than lead.

Seven of the 58 vignettes (8, 9, 12, 32, 41, 44, 50) were judged to have had negative outcomes. Six involved psychotic persons and five of these six revolved around hospital-based interventions. The involuntary hospitalization of a severely impaired person will never be a tasteful or economical decision, but fewer errors of omission will be made in this area when the ideological trappings attached to such decisions are jettisoned. The continuing fixation upon deinstitutionalization as a cause of homelessness retards progress in this area. What other field with any claims to scientific method still anchors its thinking to a policy that predates John F. Kennedy's assassination? Certainly the present unfolding of U.S. foreign policy and energy policy were irrevocably shaped by the Viet Nam War and the Arab oil embargo respectively. But it would be folly to suggest that current developments in those policy areas are directly determined by events that took place 20 years ago. The obsolescence of deinstitutionalization as an explanatory force is even implicit in the writings of those who continue to champion it. Thus, one esteemed authority recently likened his position to that of the Alec Guiness character in *Bridge Over the River Kwai.* That movie portrayed a staunch leader who, because of single-minded dedication to his cause, was the last to recognize that the broader social meanings of his work had undergone radical change. Another expert has kept deinstitutionalization alive by articulating three different aspects of it. According to this view, it is not only a fact, but also a process and a philosophy.

In truth, it is only the fact aspect of deinstitutionalization that has any heuristic value, and then only as a historical fact. When one examines the statistical facts of deinstitutionalization—as in the number of patients in public mental hospitals between 1950 and 1984 (see Torrey, 1988, p. 140)—it is immediately apparent that the bulk of census reduction was accomplished between 1960 and 1975. Homelessness as a problem of mentally impaired persons did not seize the national consciousness until the early to mid-1980s. It is more correlated in time with the disappearance of affordable housing stock than with the onset of deinstitutionalization (Kiesler, 1991). Unless we are willing to rebuild or reopen state mental institutions to conduct controlled studies of institutionalization versus not (something that no one has yet proposed in any serious fashion), progress will be better served by the forced retirement of deinstitutionalization.

If some replacement term is needed to capture the essential problems of the present, referring to the present as the civil liberties era would be more appropriate. This asserts a reality which community-based mental health programs must now grapple with as a fundamental planning principle. In the past, civil liberties were either regarded as irritants or enlisted as a mutual justification through which a community mental health program and a difficult treatment candidate tacitly agreed not to affiliate with each other. The rise of consumerism among psychotically impaired persons and the tilt from supportive housing to supported housing models were made possible by the expansion of civil liberties. Minkoff's (1987) excellent paper anticipated these developments in his proposal of a new ideology to replace deinstitutionalization. United States' psychiatry has been slow to follow his lead, although the "in need of treatment" standard of civil commitment is one exception. While many practitioners would decry relaxing the standards that govern involuntary hospitalization, the proposed "in need of treatment" standard at least recognizes that rejection of the patient role is the key problem with the psychotic street people of today.

What can explain the staying power of deinstitutionalization? It offers oversimplification and perhaps echoes with previous struggles for civil liberties that are more deeply etched in the history and collective unconscious of the United States. Bag-lady-with-shopping-cart is an evocative and compelling image with instantaneous appeal to the politicians and mass media who work the levers of public funding. Given that these two power sectors are regularly bombarded with the numbing numbers of poverty data, they too are susceptible to the availability heuristic and being disproportionately influenced by vivid imagery, for example, Lucille Ball's last television role as a bag lady.

To be sure, there are deinstitutionalized, psychotic persons who are in need of assistance. But a number of authorities have quietly observed that their absolute numbers among the New Homelessness are not nearly as large as their representations in the popular and academic literature about the New Homelessness would suggest (Kiesler, 1991; Koegel & Burnam, 1992; Koegel et al., 1990; Snow, Baker, Anderson, & Martin, 1986). And one denominator underlying the intricate, individual pathways by which homeless psychotic persons find their ways into the street culture is also common to thousands of other men and women who were not mentally impaired when they became homeless for the first time. Simply put, the New Homelessness consists of a broad, heterogeneous stratum of the lower class that has dropped down en masse to the lower quality of life associated with an inadequate supply of affordable housing. Because of their severe impairments, psychotic persons have always socially selected their ways in disproportionate numbers to the low socioeconomic strata. When the lowest stratum as a whole can no longer compete for affordable housing, its disproportionate numbers of psychotic persons are exposed to plain view. They were not thus exposed during the heydays of deinstitutionalization (1960–1975) because affordable housing was more plentiful then. The conditions of the present era are also made worse by the coming of age of the post World War II "baby boomer" generation (Caton, 1990). This has meant both larger absolute numbers of mentally impaired persons and larger absolute numbers of people competing for a diminished housing stock in 1980–1990 than was the case in 1960–1975.

Thus, the real ongoing tragedy of deinstitutionalization is this: The disproportionate attention and financial resources that are diverted to the individual pathologies of a modest subset of the homeless population are so much less that is available to devote to the socioeconomic pathology which underwrites and maintains homelessness for all street people. Those who would be rendered mentally impaired by the social causation processes associated with homelessness are actually at increased risk for same from the disproportionate diversion of resources to the social selection component of the street culture. And Kiesler (1991) is undoubtedly correct in asserting that the problems of many homeless psychotic people will be limited, if not erased, by remedying the housing problem first. A recent study of two New York state communities (Rosenfield, 1991) supports Kiesler's position. Rosenfield showed that housing was a more important factor than treatment in maintaining the community adjustment of psychiatric patients after discharge from the hospital.

In the final analysis, affordable housing is a necessary and often sufficient condition to end homelessness; mental health treatment is never a sufficient condition and not always a necessary one. Affording equal prioritization to treatment needs and housing needs brings the cart up alongside its horse, only to tangle with it and impede its progress. Those who are rightfully committed to increasing psychotic persons' access to necessary treatment resources should redirect their energies and efforts to achieving this through national health care reform, not by competing for dollars earmarked for the homelessness problem.

The 19 remaining vignettes of this book were judged to have been neutral in outcome. Most were included because they dramatized many of the culture shocks that middle class practitioners are likely to experience in street work. Thus it is not uncommon to learn of a street person's disappearance (38) or having been murdered (27b), or to learn that some street persons engage in death defiance as a matter of pride (3). There are rapes (26) and foiled rapes (33); there are drug deals (28), firearms (31), and hazing rituals (2, 21) to be endured. Sometimes the practitioner is side-tracked by failure to communicate (1), failure to comprehend (55), and failure to distance oneself properly (50). He or she must also anticipate day-to-day experiences in being caught between two cultures (1, 10, 11, 17, 31). The practitioner will encounter persons who move him or her to the depths of disgust

(42) and despair (29), while others evoke the heights of admiration (22) and wonderment (33). Through it all, he or she must monitor and manage private drifts in and out of countertransference and burnout reactions. When it is possible to do so, the practitioner will also minister to the countertransference and burnout reactions of site staff and other providers upon whom homeless persons depend (13, 24, 26, 27, 31, 37, 38, 47, 52, 57, 58).

A subset of eight vignettes were also judged as depicting neutral outcomes (7, 14, 15, 16, 18, 19, 35, 36). These represented outreach failures in which street practitioners proved unsuccessful or were rebuked in their efforts to make connections with street people. In each instance, it was the street person's intransigence that was judged to have caused the outreach failure. The inclusion of these vignettes was intended to sensitize practitioners to the fact that street persons can be abrasive and confrontational when encountered in their own territory.

Some modes of resistance hold lessons for the practitioner who would listen for them, for example, "Doctor Seven" (16) and "the spotted owl" (17). These two in particular echo themes that have spread among homeless people but which have not yet found adequate voice in the writings of practitioners and researchers. Beneath the gross effrontery of the Doctor Seven interaction resides the fact that funds earmarked for the homelessness problem during the 1980s have been channeled more to emergency measures than to long-term solutions. While the last 10 to 15 years have witnessed no appreciable gains in the availability of affordable housing (Foscarinis, 1991), they have witnessed a significant increase in the number of practitioners who intervene on behalf of homeless persons. It is an unfortunate irony that as practitioners and street institutions and programs are able minimize the more serious and telegenic miseries of homelessness, the television coverage withdraws and the pains of homelessness recede in the collective consciousness of the mainstream culture. Thus do street practitioners and others who serve homeless people contribute to the long-term normalization of homelessness, even as they put out its here-and-now fires. Each person who is effectively assisted in adapting better to his or her niche, and each person who is provided with timely respite, asylum, or hospitalization in order to prevent a life-threatening action—each such "successful" intervention effectively mutes a messenger of pain and misery that might have otherwise nudged the mainstream culture further toward effective sociopolitical action.

There are signs that homelessness is already fading as an imminent concern among the public. In 1988, the opening salvo of the presidential debates focused on homelessness. In 1992, homelessness scarcely received honorable mention among the various issues debated by the candidates. When one major party candidate stayed in a homeless shelter during his party's convention, he was mocked in the mass media for doing so. Some have questioned whether or not we are already witnessing a backlash of public sympathy toward homeless people (Furillo, 1990; Wilkerson, 1991). Recent media portrayals of homelessness depict legal perspectives on curbing panhandling and restricting street persons' access to libraries and parks. Nightclub comedians now assign "street person" to a "designated loser" role in their material, and they do so with little fear of alienating their audiences. If complacency about homelessness spreads, one will soon hear statements like "in D.C. we have shelters" among all segments of the mainstream culture.

A logical extension of this complacency will have street work become a source of stable jobs for health care practitioners and others. Such a prospect dictates that the following disclaimer be offered: a street practitioner can only occasionally accomplish more than tertiary prevention as long as the shortage of affordable housing continues. That is, while he or she is often in a position to prevent a street person's ongoing condition from getting worse, the street practitioner can seldom accomplish more than token successes in removing persons from the rolls of homelessness. In only seven (20, 40, 45, 46, 52, 55, 57) of the 58 vignettes was such secondary prevention aided or accomplished by mental health interventions. Rarely will the street practitioner be in a position to prevent a future incidence of homelessness. Such primary prevention may have been accomplished only once (30) among all of the vignettes described.

Practitioners must also guard against the side effects of specialtization in street work. Mentally impaired persons, chemically dependent persons, homeless women, veterans, families, children, and so on are increasingly seen through the prisms of their own unique needs, priorities, and advocacy positions. The emerging factionalism is detrimental to the extent that it diverts attention and resources away from primary prevention and the underlying problem that afflicts them all, the absence of affordable housing and a socioeconomic climate to support it.

Researchers are in a better position than practitioners to influence efforts at primary and secondary prevention. However, the seeds of normalization and specialtization are planted there as well. The burgeoning literature of the past 15 years has begotten a spate of journals publishing "Special Issues" on homelessness, an annotated bibliography of five hundred articles published by the American Psychological Association (Shinn et al., 1990), and most recently the *Journal of Social Issues and Homelessness.* The National Institute of Mental Health now supports the entity known as The National Resource Center on Homelessness and Mental Illness to track and organize information generated about that single subgroup of homeless people. The original NIMH demonstration projects addressing homeless mentally impaired persons have been referred to as "first generation" studies, without comment upon how many generations of such studies are projected into the future. A cursory review of abstracts from all of this scholarship yields a numbing repetition of sympathetic conclusions, plus de rigueur methodological debates about the definition and measurement of homelessness. Discussion sections of articles conclude with calls for more hands to strive for better grasps upon increasingly smaller parts of this elephant. These calls have been answered by a plenitude of comparisons of homeless subjects versus control subjects on a wide array of demographic descriptors, pathologies, and premorbid predictors.

> On one late weekday morning, the lobby of a small shelter was lined with four homeless men sitting in silence along one wall. Each was watching a professionally dressed young woman at a table in the center of the room as she administered items from the Koh's Block Design Test to another homeless man. A driver from a temporary agency popped in from the outside and announced that he needed 10 men for a job site, "a day's pay for a day's work plus transportation." None of the men against the wall so much as acknowledged his presence, and he left. A shelter staff who had observed this chuckled and said "Vacation day!" for the benefit of the psychiatrist who had just arrived. She explained that the woman was paying five dollars cash for participation in a study of homeless alcoholics, and that this amount was enough to keep a man supplied with wine for the day—otherwise at least some of the men against the wall would have answered the call of the temp driver.

It would be disingenuous to suggest that these men could not have found other means to acquire alcohol, or that eight hours of day labor represents meaningful abstinence. Nevertheless, this is an instance of a researcher enabling those whom she studies. Beyond that is the more fundamental question of whether such research should be conducted at all. Some would argue that the prevalence of brain dysfunction among homeless alcoholic persons is of significance to neurologists, neuropsychologists, public health planners, and so forth. But this study is not without its insidious effects: these alcoholic men were recruited to participate because of their poverty, their low social standing, and their disease. It is self-serving for a researcher to presume that no stigmatization occurs as the result of applying such selection criteria. A token financial gain and the pleasant attention from a professional woman because one is homeless and alcoholic cannot help but figure into one's private running commentary about oneself. This may in turn facilitate acculturation to the streets and a third-stage acceptance of street identity.

It is thus submitted here that such untoward effects of research on homeless persons warrant more stringent peer review and higher standards of scientific merit than are applied to most research with human subjects. And scientific merit would be better served by approaches that eschew specialized attention to another small patch of the elephant. The sad truth is that a decade of this piecemeal approach has contributed little thus far to the eradication of homelessness in the United States. The elephant continues to grow; none of its patches have yet disappeared, even as each one is better understood in more of its exquisite detail as illumined by our research methods. Unfortunately, if the present state of affairs is allowed to continue, ten years from now we may well see titles such as *The Left-Handed Homeless: Theory, Research, and Practice*.

There are many who believe that no further studies of *any* kind are indicated. In their view, it is not better information about homelessness that is needed but more political will to provide all with access to affordable housing (Foscarinis, 1991). Unlike the case of the spotted owl, there has been no concerted, broad-based, and well-funded effort to pressure leaders into the difficult commitments that must be made. A significant part of this problem is the disenfranchisement of street persons from the political process (Blasi & Preis, 1992). Advocacy movements begin with a core of affected and committed citizens who organize at the grassroots level first and expand upward and outward from that base into lobbying, fund-raising, and political action arms. Street persons have little free time to advocate and self-educate. They must expend considerable time and energy upon day-to-day survival behaviors. They lack reliable access to telephones and transportation. They tend to be naive in the methods of advocacy and political action. And historically, they have not voted, in part because the complexities and hurdles of residency requirements for voter registration have deterred them. Another obstacle to effective self-advocacy has been the stigma value attached to homelessness. It is a "don't look back" experience for many who escape it, and it is often the more skilled and able persons who succeed in lifting themselves out of homelessness, thus depleting the culture of potential leaders. Once having escaped the streets, many people distance themselves from the experience instead of holding on to something of their street identities and advocating for those left behind. For this, they are not to be blamed.

Neither should street practitioners be blamed for their efforts at tertiary/secondary prevention, nor researchers blamed for taking and retaking relevant pulses of the homelessness problem. At the same time, members of these two groups should not ignore their inadvertent contributions to the institutionalization of homelessness, and to the paradox that good tertiary prevention on behalf of an individual subtracts from the pressure to achieve secondary and primary prevention for the benefit of street cultures as wholes. The most responsible way to labor beneath such a paradox is to pay homage to both of its sides.

> A psychologist contracted to write a book about homelessness, for which he was to receive a standard royalty percentage from his publisher. The book addressed the special needs of one subgroup of homeless persons (the mentally impaired), and it sought to define a practitioner role ("last resort") that called for helping street people to adapt to their niches in the street culture. Recognizing that his work inadvertently contributed to the normalization and specialtization of homelessness created cognitive dissonance for him. This dissonance was resolved when he decided to donate all royalties and other profits from the book to organizations that advocate and lobby for affordable housing on behalf of homeless people.

The National Law Center for Homelessness and Poverty, the National Coalition for the Homeless, and the Low-Income Housing Coalition are a few of the national organizations whose missions are to lobby for affordable housing and an improved economic climate to sustain it. Large urban areas may have local chapters of these organizations, as well as home-grown local organizations who pursue these goals in the home community. The street practitioner may resolve his or her own dissonance by donating time, effort, and/or money to these organizations in the spirit of primary and secondary prevention.

The practitioner who owns his or her own housing might consider donating an amount linked to the government subsidy which makes his or her home more affordable. Government-subsidized housing comes to a homeowner in the form of a deduction from taxable income of interest paid on one's home mortgage. As IRS regulations are currently written, this deduction may be taken on all of the interest paid on mortgages assumed for *two* homes. According to one estimate, this deduction costs the U.S. Treasury 50 billion dollars a year (Lacayo, 1992), an amount that could otherwise provide much primary and secondary prevention for those who are presently homeless in the United States.

References

Abend, S. M. (1989). Countertransference and psychoanalytic technique. *Psychoanalytic Quarterly, 58,* 374–395.

American Psychiatric Association. (1980). *Diagnostic and Statistical Manual of Mental Disorders* (3rd ed.). DSM-III. Washington, DC: Author.

American Psychiatric Association. (1987). *Diagnostic and Statistical Manual of Mental Disorders* (3rd ed., rev.). DSM-III-R. Washington, DC: Author.

American Psychiatric Association. (1994). *Diagnostic and Statistical Manual of Mental Disorders* (4th ed.). DSM-IV. Washington, DC: Author.

Anderson, A. (1992, Aug. 31). Homeless in America. *National Review,* 25–29.

Anthony, W. A., & Jansen, M. A. (1984). Predicting the vocational capacity of the chronically mentally ill. *American Psychologist, 39,* 537–544.

Appelbaum, P. S. (1991). Advance directives for psychiatric treatment. *Hospital and Community Psychiatry, 42,* 983–984.

Arce, A. A., Tadlock, M., Vergare, M. J., & Shapiro, S. H. (1983). A psychiatric profile of street people admitted to an emergency shelter. *Hospital and Community Psychiatry, 34,* 812–817.

Armat, V. C., & Peele, R. (1992). The need-for-treatment standard in involuntary civil commitment. In H. R. Lamb, L. L. Bachrach, & F. I. Kass (Eds.), *Treating the homeless mentally ill* (pp. 183–202). Washington, DC: American Psychiatric Association.

Bach, V., & Steinhagen, R. (1987). *Alternatives to the welfare hotel.* New York: Community Service Society.

Bachrach, L. L. (1982). Young adult chronic patients: An analytical review of the literature. *Hospital and Community Psychiatry, 33,* 189–196.

Bachrach, L. L. (1992). What we know about homelessness among mentally ill persons: An analytical review and commentary. *Hospital and Community Psychiatry, 43,* 453–464.

Bachrach, L. L. (1993). The biopsychosocial legacy of deinstitutionalization. *Hospital and Community Psychiatry, 44,* 523–524.

Bachrach, L. L., Talbott, J. A., & Meyerson, A. T. (1987). The chronic psychiatric patient as a "difficult" patient: A conceptual analysis. In A. T. Meyerson (Ed.), *Barriers to treating the chronic mentally ill.* (New Directions for Mental Health Services, No. 33.) San Francisco, CA: Jossey-Bass.

Bahr, H., & Caplow, T. (1974). *Old men drunk and sober.* New York: New York University Press.

Bassuk, E. L., Rubin, L., & Lauriat, A. (1984). Is homelessness a mental health problem? *American Journal of Psychiatry, 141,* 1546–1550.

Bauerlein, M., & Farley, R. (1990, May 30). Occupied territories. *City Pages* (of the Twin Cities), 8–11.

Baxter, E., & Hopper, K. (1984). Shelter and housing for the homeless mentally ill. In H. R. Lamb (Ed.), *The homeless mentally ill* (pp. 109–140). Washington, DC: American Psychiatric Association.

Bearak, B. (1991, June 2). Despair and danger prevail at New York shelter full of victims and villains. *Minneapolis Star Tribune,* 17A–20A.

Bebout, R. R., & Harris, M. (1992). In search of pumpkin shells: Residential programming for the homeless mentally ill. In H. R. Lamb, L. L. Bachrach, & F. I. Kass (Eds.), *Treating the homeless mentally ill* (pp. 159–181). Washington, DC: American Psychiatric Association.

Belcher, J. R. (1989). On becoming homeless: A study of chronically mentally ill persons. *Journal of Community Psychology, 17,* 173–185.

Berman, J. S., & Norton, N. C. (1985). Does professional training make a therapist more effective? *Psychological Bulletin, 98,* 401–407.

Blasi, G., & Preis, J. (1992). Litigation on behalf of the homeless. In M. J. Robertson & M. Greenblatt (Eds.), *Homelessness: A national perspective* (pp. 309–322). New York: Plenum Press.

Bloom, B. L. (1981). Focused single session therapy: Initial development and evaluation. In S. H. Budman (Ed.), *Forms of brief therapy* (pp. 167–216). New York: Guilford Press.

Bloom, B. L. (1984). *Community mental health: A general introduction* (2nd ed.). Monterey, CA: Brooks/Cole.

Blumberg, L., Shipley, T., & Shandler, I. (1973). *Skid row and its alternatives.* Philadelphia, PA: Temple University Press.

Bogue, D. (1963). *Skid row in American cities.* Chicago, IL: University of Chicago Press.

Breakey, W. R. (1992). Mental health services for homeless people. In M. J. Robertson & M. Greenblatt (Eds.), *Homelessness: A national perspective* (pp. 101–108). New York: Plenum Press.

Breakey, W. R., Fischer, P. J., Kramer, M., Nestadt, G., Romanoski, A. J., Ross, A., Royall, R. M., & Stine, O. (1989). Health and mental health problems of homeless men and women in Baltimore. *Journal of the American Medical Association, 262,* 1352–1357.

Brehm, S. S., & Brehm, J. W. (1981). *Psychological reactance: A theory of freedom and control.* New York: Academic Press.

Breuer, J., & Freud, S. (1895/1957). *Studies in hysteria.* New York: Basic Books.

Burnam, M. A., & Koegel, P. (1988). Methodology for obtaining a representative sample of homeless persons: The Los Angeles skid row study. *Evaluation Review, 12,* 117–152.

Burt, M. R., & Cohen, B. E. (1988). *Feeding the homeless: Does the prepared meals provision help?* Washington, DC: The Urban Institute.

Carling, P. J. (1990). Major mental illness, housing, and supports: The promise of community integration. *American Psychologist, 45,* 969–975.

Carling, P. J. (1993). Housing and supports for persons with mental illness: Emerging approaches to research and practice. *Hospital and Community Psychiatry, 44,* 439–449.

Caton, C. L. M. (1990). *Homeless in America.* New York: Oxford University Press.

Chafetz, L. (1992). Why clinicians distance themselves from the homeless mentally ill. In H. R. Lamb, L. L. Bachrach, & F. I. Kass (Eds.), *Treating the homeless mentally ill* (pp. 95–109). Washington, DC: American Psychiatric Association.

Church, G. J. (1990, May 12). Ignore my lips. *Time,* 18–25.

Cloninger, C. R., Bohman, M., & Sigvardsson, S. (1981). Inheritance of alcohol abuse. *Archives of General Psychiatry, 38,* 861–868.

Cohen, N. L., & Marcos, L. R. (1992). Outreach intervention models for the homeless mentally ill. In H. R. Lamb, L. L. Bachrach, & F. I. Kass (Eds.), *Treating the homeless mentally ill* (pp.141–158). Washington, DC: American Psychiatric Association.

Cournos, F. (1989). Involuntary medication and the case of Joyce Brown. *Hospital & Community Psychiatry, 40,* 736–740.

Cousins, N. (1979). *The anatomy of an illness as perceived by the patient.* New York: Norton.

Craig, R., & Paterson, A. (1988). The homeless mentally ill: No longer out of sight and out of mind. *State Legislative Report* (National Conference of State Legislatures), *13,* No. 30.

Cummings, N. A., & Follette, W. (1976). Brief psychotherapy and medical utilization. In H. Dorken and Associates, *The professional psychologist today: New developments in law, health insurance, and health practice.* San Francisco, CA: Jossey-Bass.

Dahl, J. (1992, Feb. 18) Street triage: A San Diego shelter feeds the homeless with an uneven hand. *Wall Street Journal,* p. 1, A7.

Dennis, D. L., Buckner, J. C., Lipton, F. R., & Levine, I. S. (1991). A decade of research and services for homeless mentally ill persons: Where do we stand? *American Psychologist, 46,* 1129–1138.

DiMatteo, M. R., & DiNicola, D. D. (1982). *Achieving patient compliance: The psychology of the medical practitioner's role.* New York: Pergamon Press.

Dohrenwend, B. P., & Dohrenwend, B. S. (1969). *Social status and psychological disorder: A causal inquiry.* New York: Wiley.

Dowd, E. T., & Seibel, C. A. (1990). A cognitive theory of resistance and reactance: Implications for treatment. *Journal of Mental Health Counseling, 12,* 458–469.

Drake, R. E., Osher, F. C., & Wallach, M. A. (1991). Homelessness and dual diagnosis. *American Psychologist, 46,* 1149–1158.

Drake, R. E., Wallach, M. A., & Hoffman, J. S. (1989). Housing instability and homelessness among aftercare patients of an urban state hospital. *Hospital and Community Psychiatry, 40,* 46–51.

Edwards, G., Orford, J., Egert, S., Guthrie, S., Hawker, A., Hensman, C., Mitcheson, M., Oppenheimer, E., & Taylor, C. (1977). Alcoholism: A controlled trial of "treatment" and "advice." *Journal of Studies on Alcohol, 38,* 1004–1031.

Ellis, A. (1989). Using rational-emotive therapy (RET) as crisis intervention: A single session with a suicidal client. (Special Issue: Varieties of brief therapy.) *Individual Psychology, 45,* 75–81.

Farr, R., Koegel, P., & Burnam, A. (1986). *A study of homelessness and mental illness in the skid row area of Los Angeles.* Los Angeles, CA: Los Angeles County Department of Mental Health.

Fassler, D. (1985). The fear of needles in children. *American Journal of Orthopsychiatry, 55,* 371–377.

Fischer, P. J. (1992). The criminalization of homelessness. In M. J. Robertson & M. Greenblatt (Eds.), *Homelessness: A national perspective* (pp. 57–66). New York: Plenum Press.

Fischer, P. J., & Breakey, W. R. (1991). The epidemiology of alcohol, drug, and mental disorders among homeless persons. *American Psychologist, 46,* 1115–1128.

Fisher, P. (1989). Estimating the prevalence of alcohol, drug, and mental health problems in the contemporary homeless population. *Contemporary Drug Problems, 16,* 333–389.

Foscarinis, M. (1991). The politics of homelessness: A call to action. *American Psychologist, 46,* 1232–1239.

Frankl, V. E. (1967). Paradoxical intention: A logotherapeutic technique. In V. E. Frankl et al. (Eds.), *Psychotherapy and existentialism.* New York: Washington Square Press.

Freud, S. (1910/1957). The future prospects of psycho-analytic therapy. In J. Strachey (Ed.), *The standard edition of the complete works of Sigmund Freud* (Vol. 11, pp. 139–151). London: Hogarth Press.

Freud, S. (1933). *New introductory lectures on psycho-analysis.* New York: Norton.

Furillo, A. (1990, July 19). Homeless face growing hostility in nation's cities. *San Francisco Examiner/Chronicle,* pp. A1, A12.

Garfield, S. L., & Bergin, A. E. (1986). *Handbook of psychotherapy and behavior change* (3rd ed.). New York: Wiley.

Gerbner, G., Gross, L., Morgan, M., & Signorielli, N. (1981). Health and medicine on television. *New England Journal of Medicine, 305,* 901–904.

Goffman, E. (1961). *Asylum: Essays on the social situation of mental patients and other inmates.* New York: Doubleday.

Goodman, L., Saxe, L., & Harvey, M. (1991). Homelessness as psychological trauma: Broadening perspectives. *American Psychologist, 46,* 1219–1226.

Goodwin, D. W. (1986). Genetic factors in the development of alcoholism. *Psychiatric clinics of North America, 9,* 427–433.

Gounis, K., & Susser, E. (1990). Shelterization and its implications for mental health services. In N. L. Cohen (Ed.), *Psychiatry takes to the streets* (pp. 231–255). New York: Guilford Press.

Greenson, R. R. (1967). *The technique and practice of psycho-analysis* (Vol. 1). New York: International Universities Press.

Groddeck, G. (1951). *The unknown self.* New York: Funk & Wagnalls.

Grossman, C. M. (1965). Transference, countertransference, and being in love. *Psychoanalytic Quarterly, 34,* 249–256.

Groves, J. E. (1978). Taking care of the hateful patient. *New England Journal of Medicine, 298,* 883--887.

Grunberg, J., & Eagle, P. F. (1990). Shelterization: How the homeless adapt to shelter living. *Hospital and Community Psychiatry, 41,* 521–525.

Hamill, R., Wilson, T. D., & Nisbett, R. E. (1980). Insensitivity to sample bias: Generalizing from atypical cases. *Journal of Personality and Social Psychology, 39,* 578–589.

Harris, M., & Bergman, H. (Eds.). (1993). *Case management for mentally ill patients: Theory and practice.* New York: Harwood Academic Publishers.

Hartman, C. (1986). The housing part of the homelessness problem. In E. L. Bassuk (Ed.), *The mental health needs of homeless persons.* (New Directions for Mental Health Services, No. 80., pp. 71–85). San Francisco, CA: Jossey-Bass.

Hartman, C., & Reynolds, D. (1987). Resistant clients: Confrontation, interpretation, and alliance. *Social Casework, 68,* 205–213.

Hattie, J. A., Sharpley, C. F., & Rogers, H. J. (1984). Comparative effectiveness of professional and para-professional helpers. *Psychological Bulletin, 95,* 534–541.

Haynes, R. B., Taylor, D. W., & Sackett, D. L. (Eds.). (1979). *Compliance in health care.* Baltimore, MD: Johns Hopkins University Press.

Heimann, P. (1950). On counter-transference. *International Journal of Psychoanalysis, 31,* 81–84.

Hertzberg, E. L. (1988). Homeless in Hennepin County. *C.U.R.A. Reporter* (University of Minnesota), *18,* 1–6.

Horowitz, C. F. (1992, Aug. 31). Inventing homelessness. *National Review*, 25–29.

Janis, I. L. (1982). *Groupthink: Psychological studies of policy decisions and fiascoes.* Boston, MA: Houghton-Mifflin.

Jourard, S. M. (1971). *Self-disclosure: An experimental analysis of the transparent self.* New York: Wiley.

Kaffman, M. (1963). Short term family therapy. *Family Process, 2,* 216–234.

Kellner, R., Singh, G., & Irigoyen-Rascon, F. (1991). Rehearsal in the treatment of recurring nightmares in post-traumatic stress disorder and panic disorder: Case histories. *Annals of Clinical Psychiatry, 3,* 67–71.

Kennedy, C., & Manderscheid, R. W. (1993). *Mental health: United States, 1992.* Washington, DC: U.S. Government Printing Office.

Kernberg, O. (1965). Notes on countertransference. *Journal of the American Psychoanalytic Association, 13,* 38–56.

Kesey, K. (1962). *One flew over the cuckoo's nest.* New York: Viking Press.

Kiesler, C. A. (1991). Homelessness and public policy priorities. *American Psychologist, 46,* 1245–1252.

Koegel, P. (1992). Through a different lens: An anthropological perspective on the homeless mentally ill. *Culture, Medicine, and Psychiatry, 16,* 1–22.

Koegel, P., & Burnam, M. A. (1987). *The epidemiology of alcohol abuse and dependence among the homeless: Findings from inner city of Los Angeles.* Rockville, MD: National Institute on Alcohol Abuse and Alcoholism.

Koegel, P., & Burnam, M. A. (1992). Problems in the assessment of mental illness among the homeless: An empirical approach. In M. J. Robertson & M. Greenblatt (Eds.), *Homelessness: A national perspective* (pp. 77–100). New York: Plenum Press.

Koegel, P., Burnam, M. A., & Farr, R. K. (1990). Subsistence adaptation among homeless adults in the inner city of Los Angeles. *Journal of Social Issues, 46,* 83–107.

Kondratas, A. (1991). Ending homelessness: Policy challenges. *American Psychologist, 46,* 1226–1231.

Kotcher, M., & Smith, T. E. (1993). Three phases of clozapine treatment and phase-specific issues for patients and families. *Hospital and Community Psychiatry, 44,* 744–747.

Kuhlman, T. L. (1988). Gallows humor for a scaffold setting: Managing aggressive patients on a maximum security forensic unit. *Hospital and Community Psychiatry, 39,* 1085–1090.

Kuhlman, T. L. (1992). Unavoidable tragedies in Madison, Wisconsin: A third view. *Hospital and Community Psychiatry, 43,* 72–73.

Kuhlman, T. L. (1993). Humor in stressful milieus. In W. F. Fry & W. A. Salameh (Eds.), *Advances in humor and psychotherapy*. Sarasota, FL: Professional Resource Press.

Kuhlman, T. L., Green, J. A., & Sincaban, V. A. (1988). Dice therapy: Deterring suicidal behavior by a borderline patient. *Hospital and Community Psychiatry, 39,* 992–994.

Lacayo, R. (1992, May 18). Your land . . . this is my land. *Time,* 29–33.

Laing, R. D. (1960). *The divided self.* New York: Pantheon.

Laing, R. D. (1967). *The politics of experience.* New York: Ballantine Books.

Lamb, H. R. (1982). Young adult chronic patients: The new drifters. *Hospital and Community Psychiatry, 33,* 465–468.

Lamb, H. R. (Ed.). (1984). *The homeless mentally ill.* Washington, DC: American Psychiatric Association.

Lamb, H. R. (1992). Perspectives on effective advocacy for homeless mentally ill persons. *Hospital and Community Psychiatry, 43,* 1209–1212.

Lamb, H. R., Bachrach, L. L., & Kass, F. I. (Eds.). (1992). *Treating the homeless mentally ill.* Washington, DC: American Psychiatric Association.

Lamb, H. R., & Grant, R. W. (1982). The mentally ill in an urban county jail. *Archives of General Psychiatry, 39,* 17–22.

Lamb, H. R., & Grant, R. W. (1983). Mentally ill women in a county jail. *Archives of General Psychiatry, 40,* 362–368.

Lamb, H. R., & Weinberger, L. E. (1993). Therapeutic use of conservatorship in the treatment of the gravely disabled. *Hospital and Community Psychiatry, 44,* 147–150.

Lee, B. A. (1980). The disappearance of skid row: Some ecological evidence. *Urban Affairs Quarterly, 16,* 81–107.

Lefcourt, H. M., & Martin, R. A. (1984). *Humor and life stress.* New York: Springer-Verlag.

Ley, P. (1986). Cognitive variables and noncompliance. *Journal of Compliance in Health Care, 1,* 171–188.

Liotti, G. (1987). The resistance to change of cognitive structures: A counterproposal to psychoanalytic metapsychology. *Journal of Cognitive Psychotherapy, 1,* 87–104.

Littlepage, G. E., Kosloski, K. D., Schnelle, J. F., NcNees, M. P., & Gendrich, J. C. (1976). The problem of early outpatient terminations from community mental health centers: A problem for whom? *Journal of Community Psychology, 4,* 164–167.

Lorion, R. P., & Felner, R. D. (1986). Research on mental health interventions with the disadvantaged. In S. L. Garfield & A. E. Bergin (Eds.), *Handbook of psychotherapy and behavior change* (3rd ed., pp. 739–755). New York: Wiley.

Lubran, B. G. (1990). Alcohol and drug abuse among the homeless population: A national response. In M. Argeriou & D. McCarty (Eds.), *Treating alcoholism and drug abuse among the homeless: Nine community demonstration grants* (pp. 11–23). Binghamton, NY: Haworth Press.

Marcos, L. P. (1990). The politics of deinstitutionalization. In N. L. Cohen (Ed.), *Psychiatry takes to the streets* (pp. 3–15). New York: Guilford Press.

Maslow, A. H. (1970). *Motivation and personality* (2nd ed.). New York: Harper & Row.

McCarty, D., Argeriou, M., Huebner, R. B., & Lubran, B. (1991). Alcoholism, drug abuse, and the homeless. *American Psychologist, 46,* 1139–1148.

McLaughlin, M., & Pepper, B. (1990). The young and the restless: Programming for the crisis-ridden young adult patient. In N. L. Cohen (Ed.), *Psychiatry takes to the streets* (pp. 137–155). New York: Guilford Press.

Meichenbaum, D., & Gilmore, B. (1982). Resistance: From a cognitive-behavioral perspective. In P. Wachtel (Ed.), *Resistance in psychodynamic and behavioral therapies.* New York: Plenum Press.

Meichenbaum, D., & Turk, D. C. (1987). *Facilitating treatment adherence: A practitioner's guidebook.* New York: Plenum, Press.

Miller, R. D. (1992). An update on involuntary civil commitment to outpatient treatment. *Hospital and Community Psychiatry, 43,* 79–80.

Minkoff, K. (1987). Beyond deinstitutionalization: A new ideology for the post-institutional era. *Hospital and Community Psychiatry, 38,* 945–950.

Minkoff, K., & Drake, R. E. (Eds.). (1991). *Dual diagnosis of major mental illness and substance disorder.* (New Directions in Mental Health) (pp. 95–106). San Francisco, CA: Jossey-Bass.

Monohan, J. (1981). *The clinical prediction of violent behavior.* Washington, DC: U.S. Government Printing Office.

Morse, G. A. (1992). Causes of homelessness. In M. J. Robertson & M. Greenblatt (Eds.), *Homelessness: A national perspective* (pp. 3–18). New York: Plenum Press.

Nash, J. M. (1991, Apr. 5). Broken connections, missing memories: An interview with Jacob Fox. *Time,* 10–12.

Nisbett, R. E., Caputo, C., Legant, P., & Maracek, J. (1973). Behavior as seen by the actor and as seen by the observer. *Journal of Personality and Social Psychology, 27,* 154–164.

Ost, L. G. (1989). One session treatment for specific phobias. *Behavioral Research and Therapy, 27,* 1–7.

Pepper, B., Kirschner, M. C., & Ryglewicz, H. (1981). The young adult chronic patient: Overview of a population. *Hospital and Community Psychiatry, 32,* 463–469.

Policy Research Associates, Inc. (1993). Dual disorders are difficult for individuals and service systems. *Access* (The National Resource Center of Homelessness and Mental Illness), *5,* 1–9.

Reid, W. H., Pham, V. A., & Rago, W. (1993). Clozapine use by state programs: Public mental health systems respond to a new medication. *Hospital and Community Psychiatry, 44,* 733–738.

Reider, N. (1955). A type of psychotherapy based on psychoanalytic principles. *Bulletin of the Menninger Clinic, 19,* 111–128.

Reyes, L., & Waxman, L. D. (1989). *A status report on hunger and homelessness in America's cities: 1989.* Washington, DC: United States Conference of Mayors.

Ridgely, M. S., & Dixon, L. B. (1993). *Integrating mental health and substance abuse services for homeless people with co-occurring mental and substance use disorders.* Washington, DC: Federal Center for Mental Health Services.

Rivlin, L. G., & Imbimbo, J. E. (1989). Self-help effects in a squatter community: Implications for addressing contemporary homelessness. *American Journal of Community Psychology, 17,* 705–728.

Rooney, J. F. (1976). Friendship and disaffiliation among the skid row population. *Journal of Gerontology, 31,* 82–88.

Rosen, J. C., & Wiens, A. N. (1979). Changes in medical problems and use of medical services following psychological intervention. *American Psychologist, 34,* 420–431.

Rosenbaum, C. P. (1964). Events of early therapy and brief therapy. *Archives of General Psychiatry, 10,* 506–512.

Rosenfield, S. (1991). Homelessness and rehospitalization: The importance of housing for the chronic mentally ill. *Journal of Community Psychology, 19,* 60–69.

Rossi, P. H. (1989). *Down and out in America: The origins of homelessness.* Chicago, IL: University of Chicago Press.

Rossi, P. H. (1990). The old homeless and the new homelessness in historical perspective. *American Psychologist, 45*, 954–959.

Schuckit, M. A. (1987). Biological vulnerability to alcoholism. *Journal of Consulting and Clinical Psychology, 55,* 307–309.

Schutt, R. K., & Garrett, G. R. (1992). *Responding to the homeless: Policy and practice.* New York: Plenum Press.

Seagull, A. A. (1966). Must the deeply disturbed have long-term treatment? *Psychotherapy, 3,* 36–42.

Selye, H. (1976). *The stress of life.* New York: McGraw-Hill.

Shapiro, F. (1989). Efficiency of the Eye Movement Desensitization procedure in the treatment of traumatic memories. *Journal of Traumatic Stress, 2,* 199–223.

Shinn, M., Burke, P. D., & Bedford, S. (Eds.). (1990). *Homelessness: Abstracts of the Psychological and Behavioral Literature, 1967–1990* (Bibliographies in Psychology No. 7). Washington, DC: American Psychological Association.

Shore, M. F., & Cohen, M. D. (1992). Homelessness and the chronically mentally ill. In M. J. Robertson & M. Greenblatt (Eds.), *Homelessness: A national perspective* (pp. 67–76). New York: Plenum Press.

Silverman, W. H., & Beech, R. P. (1979). Are dropouts, dropouts? *Journal of Community Psychology, 7,* 236–242.

Singer, B. A., & Luborsky, L. (1977). Countertransference: The status of clinical versus quantitative research. In A. Gurman & A. Razdin (Eds.), *Effective psychotherapy* (pp. 433–451). New York: Pergamon Press.

Singer, E. (1970). *Key concepts in psychotherapy* (2nd ed.). New York: Basic Books.

Singer, J. L., Sincoff, J. B., & Kolligan, J. (1989). Counter-transference and cognition: Studying the psychotherapist's distortions as consequences of normal information processing. *Psychotherapy, 26,* 344–355.

Snow, D. A., & Anderson, L. (1987). Identity work among the homeless: The verbal construction and avowal of personal identities. *American Journal of Sociology, 92,* 1336–1371.

Snow, D. A., Baker, S. G., Anderson, L., & Martin, M. (1986). The myth of pervasive mental illness among the homeless. *Social Problems, 33,* 407–423.

Springmann, R. (1986). Countertransference: Clarifications in supervision. *Contemporary Psychoanalysis, 22,* 252–277.

Storch, R. S., & Lane, R. C. (1989). Resistance in mandated psychotherapy: Its function and management. *Journal of Contemporary Psychotherapy, 19,* 25–38.

Storms, M. D. (1973). Videotape and the attribution process: Reversing actors' and observers' point of view. *Journal of Personality and Social Psychology, 27,* 154–164.

Struening, E. L. (1987). *A study of the residents of the New York City shelter system.* New York: New York State Psychiatric Institute.

Susser, E., Goldfinger, S. M., & White, A. (1990). Some clinical approaches to the homeless mentally ill. *Community Mental Health Journal, 26,* 463–480.

Susser, E., Struening, E. L., & Conover, S. (1987). Childhood experiences of homeless men. *American Journal of Psychiatry, 144,* 1599–1601.

Susser, E., Valencia, E., & Goldfinger, S. M. (1992). Clinical care of homeless mentally ill individuals: Strategies and adaptations. In H. R. Lamb, L. L. Bachrach, & F. I. Kass (Eds.), *Treating the homeless mentally ill* (pp. 127–140). Washington, DC: American Psychiatric Association.

Swayze, F. V. (1992). Clinical case management with the homeless mentally ill. In H. R. Lamb, L. L. Bachrach, & F. I. Kass (Eds.), *Treating the homeless mentally ill* (pp. 203–220). Washington, DC: American Psychiatric Association.

Szasz, T. S. (1961). *The myth of mental illness.* New York: Harper.

Szasz, T. S. (1970). *Ideology and insanity: Essays on the psychiatric dehumanization of man.* Garden City, NY: Anchor Books.

Talbott, J. A. (Ed.). (1981). *The chronic mentally ill.* New York: Human Sciences Press.

Talmon, M. (1990). *Single-session therapy.* San Francisco, CA: Jossey-Bass.

Tannenbaum, S. A. (1919). Three brief psychoanalyses. *American Journal of Urology and Sexology, 15,* 145–151.

Tanzman, B. (1993). Housing and supports for persons with mental illness: Emerging approaches to research and practice. *Hospital and Community Psychiatry, 44,* 439–449.

Tessler, R. C., & Dennis, D. L. (1989). *A synthesis of NIMH-funded research concerning persons who are homeless and mentally ill.* Rockville, MD: National Institute of Mental Health.

Thompson, K. S., Griffith, E. E., & Leaf, P. J. (1990). A historical review of the Madison model of community care. *Hospital and Community Psychiatry, 41,* 625–633.

Toro, P. A., Trickett, E. J., Wall, D. D., & Salem, D. A. (1991). Homelessness in the United States: An ecological perspective. *American Psychologist, 46,* 1208–1219.

Torrey, E. F. (1988). *Nowhere to go: The tragic odyssey of the homeless mentally ill.* New York: Harper & Row.

Torrey, E. F. (1992, Dec. 28). The mental-health mess. *National Review,* 22–25.

Torrey, E. F. (1993). *Criminalizing the seriously mentally ill.* Washington, DC: Public Citizens' Health Research Group.

Torrey, E. F., & Wolfe, S. M. (1986). *Care of the seriously mentally ill: A rating of state programs.* Washington, DC: Public Citizens' Research Group.

Ungerleider, J. T., Andrysiak, T., Siegel, N., Tidwell, D., & Flynn, T. (1992). Mental health and homelessness: The clinician's view. In M. J. Robertson & M. Greenblatt (Eds.), *Homelessness: A national perspective* (pp. 109–116). New York: Plenum Press.

U.S. Bureau of the Census. (1983). *Annual housing survey, part C: Financial characteristics of the housing inventory.* Washington, DC: U.S. Government Printing Office.

U.S. Bureau of the Census. (1992). *Statistical abstract of the United States* (112th ed.). Washington, DC: U.S. Department of Commerce.

Wallace, S. E. (1968). The road to skid row. *Social Problems, 16,* 92–105.

Weeks, G. R., & L'Abate, L. (1982). *Paradoxical psychotherapy.* New York: Brunner-Mazel.

Wexler, D. A. (1974). A cognitive theory of experiencing, self-actualization, and therapeutic process. In D. A. Wexler & L. N. Rice (Eds.), *Innovations in client-centered therapy.* New York: Wiley.

Wilkerson, I. (1991, Sept. 2). Shift in feelings on the homeless: Empathy turns into frustration. *New York Times,* pp. A1, A10.

Williams, L. (1992). *Mourning in America: Health problems, mortality, and homelessness.* Washington, DC: National Coalition for the Homeless.

Winkleby, M. A., & White, M. (1992). Homeless adults without apparent medical and psychiatric impairment: Onset of morbidity over time. *Hospital and Community Psychiatry, 43,* 1017–1023.

Wiseman, J. P. (1987). Studying the problems of alcoholism in today's homeless (Summary). In J. Baumohl (Ed.), *The homeless with alcohol problems: Proceedings of an NIAAA-sponsored research conference* (pp. 8–9). Rockville, MD: National Institute on Alcohol Abuse and Alcoholism.

Wittman, F. D. (1992). Housing: From street to shelter to ? In R. K. Schutt & G. R. Garrett (Eds.), *Responding to the homeless: Policy and practice* (pp. 191–212). New York: Plenum Press.

Wolstein, B. (1959). *Countertransference.* New York: Grune & Stratton.

Wright, J. D., & Weber, E., (1987). *Homelessness and health.* New York: McGraw–Hill.

Author Index

Subject Index